THE **COMPLETE IDIOT'S GUIDE**® TO

Vegan Slow Cooking

by Beverly Lynn Bennett

ALPHA

A member of Penguin Group (USA) Inc.

This book is dedicated to the love of my life, Ray Sammartano, and to all vegans everywhere, as well as those who are striving to eat more vegan meals—this one's for you!

ALPHA BOOKS

Published by Penguin Group (USA) Inc.

Penguin Group (USA) Inc., 375 Hudson Street, New York, New York 10014, USA • Penguin Group (Canada), 90 Eglinton Avenue East, Suite 700, Toronto, Ontario M4P 2Y3, Canada (a division of Pearson Penguin Canada Inc.) • Penguin Books Ltd., 80 Strand, London WC2R 0RL, England • Penguin Ireland, 25 St. Stephen's Green, Dublin 2, Ireland (a division of Penguin Books Ltd.) • Penguin Group (Australia), 250 Camberwell Road, Camberwell, Victoria 3124, Australia (a division of Pearson Australia Group Pty. Ltd.) • Penguin Books India Pvt. Ltd., 11 Community Centre, Panchsheel Park, New Delhi— 110 017, India • Penguin Group (NZ), 67 Apollo Drive, Rosedale, North Shore, Auckland 1311, New Zealand (a division of Pearson New Zealand Ltd.) • Penguin Books (South Africa) (Pty.) Ltd., 24 Sturdee Avenue, Rosebank, Johannesburg 2196, South Africa • Penguin Books Ltd., Registered Offices: 80 Strand, London WC2R 0RL, England

Copyright © 2012 by Beverly Lynn Bennett

International Standard Book Number: 978-1-61564-201-4
Library of Congress Catalog Card Number: 2012935350

14   13   12   8   7   6   5   4   3   2   1

Interpretation of the printing code: The rightmost number of the first series of numbers is the year of the book's printing; the rightmost number of the second series of numbers is the number of the book's printing. For example, a printing code of 12-1 shows that the first printing occurred in 2012.

Printed in the United States of America

Note: This publication contains the opinions and ideas of its author. It is intended to provide helpful and informative material on the subject matter covered. It is sold with the understanding that the author and publisher are not engaged in rendering professional services in the book. If the reader requires personal assistance or advice, a competent professional should be consulted.

The author and publisher specifically disclaim any responsibility for any liability, loss, or risk, personal or otherwise, which is incurred as a consequence, directly or indirectly, of the use and application of any of the contents of this book.

Most Alpha books are available at special quantity discounts for bulk purchases for sales promotions, premiums, fund-raising, or educational use. Special books, or book excerpts, can also be created to fit specific needs. For details, write: Special Markets, Alpha Books, 375 Hudson Street, New York, NY 10014.

Publisher: *Mike Sanders*
Executive Managing Editor: *Billy Fields*
Senior Acquisitions Editor: *Tom Stevens*
Senior Development Editor: *Christy Wagner*
Senior Production Editor: *Kayla Dugger*
Copy Editor: *Louise Lund*

Cover Designer: *Rebecca Batchelor*
Book Designers: *William Thomas, Rebecca Batchelor*
Indexer: *Tonya Heard*
Layout: *Brian Massey*
Senior Proofreader: *Laura Caddell*

Contents

Introduction

You may be hesitant to invest in a slow cooker, but you'll be so glad you did when you discover all its advantages. No matter what your lifestyle, you'll soon appreciate the slow cooker for what it saves you and gives you, starting with easier meal preparations. All you have to do is assemble the ingredients in the slow cooker, plug it in, turn it on, and walk away! That's right, just walk away!

When you use a slow cooker, in most instances, you just fill it and forget it. Unlike stovetop cooking and oven baking—both of which require your constant attention— slow cooker cooking does the work all on its own, without requiring you to fret or fuss over it.

This means you can have your slow cooker cooking away while you're sleeping, at work, running errands, taking the kids to soccer practice, enjoying a workout at the gym, or even sitting on the couch watching TV with your feet up. And before you know it, your house will be filled with the aroma of your home-cooked meal, warm and waiting for you—and not you waiting for it or for the take-out to arrive.

In this book, you'll find more than 240 vegan slow cooker recipes that will tantalize your taste buds and provide you with plenty of creative and delicious meal ideas you can easily create in your very own kitchen. These tasty recipes run the gamut from appetizers to beverages, from early morning breakfast options to after-dinner desserts. Throughout the recipe chapters, I show you how, with the help of your slow cooker, you can prepare myriad culinary creations that will impress everyone seated at your table!

How This Book Is Organized

This book is divided into seven parts dedicated to showing you how easy—and delicious!—vegan slow cooking can be:

Part 1, Making Friends with Your Slow Cooker, provides some essential information you should know about how a slow cooker works, as well as the various advantages this handy appliance offers, including saving you precious time and money. I also share invaluable advice for helping you achieve the most success by using a slow cooker to prepare your meals, and how to convert your favorite recipes into slow cooker recipes. Finally, I teach you how to use vegan, plant-based ingredients as substitutes for animal-based ingredients and give you a few suggestions for staples to stock up on to make meal preparation easier.

Part 2, Breakfasts Worth Waking Up For, gives you plenty of breakfast ideas to help you start your day off right with a homemade breakfast. An entire chapter is devoted to easy, slow-cooked overnight oats and other hot breakfast bowls, as well as creamy grits. When you're in need of a heartier breakfast or brunch ideas, Chapter 4 offers several delicious recipes.

Part 3, Appetizers, Sauces, and More, features recipes for appetizers, snacks, spreads and toppings, gravy, and both sweet and savory sauces. This part starts with hot and bubbling dips and even vegan fondue, as well as some amazing appetizers. After that, you'll find a whole slew of sweet and savory sauces, fruit and vegetable butters, condiments, and toppings you can use both in and on top of your favorite recipes.

Part 4, Soups, Chilies, and Chowders, showcases these warm bowlfuls perfect for any season. No matter what you're in the mood for, whether it be something light and brothy, smooth and creamy, or packed with beans, veggies, rice, or pasta, you'll find these options—and a whole lot more!—in this part. If you're craving a big bowl of chunky chowder or a mild or spicy chili, you'll find it here.

Turn to **Part 5, Main Attractions,** when you find yourself hankering for a real stick-to-your-ribs meal. Sensational sandwiches, stews, casseroles, and other main dish recipes you'll be proud to serve your family and friends are all here. I also teach you how to make your own meatless meats and use them in filling sandwiches that will satisfy the hungriest of appetites. You also learn how easy it is to slow cook some classic stews, family-style casseroles, and other one-pot meals.

Part 6, Sensational Sides, provides plenty of options to round out your lunch or dinner plate with tasty veggie-, bean-, and grain-based side dishes, as well as some wholesome slow-baked breads.

Part 7, Sweet Endings, continues with your slow cooker schooling by showing you how to transform your slow cooker into a mini-oven to slow bake some delicious desserts and other sweet treats. You learn how to make some fantastic fruit-filled sweets, old-fashioned favorites like creamy and steamed puddings, and cakes that will fit whatever the occasion.

In the back of the book, I've included a glossary filled with definitions sprinkled throughout the book as well as some other technique, item, and equipment terms. Finally, I share some wonderful resources you can use to further your vegan slow cooker journey.

Extras

Throughout the book, you'll find sidebars to guide you along and offer additional information. Here's what to look for:

COOKER CAVEAT

To avoid any problems or pitfalls, be sure to heed the warnings in these sidebars.

DEFINITION

These mini-dictionaries define terms, ingredients, and techniques you might not be familiar with.

LOW AND SLOW

These helpful hints and tips touch upon certain facts and ideas presented in the text or that may be useful as you prepare a recipe.

SLOW INTERESTING

Read these sidebars for some interesting information relating to the ingredients, recipes, or other issues discussed in the book.

Acknowledgments

I would like to thank several people for all their help and assistance as I wrote this book, including Tom Stevens, Christy Wagner, Marie Butler-Knight, and the rest of the Alpha Books team who helped bring this book to fruition. Much appreciation to Marilyn Allen and her team at Allen O'Shea Literary Agency.

I'd like to extend my deepest appreciation and heartfelt thanks to all my friends and family for their love and support during the writing of this book. I would also like to thank my cat companion, Luna, for the many hours of snuggling and purring on my lap while I sat at the computer typing. And most of all, I want to thank Ray Sammartano, my partner in life as well as my co-author on two previous *Complete Idiot's Guides*, for his loving support, thoughtful suggestions, and extremely helpful insights regarding content, and most importantly, for being my chief taste-tester throughout the recipe development process for this book.

And lastly, I would like to thank all the dedicated vegan writers, cookbook authors, activists, and other folks out there who are devoted to spreading the vegan message and who strive to improve their own lives as well as the lives of the many creatures we share this planet with.

Special Thanks to the Technical Reviewer

The Complete Idiot's Guide to Vegan Slow Cooking was reviewed by an expert who double-checked the accuracy of what you'll learn here, to help us ensure that this book gives you everything you need to know about making nutritious, delicious vegan dishes in your slow cooker. Special thanks are extended to Trish Sebben-Krupka, a New Jersey–based vegan chef, culinary educator, and food writer.

Trademarks

All terms mentioned in this book that are known to be or are suspected of being trademarks or service marks have been appropriately capitalized. Alpha Books and Penguin Group (USA) Inc. cannot attest to the accuracy of this information. Use of a term in this book should not be regarded as affecting the validity of any trademark or service mark.

Making Friends with Your Slow Cooker

A slow cooker may be very simple in its design and operation, but this countertop appliance and its slow, low-temperature cooking method, is capable of helping you achieve concentrated, complex, robust, and full flavors in your finished dishes. In Chapter 1, you get acquainted with how a slow cooker works, its setting and safety considerations, and the advantages you get from using one, as well as some advice to help you decide which size and shape cooker would work best for you.

Then, in Chapter 2, you get a crash course on how to get the most out of your slow cooker, no matter what you're making, along with information on adjusting for higher altitudes, converting recipes, and even slow baking. Finally, I wrap up Part 1 with an overview of the vegan plant-based substitutions you can use to replace animal-based products, as well as the essentials you should keep stocked in your kitchen pantry, fridge, and freezer.

Slow Cooking 101

You've seen them at garage sales, on the shelves of neighborhood thrift stores, department stores, and kitchen specialty shops: that countertop appliance with its ceramic stoneware insert and see-through lid. The slow cooker. These low-tech mechanical marvels have been making mealtime easier for home cooks for more than 40 years, helping cooks create soups, stews, and one-pot meals. This beloved appliance continues to attract devotees as a way to easily get tasty, healthy meals on the table.

What's all the fuss about? Let me ask you a few questions. Do you dislike to cook, or are you intimidated by it? Do you think cooking is too time-consuming? Do you want to stretch your food budget further? Do you want to cook healthier, vegan meals for you and your family? Does your busy schedule have you hitting the drive-thru more often than you'd like?

If you answered "yes" to one or more of these questions, vegan slow cooking is for you. This unrushed style of cooking will forever change how you go about making a meal.

Slow and Steady Cooking

In 1971, the Rival Company introduced the world to the first slow cooker, affectionately called the Crock-Pot. This revolutionary cooking appliance consisted of a glazed brown stoneware insert and matching glass lid that was held in an electric heated base with handles for easy lifting. They were originally available in the infamous 1970s avocado green and harvest gold colors.

That was just the beginning of the slow cooker craze, which is well deserved for a variety of reasons. Let's take a look at some of the many benefits of cooking with slow cookers.

Effortless Eating

If you feel like there aren't enough hours in your day to get everything done, the slow cooker will soon become your best, multitasking friend. Your slow cooker and its hands-free approach to cooking makes it easy for you to do two or more things at once. It's the handy helper for busy people who want to enjoy good food with minimal effort.

Simply prep a few ingredients on the spot, at night before you go to bed, or in the morning before heading off to work or taking the kids to school. Load up your slow cooker, turn it on, and go about your business. When you return hours later, your slow cooker will have done its magic, and a warm meal will be waiting for you.

Energy Savings

Slow cookers not only save you time, but can also help save money. Compared to the stovetop or oven, slow cookers use very little electricity, even though they take a little longer to get a meal on the table. Many experts rate its energy usage as less than that of a 100-watt lightbulb.

Because a slow cooker is such a low-wattage appliance (check the bottom of your appliance for exact wattage), you can safely leave it turned on for several hours while you're not home or overnight. What's more, a slow cooker is an ideal way to cook during the hot summer months because it doesn't heat up your kitchen like an oven would.

Less Fat and More Flavor

If you're watching your weight, you'll find the slow cooker ideal for low-fat cooking because there's no need to use large amounts of added oil or margarine to prevent foods from sticking or scorching.

If you want to go no-fat, it's easy, especially if you're making a soup or chili. When you cook low and slow, you can coax out a lot more flavor from foods like beans, leafy greens, root vegetables, and pumpkin and squashes, just to name a few.

LOW AND SLOW

It never hurts to cut your consumption of added fats whenever you can, and when it comes to vegan baked goods, vegetable and fruit purées often work wonderfully as a replacement for one third to one half of the added oil or margarine in your recipe. This is one reason why many recipes in this book call for pumpkin purée or applesauce to bind, moisten, and greatly minimize the need for added oil or margarine.

However, in some instances, a little oil or margarine in the mix greatly enhances your final creation. For added depth of flavor in your sauce or stew, you may want to use a little oil for sautéing some ingredients like onions or garlic prior to adding them to the slow cooker. Or consider adding a dollop of margarine or swirl of oil to give a slight richness to your finished vegetable or grain dishes. Also, using a little margarine or sunflower oil in your desserts, breads, and baked goods yields a nice flavor and gives them a nice, moist texture.

Easier Entertaining

When you've got company coming over, let your slow cooker lend a helping hand. Not only can you prepare your soup or main or side dishes in a slow cooker, but you can also use it to keep them warm on the buffet or dining table for as long as you need. You can serve them straight from the slow cooker, which means one less dish to wash later. And for those times when you're making a big holiday or Sunday night dinner, you can free up precious space in your oven or stovetop by making and holding your side dishes or desserts in your slow cooker instead.

Some savvy manufacturers have come up with slow cooker buffet servers that consist of multiple slow cooker ceramic crock inserts contained within the same heating base, each with its own separate temperature control so you can heat and hold foods as desired. Some models have a special hinge that holds the lid open while guests serve themselves, which means no more annoying water or saucy rings left on your best tablecloth!

Portable Practicality

Unlike many other kitchen appliances, your slow cooker enables you to easily "make it and take it" from your kitchen to another location, and all you have to do when you arrive at the party, potluck, or tailgating event is plug it in to keep your food hot for hours. Also, slow cookers' relatively small size and multi-purpose capabilities make them ideal for cooking in college dorms, cozy country cabins, and even RVs.

Some manufacturers offer insulated travel bags that make it easier to take your slow cooker to get-togethers, while retaining the heat during transport.

Slow Cooking Simplified

A slow cooker, with the aid of its tight-fitting lid and low and even heat source, is perfectly designed to utilize the moist-heat methods of cooking, such as braising, poaching, steaming, and stewing. Thanks to the extremely moist environment within the confines of your slow cooker, you can prepare mouthwatering soups, stews, casseroles, and vegetable side dishes, as well as breakfast oatmeal and rice pudding for dessert.

You can also use your slow cooker to cook food without any liquid. In the mood for a baked russet or sweet potato? Forget the oven or microwave, and use your slow cooker instead. You can even use your slow cooker, rather than your oven, to slow bake quick or yeast-risen breads and your favorite cobblers, crisps, cakes, and even cheesecake! (Check out Parts 6 and 7 for recipe ideas.)

If you're using a slow cooker for the first time, remember "safety first." Be sure to thoroughly read the user's manual. Not only will you find helpful advice, but many include recipe ideas.

You should be aware that even though all slow cookers have the same basic setup, it's been my experience that cooking times can vary substantially from model to model. (I discuss this more later in this chapter.)

Slow Cooker Setup

Now let's take a look at the various parts of your slow cooker. Slow cookers are one of the most uncomplicated kitchen appliances around, and they basically have only four parts:

- See-through lid
- Ceramic crock insert
- Electrical heating base
- Temperature control knob

You place your recipe ingredients in the ceramic crock insert, put the lid on top, place the crock in the base (if it's not already there), and turn the temperature control knob to the proper setting. Now just walk away and let your slow cooker do its thing!

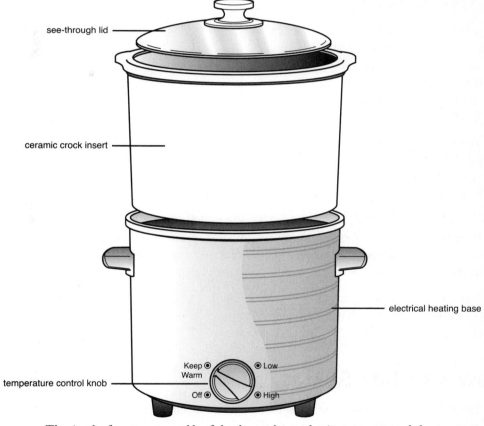

The simple, four-part assembly of the slow cooker makes it easy to use and clean.

Slow cooker lids are typically made of glass, so be careful when handling and washing them. Some lids even have an added inner rubber ring to make them more tight-fitting. Some manufacturers have added latches or bands for locking the lid in place so you can easily and safely transport your slow cooker.

The main cooking vessel, the ceramic crock insert, has a glazed, easy-to-clean finish and is easily the heaviest and bulkiest part of the appliance. Most ceramic crock inserts are microwave and oven safe and can be used to bake breads or as a casserole dish as well. They're also often dishwasher-safe, and after a brief soaking time, you should be able to easily clean them with just a little elbow grease.

COOKER CAVEAT

Be sure to follow these slow cooker don'ts: don't expose the ceramic crock insert to extreme temperature changes, or it could crack. You can take it from the fridge to the slow cooker, but not if the base has been preheated. Don't set a hot crock in the freezer or cold water to cool it down. Don't heat the crock on the stovetop. Don't immerse the base or cord in water. To clean—be sure it's unplugged and completely cool—wipe down the inner and outer surface of the base and cord with a damp sponge and thoroughly dry. With some careful use, your slow cooker will be your kitchen helper for years.

The ingenious design of the slow cooker's low-wattage, wrap-around heating coils, which are cleverly encased within the inner and outer metal walls of the base, provides an indirect heat source that cooks items without coming into direct contact with the ceramic crock insert. The coils heat up, which generates heat within the space between the base wall and the ceramic crock insert. The heat is then transferred to the insert and ultimately heats up its contents—your dinner! So even when left unattended, your slow-cooked meals will cook more evenly with little chance of burning or scorching. And because the heating coils stay on constantly, they gently and evenly heat the ceramic crock insert from both the bottom and sides, eliminating the need for constant stirring.

All slow cookers have the standard settings: off, low (about 180°F), and high (about 300°F). Some brands also include the handy "keep warm" setting, perfect for holding foods for extended periods of time.

The internal temperature of most food cooked on low remains just below the boiling point (around 180°F), which makes this setting ideal for longer cooking times (8 hours or more), like when you're at work or overnight. Recipes that like it slow and low include oatmeal or other hot cereals, soups and chilies, and foods you want to gently steam so they remain overly moist like a breakfast frittata.

On high, your foods cook at a much higher temperature, and as a result, they cook approximately twice as fast as they would on low. As a general guideline, 1 hour on high is equal to 2 to 2½ hours on low, so if you're short on time and don't have 8 hours for your soup to cook on low, crank it up to high and let it bubble away for 4 or 5 hours instead. High also seems to work best for achieving a golden brown outer crust on breads, cakes, and other baked goods, as well as for quickly heating dips.

In some instances, you might want to take a tag-team approach by starting your slow cooker on high for the first 20 to 30 minutes or so to get the cooker up to temperature quickly and then turn it down to low for the remainder of the cooking time.

SLOW INTERESTING

If you're willing to spend a little more, you can get a programmable slow cooker. You simply program the desired cooking time and temperature, and when it's done, the machine will automatically switch to the keep warm setting—handy for those nights when you're late getting home.

Just like your oven, some slow cooker brands and models run a bit hotter than others. This is especially true if you're using a new, larger-size model, which will cook your food faster than an older slow cooker made in the 1970s or 1980s. The more you use your slow cooker, the better you'll be able to assess its temperature accuracy. So consider the recommended cooking times and temperatures included with each recipe merely as a suggestion and not a steadfast rule, and adjust cook times to suit your slow cooker.

Slow Cooker Sizes and Shapes

As with many things in life, size and shape do matter, and when it comes to slow cookers, you'll have the most success when you use the proper size and shape cooker for the task at hand. Slow cookers are available in a wide range of volume capacities, from 1 quart, which is great for serving a small amount of dip, all the way up to 7 quarts, which will make enough to feed a large crowd. Most sizes come in both round and oval shapes.

All the recipes in this book include suggestions for what size slow cookers to use. Here are the recommended sizes and their capacity:

- Small: 1½-, 2-, and 2½-quart capacity

- Medium: 3-, 3½-, 4-, and 4½-quart capacity

- Large: 5-, 5½-, 6-, 6½-, and 7-quart capacity

The small, 1½-quart cookers are dandy for making and serving dips, but they're too small for making soups and stews, generally holding only enough to generously serve 1 or 2 people. The most commonly used slow cookers are the medium size, 3- or 4-quart models, which can cook a batch of stew, beans, or grains enough for feeding 3 or 4 people. If you have a larger family, or want to make enough for 2 meals, the large 5- or 6-quart capacity might better fit your needs. The even larger 7-quart capacity slow cookers are for those who like to cook in very large batches, or enough to feed 8 or more people (or those with very hearty appetites!).

In most instances, the classic, round slow cooker does a fine job of cooking main meals and desserts, and some medium and large ones can be used to make nice round loaves of bread or cake, either directly in the ceramic crock insert or in soufflé or circular casserole dishes. Most of the large, oval slow cookers are also capable of holding the average 8-inch round springform and cake pans, as well as an 8×4×2½-inch loaf pan for baking bread. For recipes that require the use of a baking pan or casserole dish, insert the empty pan into your ceramic crock insert before you fill it to ensure it fits properly without touching the lid or sides of the ceramic crock insert.

Which slow cooker is for you depends on your needs and how many people you want to serve. Like many slow cooker devotees, you may find that having more than one size and shape covers all your entertaining needs. Once you've settled into slow cooking on a regular basis, you'll be able to better determine what your needs are.

Slow Cooker Food Safety

As you now know, even on low, your slow cooker will heat your foods to around 180°F, which is above what the health department considers the "food danger zone." But what if something happens out of your control, like if the power goes out while it's cooking?

COOKER CAVEAT

Food-borne bacteria can grow in temperatures from 40°F to 140°F—the range commonly referred to within the foodservice industry as the "food danger zone." To prevent food-borne illnesses like salmonella, heed this advice: keep cold food cold, and hot food hot. Bacteria won't easily multiply in the colder temperatures of a refrigerator or freezer, or at temperatures hotter than 140°F, but they do thrive within the food danger zone. To avoid having to discard your slow-cooked meals, be sure they're not in the danger zone for more than 1 hour.

If it's near the end of the cooking time, you should be fine. Don't lift the lid, and your meal should stay hot for up to 2 hours. If it was in the middle of cooking and the power was only off briefly, you can transfer it to the stovetop or oven to finish cooking it when the power is restored.

However, if the power went out while you were at work and you're not sure for how long, forget about it. When in doubt, throw it out. Trashing some stew is a small price to pay for avoiding digestive distress.

The Least You Need to Know

- Using a slow cooker to make your meals saves you time, money, and energy.
- The slow cooker's brilliant design cooks your food using indirect heat, allowing it to be left unattended as it prepares delicious meals with little chance of burning or scorching.
- A slow cooker's low setting is about 180°F, and high is about 300°F. The option you choose is most often based on your schedule and what you're preparing.
- When choosing your slow cooker, carefully consider what size and shape best fits your needs—or get two different sizes so you can slow cook to your heart's content!

Secrets for Success

In This Chapter

- Helpful advice for using a slow cooker
- Transforming recipes for slow cooking
- Slow baking in your slow cooker
- Vegan substitution suggestions

At first glance, it may seem quite simple to use a slow cooker. All you have to do is fill it up, plug it in, and turn the knob, right? Basically, yes, but you need to take a few other things into consideration, especially if you want to slow cook something suitable for serving to company, like a bread or cake.

In this chapter, I share all the secrets for perfect slow cooker cooking, every time.

Tips for Successful Vegan Slow Cooking

Let's go over a few pointers I've learned to help you avoid any pitfalls and have greater success with your vegan slow cooking:

For easier cleanup (and as suggested in many recipes), lightly oil the ceramic crock insert with your favorite oil or vegetable cooking spray before filling it with ingredients.

Unless a recipe states otherwise, cut all vegetables into small, bite-size pieces. This helps ensure the ingredients will cook evenly.

When loading your slow cooker, it's best to layer vegetables in order according to which are most dense and take longer to cook, like potatoes and sweet potatoes, roots, and winter squashes, by placing them at the bottom of the ceramic crock insert.

If you've got the time, it's worth the extra effort to sauté aromatic vegetables like shallots, onions, carrots, garlic, and bell peppers before adding them to the slow cooker. This will tremendously boost the flavor of your finished dish.

In most instances, you should thaw frozen vegetables overnight in the refrigerator, or in a colander under running water, before adding them to the slow cooker. Otherwise, including those frozen ingredients could slow down the cooking process. However, if you'd like to add a vibrant pop of color to a nearly finished grain dish or stew, you could throw in some frozen peas or corn during the last 30 minutes of cooking time.

For optimal cooking, fill the ceramic crock insert between ½ and ¾ full, but no more than 1 inch below the outer rim, especially if cooking on high. Otherwise … oops! The rapidly simmering contents could easily spill out onto your countertop or worse yet, burn you when you lift the lid.

You can preheat an empty ceramic crock insert for recipes that use the slow cooker like an oven (when slow baking), and many recipes recommend doing so while you're prepping your ingredients. Preheating ensures that the slow cooker is at the optimal temperature for slow baking, which not only reduces the cooking time, but also helps you get the most out of your leavening agents when making baked goods.

COOKER CAVEAT

Many people like to prep their ingredients the night before and chill the loaded-up ceramic crock insert in the fridge. If you do this, do not place the ceramic crock insert into a preheated slow cooker because the sudden change of temperature could cause the insert to crack. Instead, place it in a cold slow cooker and only then turn it on so they'll slowly warm up together.

Tender vegetables like spinach, pastas, and many grains can easily be overcooked, so it's best to add them during the last 30 to 60 minutes of cooking time.

Dried herbs and spices are perfectly fine simmering for long hours at a time, but add fresh herbs at the very end. The essential oils will be immediately released and will "wake up" the flavor of the finished dish.

Don't be tempted to peek under the lid during the beginning stages of cooking. By doing so, you'll release the built-up heat and steam, which will drop the internal temperature of the slow cooker. Each time you sneak a peek, you might be adding an extra 20 minutes or more to your cooking time.

If too much liquid remains in the slow cooker at the end of the cooking time, but the food is to your desired doneness, remove the lid, crank up the temperature to high, and in less than 30 minutes, the liquid should have evaporated.

As a general rule, if you're short on time, you can cook many dishes that typically would be cooked on low on high instead, for half the time, especially those with lots of liquid ingredients. If you're not in a hurry, opt for low. Slower cooking often brings out more of the distinct flavors from your ingredients.

For safety, the cord on a slow cooker is rather short, but you can use it with a heavy-duty extension cord that has a clearly marked electrical rating appropriate for your slow cooker.

Beware that during use, the lid and handles of the ceramic crock insert do get rather hot. To avoid injury, always use potholders when handling them.

When your dish has finished cooking to your desired preference, remember to turn off the slow cooker and unplug it. The ceramic crock insert will retain heat, and with the lid on, your food will stay hot for about 2 hours.

Slow Cooking at Higher Altitudes

If you live in the mountains or at altitudes over 3,000 feet above sea level, you probably already know the higher altitude can make cooking and baking challenging. Slow cooking is no exception to this rule.

At higher altitudes, the air is less compressed, so liquids boil at lower temperatures and foods take much longer to cook. This is why it's best to prepare nearly all recipes on high, even if a recipe recommends low, and save low for keeping foods warm. On average, most foods will take up to 25 percent longer to cook at higher altitudes. If you cut your vegetables and fruits into smaller pieces than a recipe suggests, they'll cook more quickly.

LOW AND SLOW

When cooking at higher altitudes, you may want to cut back on the liquid ingredients to compensate for the lower and slower cooking temperature. Start by decreasing your liquid amount by 2 tablespoons for every 1 cup liquid called for. If you live at a very high altitude (over 7,000 feet), decrease by 4 tablespoons.

Converting Standard Recipes to Slow Cooker Recipes

Once you start using your slow cooker on a regular basis, you'll be amazed at all the things it can do. Eventually, you might want to start experimenting more and more to see what this baby can really do.

One of the first places to start is converting some of your favorite stovetop or oven-baked recipes to slow cooker recipes. The change isn't difficult, but let's discuss a few things to keep in mind when converting your favorite recipes for preparation in your slow cooker.

Make a Similar Selection

Some dishes are better suited to being made the slow cooker way than others. First, consider trying out recipes that are typically simmered in a liquid, like chili, soup, stew, and bean and vegetable side dishes.

To make things easier on yourself when converting these types of recipes to slow cooking mode, look for a similar recipe in this book and use it as a guide for how to cut and layer your ingredients, the amount of liquid you'll need, and suggestions for an approximate cooking time and temperature.

Adjust Your Liquids

When using a slow cooker, rather than cooking in a large pot on your stove, you'll notice that liquid doesn't boil away or evaporate out in the same way. This is mainly due to the fact that the water vapor accumulates and condenses on the slow cooker's lid and falls back down into the pot instead of being dispersed into the air.

The first time you try making a converted recipe, drastically cut back on your liquid ingredients to avoid overly watery dishes. You can start by using only half the amount. If your soup or bean dish comes out too thick for your liking, you can always thin it out a bit near the end of the cooking time by adding some additional water or vegetable broth as desired.

Season with Care

When you're preparing a dish that will be slow cooking for a long time, it's best to use dried herbs rather than fresh. However, the long, slow cooking process can concentrate the flavor of your dried herbs and spices, and as a result, they may become bitter or overpowering in the final dish. You may want to start by adding only half the amount you would normally use, or add them during the last hour of cook time. And again, to fully appreciate the flavor of your fresh herbs, add them only at the end.

LOW AND SLOW

When it comes to seasonings, you can always add, but you can't take away. Adding too much of some seasonings, especially salt, can ruin the flavor of your food and may even make it unpalatable. So in the initial stages of cooking, it's better to err on the lighter side with your seasonings. When your dish is done, give it a taste. If you think it's a little bland, you can always add more seasonings.

Unless you're cooking dried beans (see Chapter 15), you can add salt and black pepper at the beginning of the cooking time. But again, you might want to go a little light on these and add more later.

And lastly, as any good chef will attest, you should always taste your food before you serve it, which is why in many recipes you'll see the recommendation to taste and adjust the seasonings as desired. We all appreciate flavors differently based on our own individual taste buds and preferences, and you'll enjoy your meal more when it's seasoned to perfection and just the way you like it!

Suggestions for Slow Baking

Yes, that's right! You can use your slow cooker for baking—or as I like to call it, slow baking. The inside of your slow cooker virtually becomes a mini-oven that can be used for baking some of your favorite breads, cakes, desserts, and other sweet treats.

However, there is a limit to what you can successfully slow bake, and you should know that slow-baked items don't always brown as nicely on top as they do on the bottom and sides. So forget about trying to slow bake a pie or quiche with a bottom pastry-style crust.

But you can make an upside-down version with a biscuit-style crust on top, like the Mixed Berry Cobbler in Chapter 18, or the Crustless Tofu-Vegetable Quiche in Chapter 4. Throughout this book, you'll find a wide assortment of recipes that have been revamped for slow baking.

Preheat Pointers

When you bake in your oven, nearly all recipes call for preheating the oven to get it up to the proper temperature before you set your baking pan or casserole dish inside.

Preheating is also important when slow baking. While you prep your ingredients (at least 10 minutes), preheat your slow cooker to get it nice and hot before you add your foods to be slow baked. A hot slow cooker starts to work slow baking your item immediately, which is very important for recipes that rely on chemical leaveners like baking powder or soda to give them lift and height in the final product.

Opt for a Pan

In some slow-baked recipes, like the Pull-Apart Whole-Wheat Rolls in Chapter 17 and the fruit-based desserts in Chapter 18, you will slow bake your mixture directly in the ceramic crock insert. Using this direct approach, or slow baking directly inside the confines of the slow cooker, can have mixed results and may even lead to baked goods that are overcooked and undercooked at the same time. To rectify this situation, you may want to do some experimenting to better determine what you can and cannot successfully slow bake inside the ceramic crock insert of your particular slow cooker.

In fact, with a majority of my slow-baked goods, I have better results when I use a pan inside my slow cooker. Fortunately, many of my smaller, ovenproof baking pans and casserole dishes fit rather well inside my large oval slow cooker. If you only have a medium cooker, you'll probably need to use a smaller pan than suggested. You might have to cut the recipe ingredients in half, too.

COOKER CAVEAT

Before attempting any of the recipes that call for slow baking with the use of a pan, first do a bit of investigative work to avoid running into problems later. Place your baking pan or casserole dish inside the ceramic crock insert to be sure it actually fits, and check to be sure the lid won't come into direct contact with the panned product.

The Props: Trivets and Foil Rings

When using a pan or dish, you need to somehow prop up the pan to keep it off the bottom of the crock insert and away from the sides. This ensures that the heat circulates evenly around the pan or dish. Plus, direct contact between the two can lead to overbrowning on the bottom and sides of your slow-baked items.

To help prop up your pan, I offer two options: use a stainless-steel or cast-iron trivet, or use a homemade aluminum foil ring.

You can make the latter quickly and easily by crumpling up an 8-inch-long piece of foil into a log, bend it into a ring, and flatten the ring slightly so your pan sits flatly on top of it. You don't need to discard your foil ring after you use it. Because it doesn't come into direct contact with your food, it can be reused continuously. If you do get some dripped cake batter or other such food mess on it, clean it or recycle it.

Vent and Tent

As you know, your slow cooker gets quite steamy inside, which can be advantageous when you're making soups and stews or trying to give some rise to a yeast-based bread. However, too much contained steam can cause condensation to collect and eventually drip off the slow cooker's lid, which can damage your slow-baked quick breads, cakes, and other sweet treats.

To help this steam or accumulating condensation slowly escape, you can vent or tent. You can either slightly vent the slow cooker lid by using a toothpick, chopstick, or handle of a wooden spoon to slightly prop it up, or you can make a tentlike covering with a clean kitchen towel placed just under the lid to help capture the accumulating condensation and prevent it from falling back down on the top of your item.

Vegan Substitutions and Staples

Now that you know the basic ins and outs of using a slow cooker, there's just one last subject to cover before we delve into the recipe chapters.

Let's take a brief overview of the various vegan, plant-based ingredients you can use in your meal preparations. If you're a long-time vegan, you're probably already aware of many of the animal-free alternatives available to replace meats, chicken, fish, eggs, and dairy products. But if you're a new vegan, or just veg-curious and trying to incorporate more plant-based meals into your diet, the vegan staples and substitution suggestions in this section should prove very enlightening.

For a more in-depth discussion about vegan substitutions, check out my other books, *The Complete Idiot's Guide to Vegan Living*, now in its second edition, and *The Complete Idiot's Guide to Vegan Cooking*.

Meatless Alternatives

Many plant-based ingredients—nuts and seeds, legumes (beans, peas, and lentils), mushrooms, tofu, tempeh, and seitan—can help you deliciously fulfill your body's protein needs and be used to replace meat, fish, and fowl in your vegan recipes. These tasty ingredients can be used to add a lot of flavor, chewiness or texture, and even bulk, to your soups, chilies, stews, and main and side dishes.

> **SLOW INTERESTING**
>
> As a vegan, you don't really need to get hung up on where to get protein. You can easily meet and even exceed your protein needs simply by eating a variety of plant-based foods, including plenty of legumes and soy-based products, whole grains, nuts and seeds, and fiber-rich leafy and dark green vegetables. As an added benefit, plant-based proteins are cholesterol free!

If you have limited experience with using these ingredients, have no fear, the Vegan Chef is here! In the upcoming recipe chapters, I show you how easy it is to replace or mimic meats, as well as other similar animal-based proteins. You can also combine many of these plant-based proteins with other vegan staples to create some fantastic homemade breakfast items (like Chapter 4's Easy Cheesy Tofu Scramble or Florentine Frittata), light lunches, super sandwiches (like Chapter 11's Lentil Sloppy Joes or Portobello Mushroom Fajitas), and even hearty and filling main dishes (like Chapter 12's Sweet-and-Sour Tempeh, or Chapter 13's Veggie Lasagna or Stuffed Seitan Roast).

Nondairy Necessities

As they say, "practice makes perfect," and the more you experiment with nondairy alternatives, the sooner you'll discover that going dairy free isn't as difficult or daunting a task as one might think. In the last decade, a plethora of nondairy vegan products has flooded the market, and now you can find them alongside their animal-based counterparts in stores from coast to coast.

Here are just a few of the wonderful nondairy products you can find: plant-based milks (like soy, coconut, rice, hemp, sunflower, oat, multi-grain, almond, hazelnut, and other nuts); soy and coconut-based liquid creamers; vegan yogurts, kefir, and sour cream; vegan cheeses and cream cheese; nondairy ice creams; and even fluffy vegan whipped toppings.

Vegan nondairy milks and creamers come in a wide variety of flavors, and having so many options can be good when making desserts, breads, and sweet treats. But when you're making a savory dish, you should use a plain or unsweetened product, so be sure to check the ingredients list to avoid unwanted flavorings like vanilla, sugar and other sweeteners, or other similar add-ins that might affect the flavor of your finished dish.

Eggless Alternatives

When it comes to cooking and baking, eggs are typically used as a binder, thickener, or leavening agent or simply to add some moisture to a recipe. Vegans have several options for replacing eggs, and which one you choose to go with often depends on the results you're trying to achieve.

Here are some simple suggestions for replacing 1 egg in your veganized recipes:

- ¼ cup vegan yogurt or puréed silken, firm, or extra-firm tofu

- ¼ cup applesauce, mashed or puréed bananas, pumpkin or winter squash purée, or other fruit or vegetable purées, with ½ teaspoon aluminum-free baking powder added

- 2 tablespoons tahini, peanut butter, or other nut or seed butter

- 2 tablespoons arrowroot, cornstarch, tapioca starch, or flour mixed with 2 tablespoons water or other liquid

- 1 tablespoon ground flaxseeds (or flaxseed meal) blended or whisked together with 3 tablespoons water; let sit for 5 minutes before using

- 1 tablespoon *Ener-G Egg Replacer* (double the package recommendations) whisked together with 2 tablespoons water until very frothy (like beaten egg whites)

DEFINITION

Ener-G Egg Replacer is a commercial egg replacer product made of potato starch, tapioca starch, and leavening agents. It can be used as a substitute for eggs in your baked goods and other sweet and savory dishes. Look for it prepackaged and in bulk bins in most grocery and natural foods stores.

For binding or thickening baked goods or savory dishes, try vegan yogurt or puréed tofu, a fruit or vegetable purée, nut or seed butter, or the starch/flour and water or flaxseed and water combos. With the exception of the flaxseeds and starch/flour and water combos, these suggestions also help add moisture to your recipe.

To boost the leavening (or rise) in your baked good recipes when using one of these suggestions, you might need to add an additional ½ teaspoon baking powder or other leavening agent. You'll find more specific examples of how to use these eggless alternatives in the recipes throughout this book.

Stock-Up Staples

If you want to make delicious, healthy meals for you and your family and friends, you need to set yourself up for success by keeping your pantry, fridge, and freezer stocked with your favorite ingredients and the ones you use most often.

At the farmers' market or corner store, grab plenty of fresh fruits, veggies, garlic, ginger, and herbs (and also frozen favorites, too!), whole grains, breads and pastas, dried and canned legumes, canned tomatoes and other canned goods, as well as your most commonly used oils, vinegars, and other condiments and flavoring agents.

Also, stock up on fruit juices, plant-based milks, dairy-free cheeses and cream cheese, vegan yogurt and sour cream, and other such products, along with some packages of tofu and tempeh.

Don't forget to fill up on the dried herbs and spices, dried fruits, nuts and seeds, assorted granular and liquid sweeteners, and flours and starches you use most often.

All these vegan plant-based ingredients—plus a whole lot more—are readily available in most grocery and natural foods stores. Keeping these and other staple ingredients on hand guarantees you'll be eating more wholesome, homemade meals, breads, and sweet treats.

You'll find additional ingredient and product information, as well as helpful hints to help you get the most out of your slow cooker, throughout the recipe chapters. Are you ready? Roll up your sleeves, and let's begin your vegan slow cooking adventure!

The Least You Need to Know

- Armed with a few tips for achieving the most success with your vegan slow cooking, you'll get off to a delicious start with your new best friend in the kitchen.

- When converting your favorite recipes for the slow cooker, use a similar recipe as a guide, adjust your liquid amounts accordingly, and go easy on the seasonings.

- Your slow cooker can be used like a mini-oven for slow baking your favorite baked goods.

- For easier meal preparations, keep your pantry, fridge, and freezer well stocked with your favorite vegan ingredients.

Breakfasts Worth Waking Up For

Breakfast is the most important meal of the day, and a good one can help get your day off to a good start. Even if you prefer to sleep in and skip breakfast or you "don't have time" to eat breakfast, you'll find the concept of having a hot breakfast like those in Part 2 waiting for you hard to resist. Those who like a bowl of fruit-topped steel-cut oats or creamy grits will love the hot breakfast cereal in Chapter 3, especially when you learn that you can make a batch without having to constantly stir it—and in fact, you don't even need to be awake while it cooks!

In Chapter 4, things move past the bowl and onto the plate. These home-style breakfasts and brunches assemble quickly and cook in less time than the overnight oats. So you may want to make many of the recipes, such as the Breakfast Hash Brown Casserole, Morning Migas, and California Vegetable and Cheese Strata, as a late-morning weekend breakfast or for brunch. Several of them make use of companion recipes that appear in other chapters of the book and are meant to inspire you to find ways to reinvent your slow cooker recipe leftovers into something new and equally delicious. No matter which recipe you choose, you're sure to agree that because it's hot, fresh, and homemade, it's definitely a breakfast worth getting up for!

Breakfast by the Bowlful

In This Chapter

- Hot cereal selections
- Southern staples
- Overnight oats
- Stick-to-your-rib grits

Generations of mothers have spent long (and often hot!) hours over the stove, stirring pots filled with simmering porridges. Perhaps this explains why one of the most popular uses for slow cookers today is making creamy oatmeal and other hot breakfast cereals. The slow and steady moist heat a slow cooker produces is ideal for cooking whole grains and their milled, morning meal minions.

Grains provide beneficial dietary fiber, and what better way to add more to your diet than by eating a bowlful for breakfast? Invest a few minutes loading your slow cooker before going to bed, turn it on low, and let it do its thing overnight. In the morning, you'll awaken to a nutritious, hot breakfast. You can store any extra servings of hot breakfast cereals in an airtight container in the refrigerator or freezer.

In this chapter, I share recipes for breakfasts using good-for-you grains, from amaranth to oats. Be sure to check out other tasty whole-grain, rolled flake options, too, such as barley, brown rice, kamut, quinoa, rye, spelt, triticale, and wheat. Experiment by swapping them for rolled oats in these or your other favorite recipes.

Autumn Amaranth Porridge

Apples, raisins, cinnamon, and freshly toasted pecans are the perfect accompaniments to the nutty flavor of *amaranth* in this hearty porridge.

Yield:	Prep time:	Cook time:	Serving size:
6 cups	5 to 7 minutes	6 or 7 hours or overnight	1 cup

2 large Gala or other apples, cored and diced

1½ cups amaranth

¾ cup raisins or dried cranberries

1½ tsp. ground cinnamon

6 cups apple juice or water (or 3 cups each)

¾ cup toasted pecans, roughly chopped

Soy or other nondairy milk (optional)

Maple syrup or sorghum syrup (optional)

1. In a medium slow cooker, combine Gala apples, amaranth, raisins, and cinnamon, and stir well to coat. Pour in apple juice.

2. Cover and cook on low for 6 or 7 hours or overnight.

3. Serve hot, garnishing individual servings with 1½ tablespoons toasted pecans, plus ¼ or ⅓ cup soy milk (if using) or 1 or 2 teaspoons maple syrup (if using).

Variation: Other fresh or frozen pears, peaches, or berries, or dried chopped dates, dried cherries, or dried cranberries work well in place of the apples and raisins. To make **Mapley Millet Mush,** replace the amaranth with 1½ cups millet, and instead of 6 cups apple juice, cook the millet in a combination of 4 cups water, 2 cups soy milk or other nondairy milk, and ½ cup maple syrup or maple sugar.

DEFINITION

Amaranth is a member of the pigweed family and has been cultivated and consumed for centuries by the indigenous people of Asia, Africa, and North and Central America. The plant's tiny seeds are most widely used. Amaranth is an excellent source of plant-based protein and can be cooked in liquid much like quinoa, or ground into flour for use in making pancakes, pasta, breads, and other baked goods.

Breakfast Couscous with Yogurt, Apricots, Dates, and Pistachios

You'll be pleasantly surprised by how well the flavors of the hot, cardamom and citrus-scented couscous plays off the creamy richness of coconut yogurt, chewy dried fruit, and crunchy nuts.

Yield:	Prep time:	Cook time:	Serving size:
6 or 7 cups	7 to 10 minutes	6 or 7 hours or overnight	1¼ cups

1 cup regular or whole-wheat couscous

6 TB. date sugar or light brown sugar, packed

1 TB. orange zest (optional)

¾ tsp. ground cardamom

1½ cups water

1½ cups fresh orange juice

1½ cups coconut or other vegan yogurt

6 TB. date pieces coated with oat flour or pitted dates, cut into ½-in.-long strips

6 TB. dried apricots (about 6), cut into ½-in.-long strips

6 TB. raw or toasted pistachios, roughly chopped

1. In a medium slow cooker, combine couscous, date sugar, orange zest (if using), and cardamom, and stir well to coat. Pour in water and orange juice.

2. Cover and cook on low for 6 or 7 hours or overnight.

3. Serve hot, garnishing individual servings with ¼ cup coconut yogurt, 1 tablespoon dates, 1 tablespoon apricots, and 1 tablespoon pistachios.

Variation: For a gluten-free version, replace the couscous with an equal amount of quinoa or millet.

LOW AND SLOW

I highly recommend using freshly ground cardamom whenever possible. It's quite easy to grind your own, and the payoff is an almost intoxicating, perfumelike aroma and flavor. To remove the tiny seeds from the green cardamom pods, place them in a mortar and pestle, and pound them until each is slightly cracked open. Or place the cardamom pods on a cutting board, and, using a rocking motion, firmly press down on them using the bottom of a saucepan to crack open the cardamom pods. Pulverize the seeds to a fine powder using the mortar and pestle or a spice grinder.

Creamy Corn Grits

For those living south of the Mason-Dixon Line, breakfast just isn't breakfast without a helping of grits. This version is creamy, buttery, and cooked to perfection, thanks to the slow cooker.

Yield:	Prep time:	Cook time:	Serving size:
6 cups	5 minutes	6 or 7 hours or overnight	1 cup

1½ cups stone-ground or coarse *corn grits*

1 tsp. sea salt

5 cups water

1 cup plain soy creamer, soy milk, or other nondairy milk, plus more for garnish

3 TB. nonhydrogenated margarine, plus more for garnish

Maple syrup or sorghum syrup (optional)

1. Lightly coat a medium slow cooker's ceramic crock insert with vegetable cooking spray or oil of choice.

2. In the slow cooker, combine stone-ground corn grits and sea salt. Pour in water, and stir well to combine.

3. Cover and cook on low for 6 or 7 hours or overnight.

4. Before serving, stir in soy creamer and nonhydrogenated margarine. Serve hot, garnishing individual servings with 2 or 3 tablespoons soy creamer, 1 or 2 teaspoons nonhydrogenated margarine, and 1 or 2 teaspoons maple syrup (if using).

Variations: For **Southern-Style Grits,** replace the stone-ground corn grits with 1½ cups *hominy grits.* For **Cheezy Corn Grits,** stir 1 cup shredded vegan cheddar or Monterey Jack cheese into the full batch of grits, and top individual servings with 1 or 2 tablespoons shredded cheese as desired.

DEFINITION

Corn grits are basically coarsely ground cornmeal. Cooking in liquid transforms the corn grits into a porridgelike hot cereal. They're also used to make Italian polenta. **Hominy grits** are made from coarsely ground dried hominy. Hominy is dried white or yellow corn that's been soaked in an alkali solution, like baking soda or lye, which causes the corn kernels to soften and swell to nearly double their size. The hull and germ are then removed, and the hominy is dried again before being ground into hominy grits.

Jalapeño and Green Chile Grits

Take the flavor of your grits from mild to wild by adding vegan pepper Jack cheese, spicy jalapeño peppers, green chiles, and chipotle chile powder.

Yield:	Prep time:	Cook time:	Serving size:
6 cups	5 minutes	6 or 7 hours or overnight	1 cup

1½ cups stone-ground or coarse corn grits

½ cup green onions, white and green parts, thinly sliced

2 medium jalapeño peppers, ribs and seeds removed, and finely diced

1 (4-oz.) can diced mild green chiles, with liquid

1 tsp. sea salt

½ tsp. chipotle chile powder

½ tsp. freshly ground black pepper

5 cups water

1 cup shredded vegan pepper Jack or cheddar cheese, plus more for garnish

2 TB. nonhydrogenated margarine

1 TB. nutritional yeast flakes

Hot pepper sauce (optional)

1. Lightly coat a medium slow cooker's ceramic crock insert with vegetable cooking spray or oil of choice.

2. In the slow cooker, combine stone-ground corn grits, green onions, jalapeño peppers, mild green chiles, sea salt, chipotle chile powder, and black pepper. Pour in water, and stir well to combine.

3. Cover and cook on low for 6 or 7 hours or overnight.

4. Stir in pepper Jack cheese, nonhydrogenated margarine, and nutritional yeast flakes.

5. Serve hot, garnishing individual servings with 1 or 2 tablespoons pepper Jack cheese and a few drops hot pepper sauce (if using).

Variation: For **Spicy Sausage Grits,** add 2 Seitan Chorizo Sausages (recipe in Chapter 11), thinly sliced, to the cooking grits mixture.

COOKER CAVEAT

Be very careful and try to avoid touching or rubbing your eyes when working with chiles and other hot peppers. The volatile oils from the seeds and inner ribs can cause your eyes to burn and water. For added protection, you may want to wear a pair of vinyl food handler's gloves.

By-the-Numbers Banana-Coconut Hot Cereal

Whether you opt for a 5-, 7-, or 9-grain (or more) hot cereal blend is entirely up to you, but whichever you choose will taste fantastic when it's cooked with creamy coconut milk and banana slices and lightly dusted with toasted, shredded coconut.

Yield:	Prep time:	Cook time:	Serving size:
6 cups	5 to 7 minutes	6 to 7 hours or overnight	1 cup

3 cups dry 5-grain hot cereal blend (or other multigrain blend)

2 large bananas, peeled and thinly sliced

½ cup agave nectar or maple syrup

½ TB. vanilla extract

½ tsp. sea salt

6 cups water

3 cups plain or vanilla coconut milk beverage or other nondairy milk

9 TB. unsweetened shredded coconut, toasted

1. In a medium slow cooker, combine 5-grain hot cereal blend, bananas, agave nectar, vanilla extract, and sea salt. Pour in water and coconut milk beverage.

2. Cover and cook on low for 6 or 7 hours or overnight.

3. Serve hot, garnishing individual servings with 1½ tablespoons toasted shredded coconut.

Variation: For **Berry-Banana Hot Cereal,** use only 1 banana and add 2 cups fresh or frozen strawberries, sliced (or fresh or frozen blueberries, raspberries, and/or blackberries).

LOW AND SLOW

Most grocery stores carry packaged multigrain hot cereal blends, but I find the best bargains in the bulk department. For easy preparation, I make a note on the twist-tie tag (or brown bag) that includes the suggested cereal-to-liquid ratio and the cooking instructions. These usually appear on the bulk bin's product description label.

Creamy Old-Fashioned Cinnamon-Sugar Oatmeal

Brown sugar and cinnamon are the perfect combination for transforming ordinary rolled oats into this lightly sweetened and spiced oatmeal.

Yield:	Prep time:	Cook time:	Serving size:
6 cups	5 minutes	6 or 7 hours or overnight	1 cup

3 cups old-fashioned or regular rolled oats

¾ cup light brown or muscovado sugar, packed

2 tsp. ground cinnamon

½ TB. vanilla extract

½ tsp. sea salt

3½ cups water

3 cups plain or vanilla soy or other nondairy milk

1. In a medium slow cooker, combine old-fashioned rolled oats, light brown sugar, cinnamon, vanilla extract, and sea salt, and stir well to coat. Pour in water and soy milk.

2. Cover and cook on low for 6 or 7 hours or overnight.

3. Serve hot as is, or top with some dried fruit or chopped or sliced fresh or frozen fruit or berries (thawed).

Variation: Don't try to use quick-cooking rolled oats or instant oatmeal in this recipe. They won't hold up well to the long hours of slow cooking. You can replace the brown sugar with ¾ cup maple syrup. If you like your oatmeal really thick, add only 3 cups water. Feel free to top individual servings of oatmeal with chopped fruit, fresh or frozen berries, dried fruit, or chopped nuts and seeds as desired. For **Multigrain Porridge,** replace the rolled oats with 1½ cups barley flakes and 1½ cups wheat flakes. Or use a combination of other varieties of whole-grain rolled flakes, such as kamut, quinoa, spelt, or triticale, and add additional brown sugar as desired.

SLOW INTERESTING

Old-fashioned or *regular rolled oats* are oat groats that have been steamed and then rolled between rollers (or flattened) into flakes. *Steel-cut oats* are oat groats that have been coarsely cut into several pieces using steel blades, resulting in a chewy and slightly nutty texture. *Quick-cooking rolled oats* are steel-cut oats that have been steamed and then rolled and flattened into flakes. *Instant oatmeal* is precooked, dried, and rolled to make very thin, fine flakes. Some brands also add sugar, salt, and other ingredients to the finished product.

Trail Mix–Topped Steel-Cut Oats

Many (this Irish gal included) consider steel-cut oats the best oat variety for making oatmeal, and my favorite way to eat them is topped with some trail mix for a little added crunch.

Yield:	Prep time:	Cook time:	Serving size:
6 cups	5 minutes	7 or 8 hours or overnight	1 cup

1½ cups steel-cut oats

⅔ cup light brown sugar, packed, or ⅓ cup maple syrup

½ TB. vanilla extract

¾ tsp. sea salt

6 cups water

1½ cups trail mix (choose one with an assortment of dried fruit, nuts, and seeds)

6 TB. ground flaxseeds or flaxseed meal

3 TB. hemp seeds

1. In a medium slow cooker, combine steel-cut oats, light brown sugar, vanilla extract, and sea salt, and stir well to coat. Pour in water.

2. Cover and cook on low for 7 or 8 hours or overnight.

3. Serve hot, garnishing individual servings with ¼ cup trail mix, 1 tablespoon ground flaxseeds, and ½ tablespoon hemp seeds.

Variation: For a creamier version, replace 3 cups water with 3 cups vanilla almond or other nondairy milk. You can also replace the trail mix topping with your favorite dried fruit, such as raisins, dried blueberries or cranberries, goji berries, or chopped dates.

SLOW INTERESTING

Steel-cut oats (also called Irish oats or oatmeal) are notorious for taking a long time to cook on the stove, but the slow cooker makes this job simple if you let it work overnight.

Pumpkin Patch Steel-Cut Oats

Capture all the colors and flavors associated with autumn with a bowl of these steel-cut oats, which owe their golden color and slight sweetness to a blend of pumpkin pie fixins, maple syrup, and a delightful raisin, cranberry, and pecan topping.

Yield:	Prep time:	Cook time:	Serving size:
6 cups	5 to 7 minutes	7 or 8 hours or overnight	1 cup

3 cups water

2 cups vanilla almond or other nondairy milk

1 (15-oz.) can pumpkin purée

1½ cups steel-cut oats

½ cup maple syrup, plus more for garnish

2 tsp. pumpkin pie spice

½ TB. vanilla extract

½ tsp. sea salt

9 TB. raisins

9 TB. dried cranberries

9 TB. raw or toasted pumpkin seeds or toasted pecans, roughly chopped

1. In a medium slow cooker, whisk together water, vanilla almond milk, and pumpkin purée. Add steel-cut oats, maple syrup, pumpkin pie spice, vanilla extract, and sea salt, and stir well to combine.

2. Cover and cook on low for 7 or 8 hours or overnight.

3. Serve hot, garnishing individual servings with 1½ tablespoons raisins, 1½ tablespoons dried cranberries, and 1½ tablespoons pumpkin seeds and drizzling 1 tablespoon maple syrup over all.

Variation: Instead of canned pumpkin purée, you can use 2 cups Pumpkin Purée (variation in Chapter 7). Easily change the flavor of these steel-cut oats by replacing the Pumpkin Purée with Sweet Potato Purée (variation in Chapter 7) or Wonderful Winter Squash Purée (recipe in Chapter 7). If you don't have pumpkin pie spice, replace it with 1 teaspoon ground cinnamon, ½ teaspoon ground ginger, ¼ teaspoon freshly grated nutmeg, and ¼ teaspoon ground cloves.

SLOW INTERESTING

By nature, oats are gluten free, but often they're processed and packaged on equipment that has also been used for wheat, barley, and other gluten-containing grains. Fortunately for celiac sufferers, you can find certified 100 percent gluten-free oats in most grocery and natural foods stores.

Hearty Breakfast Fare

In This Chapter

- Tasty hash brown casserole
- Sausage gravy–covered biscuits
- Scrambled and cubed tofu options
- Eggless quiche, frittata, and strata

When you're in the mood for a heartier breakfast, this is the chapter for you. Luckily, they're also pretty quick to prepare—many take only 2 to 4 hours to slow cook. Prep and get these recipes slow cooking away in the morning, and by brunch, they'll be ready to enjoy.

Also in this chapter are recipes that use a slow cooker as a mini-oven. For optimal results with the quiche and frittata recipes, bake them in an 8-inch cake pan or a 6-cup or larger casserole dish (whichever fits your slow cooker), and use a large, oval slow cooker. If you only have a medium slow cooker, you'll probably need to use a smaller pan, and to avoid any overflowing or spillage problems, reduce the ingredient amounts by $1/3$ or $1/2$, depending on the size of your baking pan.

Tofu plays a key role in many of these recipes. This protein-rich powerhouse is scrambled, cubed, and blended to create some truly rave-worthy breakfasts to get your and your family's mornings started off right!

Breakfast Hash Brown Casserole

Frozen shredded hash brown potatoes never had it so good. This creamy casserole of shredded potatoes and aromatic vegetables is as flavorful as it is filling and will have your family clamoring for seconds.

Yield:	Prep time:	Cook time:	Serving size:
6 cups	7 to 10 minutes	2½ to 3 hours	1 cup

1 (12-oz.) pkg. firm or extra-firm *silken tofu*

⅔ cup soy or other nondairy milk

⅔ cup water

3 TB. nutritional yeast flakes

3 TB. cornstarch or tapioca starch

1½ tsp. dried thyme

1 tsp. garlic powder or garlic granules

1 tsp. onion powder

1 tsp. seasoning salt (such as Herbamare)

½ tsp. freshly ground black pepper

1 (16-oz.) pkg. frozen hash brown potatoes

⅔ cup red onion, diced

⅔ cup green bell pepper, ribs and seeds removed, and diced

½ cup green onions, white and green parts, thinly sliced

⅓ cup chopped fresh parsley

Smoked or sweet paprika

1. Lightly coat a medium slow cooker's ceramic crock insert with vegetable cooking spray or oil of choice.

2. In a food processor fitted with an S blade, process silken tofu, soy milk, water, nutritional yeast flakes, cornstarch, thyme, garlic powder, onion powder, seasoning salt, and black pepper for 1 minute. Scrape down the sides of the container with a spatula, and process for 1 more minute or until very creamy.

3. In the slow cooker, combine hash brown potatoes, red onion, green bell pepper, green onions, and parsley. Add tofu mixture, and stir well to combine. Sprinkle a little smoked paprika over top for added color.

4. Cover and cook, stirring occasionally, on high for 2½ to 3 hours, on low for 5 or 6 hours, or until hot and lightly browned around the edges. Taste and adjust seasonings as desired, and serve hot.

Variation: You can also prepare this recipe using 4 cups shredded raw potatoes, packed, instead of the frozen hash browns. For **Cheesy Hash Brown Breakfast Casserole,** add 1½ cups shredded vegan Monterey Jack, pepper Jack, or cheddar cheese.

> **DEFINITION**
>
> **Silken tofu** is made from soybeans and has a creamy and velvety-smooth texture. The process for making silken tofu differs slightly from regular tofu in that the soy milk curds and excess water are not separated during production. Depending on the silken tofu's final texture, it's labeled soft, firm, or extra firm. Silken tofu is often blended for making sauces, salad dressings, beverages, desserts, and baked goods.

Biscuits with Country Sausage Gravy

Now this is a real down-home breakfast! Biscuit wedges are topped with creamy gravy bursting with chunks of spicy vegan sausage and with a nice peppery bite.

Yield:	Prep time:	Cook time:	Serving size:
8 biscuits and 2½ cups gravy	5 minutes	1 to 1½ hours	1 biscuit wedge and ⅓ cup gravy

2 cups soy or other nondairy milk

1 tsp. onion powder

¾ tsp. sea salt

½ tsp. freshly ground black pepper

3 TB. white whole-wheat or other flour

3 TB. water

1 TB. olive or other oil

½ (14-oz.) pkg. Gimme Lean Sausage

1 batch Biscuits in the Round (recipe in Chapter 17)

1. In a small slow cooker, combine soy milk, onion powder, sea salt, and black pepper.

2. Cover and cook on high for 1 to 1½ hours, on low for 2 or 3 hours, or until hot and bubbling around edges.

3. In a small bowl, stir together whole-wheat flour and water. Add to the slow cooker, and cook for 5 to 10 more minutes or until gravy thickens.

4. Meanwhile, in a medium nonstick or cast-iron skillet over medium heat, add olive oil. Using your fingers, crumble Gimme Lean Sausage into the skillet, and cook, stirring often, for 5 to 7 minutes or until golden brown. Remove the skillet from the heat.

5. Add browned Gimme Lean Sausage to the slow cooker. Cover, and cook for an additional 5 minutes. Taste and adjust seasonings as desired.

6. Split Biscuits in the Round into wedges, top with sausage gravy, and serve.

Variation: You can also serve the sausage gravy over Marvelous Mashed Potatoes (recipe in Chapter 14).

 LOW AND SLOW

Gimme Lean Sausage, made by Lightlife Foods, comes in a 14-ounce log and can be found in the refrigerated case of most natural foods stores. It can be crumbled or formed into patties and then browned in an oiled skillet for use in recipes. Lightlife Foods also makes several other vegan meatless alternative products, like crumbles, deli- and bacon-style slices, burgers, hot dogs, and sausage links.

Easy Cheesy Tofu Scramble

Tofu scrambles are one of the most popular vegan breakfast options around, and this simple and straightforward version is flavored with bits of shredded vegan cheese.

Yield:	Prep time:	Cook time:	Serving size:
4 cups	5 minutes	2½ to 3½ hours	1 cup

2 TB. nutritional yeast flakes	1 lb. extra-firm or *super-firm tofu*
1 TB. tamari, shoyu, or Bragg Liquid Aminos	½ cup Homemade Vegetable Broth (recipe in Chapter 8)
¾ tsp. onion powder	⅔ cup shredded vegan cheddar cheese or other variety
¾ tsp. garlic powder or garlic granules	Sea salt
½ tsp. turmeric	Freshly ground black pepper

1. Lightly coat a small or medium slow cooker's ceramic crock insert with vegetable cooking spray or oil of choice.

2. In a small bowl, combine nutritional yeast flakes, tamari, onion powder, garlic powder, and turmeric.

3. Using your fingers, crumble extra-firm tofu into the slow cooker. Sprinkle nutritional yeast mixture over top, and stir well to evenly coat tofu. Pour in Homemade Vegetable Broth.

4. Cover and cook on high for 2½ to 3½ hours, on low for 5 or 6 hours, or until desired doneness and all liquid is absorbed. For a softer tofu scramble, cook it for only 2½ hours. For a firmer texture, cook for 3 to 3½ hours.

5. Uncover, add cheddar cheese, cover, and let sit for 5 minutes or until cheese has melted.

6. Taste and season with sea salt and black pepper as desired, gently stir with a fork to combine, and serve hot.

Variation: You can also add chopped veggies and fresh herbs to your tofu scramble if you like. For a **Spanish-Style Tofu Scramble,** add 1 teaspoon smoked or sweet paprika to the spice mixture, and add 1 cup finely diced red-skinned potatoes, ¹/₂ cup diced onion, and 1 Seitan Chorizo Sausage (recipe in Chapter 11), cut into quarters lengthwise, and thinly sliced.

> **DEFINITION**
>
> **Super-firm tofu** is tofu that's had most of the water pressed out of it prior to packaging, which gives the block of tofu an extremely dense texture. Super-firm tofu can be used in many dishes, especially in recipes that call for marinating, grilling, baking, or frying the tofu.

Morning Migas

Migas is a Tex-Mex dish made by scrambling eggs with strips of fried corn tortillas. This vegan version is made with salsa-infused cubes of tofu, bell peppers, and jalapeño pepper. Just before serving, add some crumbled tortilla chips and a few other tasty accoutrements.

Yield:	Prep time:	Cook time:	Serving size:
5 or 6 cups	10 to 15 minutes	3 to 3½ hours	1¼ cups

2 TB. nutritional yeast flakes

1 TB. tamari, shoyu, or Bragg Liquid Aminos

¾ tsp. onion powder

¾ tsp. garlic powder or garlic granules

¾ tsp. chili powder

¼ tsp. chipotle chile powder or cayenne

1 lb. extra-firm or super-firm tofu, cut into ½-in. cubes

1 cup yellow onion, diced

²/₃ cup green bell pepper, ribs and seeds removed, and diced

²/₃ cup red bell pepper, ribs and seeds removed, and diced

1 medium jalapeño pepper, ribs and seeds removed, and finely diced

¼ cup salsa, plus more for garnish

¼ cup water

3 cups tortilla chips

²/₃ cup shredded vegan cheddar cheese or other variety

¹/₃ cup green onions, white and green parts, thinly sliced

¹/₃ cup chopped fresh cilantro

¹/₃ cup black olives, pitted and roughly chopped

Sea salt

Freshly ground black pepper

1 large Hass avocado, peeled, pitted, and diced

1. Lightly coat a medium slow cooker's ceramic crock insert with vegetable cooking spray or oil of choice.

2. In a medium bowl, combine nutritional yeast flakes, tamari, onion powder, garlic powder, chili powder, and chipotle chile powder. Add extra-firm tofu, and stir well to coat.

3. In the slow cooker, combine coated tofu cubes, yellow onion, green bell pepper, red bell pepper, and jalapeño pepper. Add salsa and water.

4. Cover and cook on high for 3 to 3½ hours, on low for 6 or 7 hours, or until desired doneness and all liquid is absorbed.

5. Uncover and crumble tortilla chips over top. Add cheddar cheese, green onions, cilantro, and black olives, and gently stir with a fork to combine. Cover and let sit for 5 minutes.

6. Taste and season with sea salt and black pepper as desired. Serve hot, garnishing individual servings with more salsa and diced Hass avocado as desired.

Variation: For a real Tex-Mex-style meal, serve some savory beans along with your migas, like Tex-Mex Pinto Beans (recipe in Chapter 15) or Refried Pinto Bean Dip (recipe in Chapter 5).

SLOW INTERESTING

Not all packaged vegan cheeses are equal, especially when it comes to melting down to ooey gooey yumminess (some do and some don't). One of the most popular brands of meltable vegan cheese is Daiya, and not only is it made with all plant-based ingredients, but it also doesn't contain many of the common allergens like soy, dairy, gluten, eggs, peanuts, and/or tree nuts (excluding coconut).

Crustless Tofu-Vegetable Quiche

This eye-catching eggless and crustless quiche is made with blended tofu and a colorful assortment of veggies and works equally as well for brunch or paired with salad for a light supper.

Yield:	Prep time:	Cook time:	Serving size:
1 (8-inch) quiche	10 to 15 minutes	3 to 3½ hours	1 piece

1 lb. firm or extra-firm tofu

¼ cup arrowroot or cornstarch

¼ cup soy or other nondairy milk

¼ cup nutritional yeast flakes

1 TB. tamari, shoyu, or *Bragg Liquid Aminos*

½ TB. Dijon mustard

1 tsp. onion powder

1 tsp. garlic powder or garlic granules

1 tsp. dried basil

1 tsp. dried oregano

½ tsp. turmeric

½ tsp. smoked or sweet paprika

½ tsp. seasoning salt

½ tsp. freshly ground black pepper

⅓ cup chopped fresh Italian flat-leaf parsley

½ cup crimini or white button mushrooms, cut in ½ and thinly sliced

½ cup red onion, diced

½ cup zucchini, diced

1. Lightly coat an 8-inch cake pan or 6-cup or larger casserole dish (whichever fits a large, oval slow cooker) with vegetable cooking spray or oil of choice. Place a trivet or foil ring in the bottom of the ceramic crock insert. Preheat the slow cooker to high (or low for longer baking time).

2. In a food processor fitted with an S blade, process firm tofu, arrowroot, soy milk, nutritional yeast flakes, tamari, Dijon mustard, onion powder, garlic powder, basil, oregano, turmeric, smoked paprika, seasoning salt, and black pepper for 1 minute. Scrape down the sides of the container with a spatula, add Italian flat-leaf parsley, and process for 1 more minute or until very creamy.

3. Pour ½ of tofu mixture into the prepared pan or casserole dish, top with crimini mushrooms, red onion, and zucchini, followed by remaining tofu mixture. Using a spatula or spoon, gently swirl two mixtures together and smooth the top.

4. Place the pan or casserole dish on top of the trivet or foil ring. Cover and cook on high for 3 to 3½ hours, on low for 6 or 7 hours, or until filling is firm to the touch.

5. Uncover and allow quiche to cool inside the ceramic crock insert for 15 minutes before carefully removing the pan from the ceramic crock insert. Serve warm, cold, or at room temperature.

Variation: Feel free to add additional fresh herbs or chopped vegetables as you like.

DEFINITION

Bragg Liquid Aminos is made from soybeans and water, with a salty, rich flavor similar to tamari or other soy sauce. It's commonly used as a condiment and flavor enhancer, and it contains large amounts of dietary essential and nonessential amino acids.

Florentine Frittata

A frittata is the Italian version of a crustless quiche, but with a much firmer texture. This version features a delightful combination of spinach and spaghetti.

Yield:	Prep time:	Cook time:	Serving size:
1 (8-inch) frittata	10 to 15 minutes	3 to 3½ hours	1 piece

1 lb. firm or extra-firm tofu

¼ cup arrowroot or cornstarch

¼ cup soy or other nondairy milk

¼ cup nutritional yeast flakes

1 TB. tamari, shoyu, or Bragg Liquid Aminos

1 TB. minced garlic

½ TB. Dijon mustard

1 tsp. onion powder

1 tsp. garlic powder or garlic granules

1 tsp. dried oregano

1 tsp. crushed red pepper flakes

½ tsp. turmeric

½ tsp. seasoning salt

½ tsp. freshly ground black pepper

¼ cup fresh basil, cut chiffonade

¼ cup chopped fresh Italian flat-leaf parsley

2 cups spinach, stems removed, and cut chiffonade

1½ cups cooked whole-wheat spaghetti, cut into 3-in. pieces

⅓ cup green onions, white and green parts, thinly sliced

1. Lightly coat an 8-inch cake pan or 6-cup or larger casserole dish (whichever fits a large, oval slow cooker) with vegetable cooking spray or oil of choice. Place a trivet or foil ring in the bottom of the ceramic crock insert. Preheat the slow cooker to high (or low for longer baking time).

2. In a food processor fitted with an S blade, process firm tofu, arrowroot, soy milk, nutritional yeast flakes, tamari, garlic, Dijon mustard, onion powder, garlic powder, oregano, crushed red pepper flakes, turmeric, seasoning salt, and black pepper for 1 minute. Scrape down the sides of the container with a spatula. Add basil and Italian flat-leaf parsley, and process for 1 more minute or until very creamy.

3. Transfer tofu mixture to a large bowl. Add spinach, whole-wheat spaghetti, and green onions, and stir well to combine. Transfer tofu mixture to the prepared pan or casserole dish, and smooth the top.

4. Place the pan or casserole dish on top of the trivet or foil ring. Cover and cook on high for 3 to 3½ hours, on low for 6 or 7 hours, or until filling is firm to the touch.

5. Uncover and allow frittata to cool inside the slow cooker for 15 minutes before carefully removing the pan from the slow cooker. Serve warm, cold, or at room temperature.

Variation: To further accentuate the greenness of the frittata, you can prepare this recipe using spinach-flavor spaghetti.

 LOW AND SLOW

If you want to make a gluten-free frittata, simply swap the whole-wheat spaghetti for your favorite plain or flavored gluten-free spaghetti and use wheat-free tamari to season the tofu mixture.

California Vegetable and Cheese Strata

This slowly baked, casserole-like dish is a tasty mish-mash of ingredients. You'll be pleasantly surprised by how well the savory tofu-based custard mixture mingles with layers of colorful veggies and bread cubes to create this brunch dish.

Yield:	Prep time:	Cook time:	Serving size:
8 cups	10 to 15 minutes, plus overnight for air-drying bread	4 to 4½ hours	1½ cups

6 cups Hearty Herb Bread (recipe in Chapter 17) or Scarborough Fair Bread (variation in Chapter 17), cut into 1-in. cubes

1 (12-oz.) pkg. firm or extra-firm silken tofu

1½ cups soy or other nondairy milk

¼ cup nutritional yeast flakes

2 TB. cornstarch

½ TB. Dijon mustard

1 tsp. onion powder

1 tsp. garlic granules or garlic powder

1 tsp. dried basil

1 tsp. dried oregano

1 tsp. sea salt

½ tsp. freshly ground black pepper

¼ tsp. turmeric

⅓ cup chopped fresh parsley

2 TB. chopped fresh dill or 1 tsp. dried dill weed

1 (10-oz.) pkg. frozen California blend vegetables (broccoli, cauliflower, and carrots), thawed

⅔ cup red bell pepper, ribs and seeds removed, and diced

⅔ cup yellow onion, diced

⅔ cup shredded vegan cheddar cheese

1. Place Hearty Herb Bread cubes on a cookie sheet, cover with a towel, and set aside to air-dry overnight. (Alternatively, bake bread cubes in a 325°F oven for 20 to 25 minutes or until lightly toasted and dry. Remove from the oven and set aside to cool.)

2. Lightly coat a medium slow cooker's ceramic crock insert with vegetable cooking spray or oil of choice.

3. In a food processor fitted with an S blade, process firm silken tofu, soy milk, nutritional yeast flakes, cornstarch, Dijon mustard, onion powder, garlic granules, basil, oregano, sea salt, black pepper, and turmeric for 1 minute. Scrape down the sides of the container with a spatula. Add parsley and dill, and process for 1 more minute or until very creamy.

4. Place ½ of bread cubes in the bottom of the slow cooker, top with ½ of California blend vegetables, ½ of red bell pepper, ½ of yellow onion, and ½ of cheddar cheese. Repeat layers.

5. Pour blended tofu mixture over top, and press with a spatula to assure bread cubes are thoroughly moistened.

6. Cover and cook on low for 4 to 4½ hours or until all liquid is absorbed and *strata* is slightly puffed up. Serve hot or warm.

Variation: Feel free to replace the California blend vegetables with another variety of frozen vegetable blend or 3 cups assorted fresh veggies, roughly chopped. Also, you can prepare this recipe using a large slow cooker (preferably an oval one) and an oiled 10-cup or larger casserole dish (whatever fits your slow cooker). Place the casserole dish on top of a trivet or foil ring in the bottom of the ceramic crock insert.

DEFINITION

A **strata** is much like a savory bread pudding, and like so many peasant-style dishes, it was developed as a way to use stale bread. It's commonly made with layers of bread cubes, veggies, and often cheese, which are then covered with a rich, custardlike blend of eggs and milk or cream.

Appetizers, Sauces, and More

If you like to be the "host with the most" and your idea of entertaining people in your home revolves around putting out a nice spread, the slow cooker can assist you in several ways.

A small slow cooker is perfect for preparing hot and bubbling dips and fondue—all of which can be served straight from the slow cooker so you can effortlessly keep them warm all through the party. A larger cooker works well to make toppings for some yummy appetizers. Many of the sweet, fruity, and tangy sauces, butters, purées, and condiments featured in Part 3 can be used as sparingly or liberally as you desire to spruce up your vegan meals and slow cooker creations.

Delicious Dips and Appetizers

In This Chapter

- Fabulous fondues
- Hot and bubbling cheesy dips
- Bold and beany dips
- Luscious layered appetizers

There's just something enticing about dunking a big hunk of bread or chip into a dip—especially one that's been warmed to perfection in your slow cooker. Whether you prefer a bubbling fondue, a tangy cream cheese concoction, or spicy refried bean dips, you'll be busting out some delectable dip in no time.

And not only can you prepare many of your favorite dips using the slow cooker, but you can serve them directly from it as well—with the added bonus that it will stay warm all night, without burning, on low or "keep warm." With this in mind, the dip recipes here call for a small slow cooker. If you're entertaining a crowd, double or triple the ingredients and use a medium slow cooker instead.

Also included in this chapter are recipes for making marvelous, multi-layered appetizers, many of which utilize toppings made in the slow cooker. Let's get snacking!

Wine Is Fine Fondue

The mild flavor of this cheese fondue is thanks to the commingling of fruity white wine with nutritional yeast flakes, plus vegan mozzarella and Monterey Jack cheeses.

Yield:	Prep time:	Cook time:	Serving size:
3 cups	10 to 15 minutes	1½ to 2 hours	¼ cup

1½ cups white wine (such as Riesling, Pinot Grigio, or Chardonnay)

1 cup water

1 cup shredded vegan mozzarella cheese

1 cup shredded vegan Monterey Jack cheese

¼ cup nutritional yeast flakes

1½ TB. tapioca starch or cornstarch

1 tsp. garlic powder or garlic granules

1 tsp. onion powder

¼ tsp. white pepper or freshly ground black pepper

Pinch freshly grated nutmeg

1. Lightly coat a small slow cooker's ceramic crock insert with vegetable cooking spray or oil of choice.

2. In the slow cooker, combine white wine and water. Cover and cook on high for 30 minutes.

3. In a large bowl, place mozzarella cheese and Monterey Jack cheese. Sprinkle nutritional yeast flakes, tapioca starch, garlic powder, onion powder, and white pepper over top, and using your hands, toss to coat.

4. When white wine mixture is hot, while stirring, slowly add cheese mixture, 1 handful at a time, letting each addition melt slightly before adding more. Stir in nutmeg.

5. Cover, reduce heat to low, and cook for 1 hour or until hot and bubbling and both cheeses are thoroughly melted.

6. Uncover and turn slow cooker to "keep warm" while serving with crackers, bread cubes, fruit slices, or vegetable crudités for dipping.

Variation: For **Mellow Cheese Fondue,** replace white wine with 1½ cups soy or other nondairy milk.

LOW AND SLOW

The cheeses are tossed with the tapioca starch and seasonings to prevent lumps from forming, which could happen if they were added directly into the hot wine. The tapioca starch also helps keep the finished fondue emulsified.

English Pub Beer-n-Cheddar Fondue

Make this for your beer-loving friends because they're sure to love how well the smooth flavors of the hops play off the sharpness of cheddar cheese.

Yield:	Prep time:	Cook time:	Serving size:
3½ to 4 cups	10 to 15 minutes	1½ to 2 hours	¼ cup

½ cup red onion, diced

¼ cup water

2 cloves garlic

2 (12-oz.) bottles pale ale or amber brown beer

2½ cups shredded vegan cheddar cheese

2 TB. *nutritional yeast flakes*

1½ TB. tapioca starch or cornstarch

1 tsp. dry mustard

1 tsp. smoked paprika

¼ tsp. freshly ground black pepper

Dash vegetarian Worcestershire sauce

1. Lightly coat a small slow cooker's ceramic crock insert with vegetable cooking spray or oil of choice.

2. In a food processor fitted with an S blade, process red onion, water, and garlic for 1 minute. Scrape down the sides of the container with a spatula, and process for 30 more seconds or until smooth. Transfer mixture to the slow cooker.

3. Add pale ale, and stir to combine. Cover and cook on high for 30 minutes.

4. In a large bowl, place cheddar cheese. Sprinkle nutritional yeast flakes, tapioca starch, dry mustard, smoked paprika, and black pepper over top, and using your hands, toss well to coat.

5. When beer mixture is hot, while stirring, slowly add cheddar cheese mixture, 1 handful at a time, letting each addition melt slightly before adding more. Stir in vegetarian Worcestershire sauce.

6. Cover, reduce heat to low, and cook for 1 hour or until hot and bubbling and both cheeses are thoroughly melted.

7. Uncover and turn slow cooker to "keep warm" while serving with crackers, pretzels, bread cubes, or vegetable crudités for dipping.

Variation: You can prepare this recipe using nonalcoholic beer. For **Bold Beer-N-Cheese Fondue,** use 2 bottles of dark beer or vegan stout, use only 1 cup shredded vegan cheddar cheese, and add $1^{1}/_{2}$ cups shredded vegan pepper Jack cheese.

DEFINITION

Nutritional yeast flakes are an inactive yeast with a nutty, almost cheeselike flavor, which is why it's commonly used as an imitation cheese flavoring for foods and nondairy cheese products. It's an excellent way for vegans to get their recommended daily dose of vitamin B_{12}. Do not confuse nutritional yeast flakes with active yeast, the type used for making breads and baked goods.

Hot Vegetable Confetti Cream Cheese Dip

A colorful assortment of finely chopped vegetables are lightly sautéed to bring out their natural sweetness and then combined with fresh herbs and vegan cream cheese, sour cream, and mayo to create this well-seasoned dip.

Yield:	Prep time:	Cook time:	Serving size:
3 to 3½ cups	5 to 7 minutes	1½ to 2 hours	¼ cup

1 (8-oz.) pkg. vegan cream cheese

1 cup vegan sour cream

1 cup vegan mayonnaise

3 TB. nutritional yeast flakes

1 tsp. seasoning salt (such as Herbamare)

½ tsp. freshly ground black pepper

⅓ cup carrots, finely diced

⅓ cup green bell pepper, ribs and seeds removed, and finely diced

⅓ cup red bell pepper, ribs and seeds removed, and finely diced

⅓ cup red onion, finely diced

½ TB. olive oil

1 TB. minced garlic

¼ cup green onions, white and green parts, thinly sliced

⅓ cup chopped fresh basil

⅓ cup chopped fresh parsley

1. Lightly coat a small slow cooker's ceramic crock insert with vegetable cooking spray or oil of choice.

2. In a food processor fitted with an S blade, process cream cheese, sour cream, mayonnaise, nutritional yeast flakes, seasoning salt, and black pepper for 1 minute. Scrape down the sides of the container with a spatula, and process for 1 more minute or until very creamy. Transfer mixture to the slow cooker.

3. In a small, nonstick skillet over medium heat, add carrots, green bell pepper, red bell pepper, red onion, and olive oil, and sauté, stirring often, for 3 minutes.

4. Add garlic, and sauté, stirring often, for 30 seconds. Remove the skillet from heat.

5. Add sautéed vegetable mixture, green onions, basil, and parsley to the slow cooker, and stir well to combine.

6. Cover and cook on low for 2 to 2½ hours, stirring occasionally, or until hot and bubbling. Taste and adjust seasonings as desired.

7. Uncover and turn slow cooker to "keep warm" while serving with crackers, bread slices, or vegetable crudités for dipping.

Variation: This hot dip is also tasty as a spread for toasted bagels or on sandwiches. For more flavor, add 1 cup shredded vegan Monterey Jack or cheddar cheese.

LOW AND SLOW

You can find vegan cream cheese and sour cream alongside their dairy-based counterparts in the refrigerated dairy case of most grocery and natural foods stores. This is also where you may find jars of vegan mayonnaise because some brands require constant refrigeration.

Hot Artichoke Dip with Buttery Breadcrumbs

This ultra-creamy savory dip will win you rave reviews. Under toasted breadcrumbs lies a luscious base made with whipped vegan cream cheese, chopped artichoke hearts and green onions, oozing mozzarella cheese, and a touch of hot pepper sauce for some kick.

Yield:	Prep time:	Cook time:	Serving size:
3 to 3½ cups	5 to 7 minutes	1½ to 2 hours	¼ cup

2 (14-oz.) cans artichoke hearts packed in water, drained, or 1 (16-oz.) pkg. frozen artichoke hearts, thawed

1 (8-oz.) pkg. vegan cream cheese

½ cup vegan mayonnaise

¼ cup nutritional yeast flakes

1 TB. Dijon mustard

1 TB. fresh lemon juice

1 tsp. dried basil

1 tsp. seasoning salt (such as Herbamare)

½ tsp. freshly ground black pepper

½ tsp. hot pepper sauce

1 cup shredded vegan mozzarella cheese

⅓ cup green onions, white and green parts, thinly sliced

⅔ cup fresh breadcrumbs

1 TB. nonhydrogenated margarine or olive oil

Smoked or sweet paprika

1. Lightly coat a small slow cooker's ceramic crock insert with vegetable cooking spray or oil of choice.

2. In a food processor fitted with an S blade, process artichoke hearts for 30 to 60 seconds or until coarsely chopped. Transfer to a small bowl, and set aside.

3. In the food processor, process cream cheese, mayonnaise, nutritional yeast flakes, Dijon mustard, lemon juice, basil, seasoning salt, black pepper, and hot pepper sauce for 1 minute. Scrape down the sides of the container with a spatula, and process for 1 more minute or until very creamy. Transfer mixture to the slow cooker.

4. Add artichoke hearts, mozzarella cheese, and green onions, and stir well to combine.

5. Cover and cook on low for 2 to 2½ hours, stirring occasionally, or until hot and bubbling. Taste and adjust seasonings as desired.

6. Meanwhile, in a small, nonstick skillet over medium heat, cook breadcrumbs and nonhydrogenated margarine, stirring often, for 3 to 5 minutes or until golden brown.

7. Uncover and turn slow cooker to "keep warm" setting. Spoon breadcrumbs evenly over top of dip and sprinkle smoked paprika over top for added color. Serve with crackers, bread slices, or vegetable crudités for dipping.

Variation: For **Hot Artichoke-Spinach Dip,** reduce the artichoke hearts to 1 (14-ounce) can and add 3 cups fresh spinach, washed well, stems removed, and cut chiffonade (or ¾ cup frozen chopped spinach, thawed and squeezed dry).

LOW AND SLOW

When serving hot dips and fondues, don't forget to ready your dunkable items. Some can't-go-wrong options include bread slices or cubes, pita breads, crackers, tortilla chips, apple and pear slices, and the never-fail vegetable crudités of carrot and celery sticks, pepper strips, cherry tomatoes, and broccoli and cauliflower florets, and so on.

Chili Con Queso

Juicy fresh tomatoes, red onions, green onions, jalapeño pepper, and cilantro transform Mellow Cheese Fondue into a spicy, cheesy chili con queso dip perfect for serving with your favorite tortilla chips.

Yield:	Prep time:	Cook time:	Serving size:
3 to 3½ cups	5 to 7 minutes	1½ to 2 hours	¼ cup

1½ cups Mellow Cheese Fondue (variation earlier in this chapter)	1 medium jalapeño pepper, ribs and seeds removed, and finely diced
1 tsp. chili powder	⅓ cup red onion, finely diced
½ tsp. ground cumin	1 tsp. olive oil
¼ tsp. chipotle chile powder or cayenne	1 cup tomatoes, diced
¼ tsp. freshly ground black pepper	¼ cup green onions, white and green parts, thinly sliced
	¼ cup chopped fresh cilantro

1. Lightly coat a small slow cooker's ceramic crock insert with vegetable cooking spray or oil of choice.

2. In the slow cooker, combine Mellow Cheese Fondue, chili powder, cumin, chipotle chile powder, and black pepper.

3. In a small, nonstick skillet over medium heat, add jalapeño pepper, red onion, and olive oil, and sauté, stirring often, for 3 minutes. Remove the skillet from heat.

4. Add sautéed jalapeño mixture, tomatoes, green onions, and cilantro to the slow cooker, and stir well to combine.

5. Cover and cook on low for 2 to 2½ hours, stirring occasionally, or until hot and bubbling. Taste and adjust seasonings as desired.

6. Uncover and turn slow cooker to "keep warm" while serving with tortilla chips, crackers, or vegetable crudités for dipping.

Variation: For a milder flavor, replace the jalapeño pepper with ½ cup green bell pepper, ribs and seeds removed, and finely diced. For **Easy, Extra-Cheesy Chili Con Queso,** replace the jalapeño mixture and tomatoes with 1 (14-ounce) can diced tomatoes with green chiles and add ¾ cup shredded vegan cheddar or pepper Jack cheese.

SLOW INTERESTING

Cheesy and peppery *chili con queso,* which literally translates in Spanish to "chili with cheese," is commonly served as an appetizer or side dish along with tortilla chips in Southwestern, Mexican, and Tex-Mex restaurants.

Refried Pinto Bean Dip

This spicy Mexican-inspired dip is a mixture of mashed pinto beans, sautéed yellow onion and jalapeño pepper, and an ample assortment of herbs and spices. ¡Olé!

Yield:	Prep time:	Cook time:	Serving size:
4 cups	8 to 10 minutes	1½ to 2 hours	¼ cup

1 cup yellow onion, diced
2 medium jalapeño peppers, ribs and seeds removed, and finely diced
½ TB. olive oil
1½ TB. minced garlic
2 tsp. dried oregano
2 tsp. chili powder
2 tsp. ground cumin
1 tsp. ground coriander

1 tsp. sea salt
½ tsp. freshly ground black pepper
3 cups cooked pinto beans, or 2 (15-oz.) cans pinto beans, drained and rinsed
⅔ cup water
2 TB. fresh lime juice
1½ TB. nutritional yeast flakes
½ cup shredded vegan cheddar or pepper Jack cheese (optional)

1. Lightly coat a small slow cooker's ceramic crock insert with vegetable cooking spray or oil of choice.

2. In a medium nonstick skillet over medium heat, combine yellow onion, jalapeño peppers, and olive oil, and sauté, stirring often, for 3 minutes.

3. Add garlic, oregano, chili powder, cumin, coriander, sea salt, and black pepper, and sauté, stirring often, for 1 minute. Remove the skillet from heat.

4. In a large bowl, combine pinto beans, water, and lime juice. Using a potato masher, mash bean mixture until completely smooth or a slightly chunky consistency, as desired. Add sautéed onion mixture and nutritional yeast flakes, and stir well to combine. (Alternatively, in a food processor fitted with an S blade, combine sautéed onion mixture, pinto beans, water, lime juice, and nutritional yeast flakes, and process for 1 or 2 minutes or until completely smooth.) Transfer mixture to the slow cooker.

5. Cover and cook on low for 1 to 1½ hours, stirring occasionally, or until hot.

6. Taste and adjust seasonings as desired. Sprinkle cheddar cheese (if using) over top.

7. Uncover and turn slow cooker to "keep warm" while serving with your favorite salsa and tortilla chips, crackers, or vegetable crudités for dipping. You can also serve this dip at room temperature.

Variation: For a less-spicy bean dip, use only 1 jalapeño pepper, or omit the jalapeño peppers altogether. For **Refried Black Bean Dip,** replace the pinto beans with 3 cups cooked black beans or 2 (15-ounce) cans black beans, drained and rinsed.

LOW AND SLOW

You can use this tasty dip as a filling for burritos, enchiladas, or tacos or serve as a side dish as part of a Mexican-style meal.

Gettin' Saucy!

In This Chapter

- Thick and fruity sauces
- Sauces for sweet treats
- Savory sauces
- Rich and flavorful gravy

Knowing how to make a good sauce is an essential cooking skill, and using a slow cooker to prepare your sauce makes smart sense. Gone are the hours of stirring sauces to prevent them from scorching or bubbling over. Instead, when you leave your sauce to simmer away in a slow cooker, in most instances, you only have to stir the ingredients at the beginning and you can leave it undisturbed almost until it's time to serve.

When you're looking for something to spruce up your meals or dress up your dessert, the sauces in this chapter fit the bill. You'll find fruit-filled sauces, delicious toppings for your breakfast and dessert offerings, along with luscious butterscotch and hot fudge sauces perfect for ladling over your favorite sweet treats. Rounding out the chapter are a rich gravy and savory barbecue and marinara sauces that can dress up your favorite vegetables, grains, and pasta dishes.

Apple Juice–Sweetened Applesauce

Most brands of store-bought applesauce are sweetened with tons of sugar, or worse yet, high-fructose corn syrup! But by cooking your apples in apple juice and a bit of cinnamon, you'll get to fully enjoy the delicate sweetness of the apples.

Yield:	Prep time:	Cook time:	Serving size:
6 cups	7 to 10 minutes	2½ to 3 hours	1 cup

8 or 10 large apples of choice (4 lb.), peeled, cored, and sliced (about 12 cups)

2 cups apple juice

1 TB. ground cinnamon

1. In a medium slow cooker, combine apples, apple juice, and cinnamon.

2. Cover and cook on high for 2½ to 3 hours, on low for 5 or 6 hours, or until apples are very soft.

3. Serve hot, warm, or cold as a side dish or atop waffles, cakes, or your favorite desserts. Store applesauce in an airtight container in the refrigerator for up to 7 days or in the freezer for up to 3 months.

Variations: If you like your applesauce chunky, serve as is, but if you prefer smooth applesauce, mash the apples with a potato masher. Feel free to replace the apple juice with apple cider. For **Pink Applesauce,** add 1½ cups fresh or frozen red raspberries. For **Spiced Pear Applesauce,** replace the apple juice with 2 cups spiced cider; use a combination of 6 cups apples and 6 cups Anjou or Bosc pears, peeled, cored, and sliced; and add 1 teaspoon ground cardamom or ground ginger.

SLOW INTERESTING

Some of the best varieties of apples for making applesauce include Braeburn, Cameo, Cortland, Fuji, Gala, Gravenstein, Pippin, McIntosh, and Rome.

Citrusy Cranberry Sauce

A combination of sugar and fresh orange juice and zest help balance the tart flavor of whole cranberries in this Thanksgiving dinner staple.

Yield:	Prep time:	Cook time:	Serving size:
4 cups	5 to 7 minutes	2 to 2½ hours	½ cup

2 (12-oz.) bags whole fresh or frozen cranberries

¾ cup water

¾ cup fresh orange juice

1 cup unbleached cane sugar

½ cup light brown or *muscovado sugar,* packed

Zest of 2 large oranges

¾ tsp. ground cinnamon

½ tsp. ground ginger

¼ tsp. ground cloves or freshly grated nutmeg

1. In a small slow cooker, combine cranberries, water, orange juice, unbleached cane sugar, light brown sugar, orange zest, cinnamon, ginger, and cloves.

2. Cover and cook on high for 2 to 2½ hours, on low for 4 or 5 hours, or until cranberries have popped and sauce is thickened.

3. Serve as a side dish hot, warm, or cold as desired. Store cranberry sauce in an airtight container in the refrigerator for up to 7 days or in the freezer for up to 3 months.

Variation: For **Maple-Walnut Cranberry Sauce,** replace the unbleached cane sugar and light brown sugar with 1 cup maple syrup, and stir ¾ cup toasted walnuts, roughly chopped, into the finished cranberry sauce.

DEFINITION

Muscovado sugar (often referred to as Barbados sugar) is a type of cane sugar produced in Barbados, Mauritius, and the Philippines that has a moist texture and a pronounced molasses flavor. It's available in both light and dark varieties, and both are an excellent substitute for light or dark brown sugar in breads and baked goods.

Warm Mixed Berry Sauce

Sweet and juicy blueberries, strawberries, and red raspberries are combined with cranberry-raspberry juice in this luscious sauce flavored with some brown sugar and spices.

Yield:	Prep time:	Cook time:	Serving size:
4 cups	5 to 7 minutes	2½ to 3 hours	⅓ to ½ cup

1 pt. fresh strawberries, hulled and sliced

1 pt. fresh blueberries

1 pt. fresh red raspberries

1 cup cranberry-raspberry or apple juice

⅔ cup unbleached cane or light brown sugar, packed

¾ tsp. ground cinnamon

½ tsp. ground cardamom or ground ginger

2 TB. cornstarch

2 TB. water

1. In a small slow cooker, combine strawberries, blueberries, red raspberries, cranberry-raspberry juice, unbleached cane sugar, cinnamon, and cardamom.

2. Cover and cook on high for 2½ to 3 hours, on low for 5 or 6 hours, or until berries are very soft.

3. In a small bowl, stir together cornstarch and water, add to the slow cooker, and cook for 5 to 10 more minutes or until sauce thickens slightly.

4. Serve hot, warm, or cold as a topping for waffles, pancakes, nondairy ice cream, cakes, and your other favorite desserts. Store mixed berry sauce in an airtight container in the refrigerator for up to 7 days or in the freezer for up to 3 months.

Variation: Feel free to replace each pint of fresh berries with 1 (10-ounce) bag frozen berries, thawed, or swap out all the fresh berries with 2 (16-ounce) bags frozen mixed berries, thawed.

LOW AND SLOW

If you have a corn allergy, you can use arrowroot to thicken the sauce instead of using cornstarch.

Butterscotch Sauce

This thick and decadent golden syrup achieves a caramel-like flavor simply by combining soy creamer, several sweeteners, and vanilla. Margarine gives the sauce its buttery richness.

Yield:	Prep time:	Cook time:	Serving size:
3 cups	5 minutes	1½ to 2 hours	¼ cup

2½ cups vanilla soy or coconut creamer

1½ cups light brown or muscovado sugar, packed

¾ cup *brown rice syrup*

½ cup nonhydrogenated margarine

1 TB. vanilla extract

Pinch sea salt

2 TB. cornstarch

2 TB. water

1. In a small slow cooker, whisk together vanilla soy creamer, light brown sugar, brown rice syrup, nonhydrogenated margarine, vanilla extract, and sea salt.

2. Cover and cook on high for 1½ to 2 hours, on low for 3 or 4 hours, or until sauce is hot and bubbling around the edges.

3. In a small bowl, stir together cornstarch and water. Add to the slow cooker, stir to combine, and cook for 5 to 10 more minutes or until sauce thickens slightly.

4. Serve hot, warm, or cold as a topping for nondairy ice cream, cakes, and your other favorite desserts. Store butterscotch sauce in an airtight container in the refrigerator for up to 7 to 10 days.

Variation: For **Boozy Butterscotch Sauce,** add 2 tablespoons Scotch, bourbon, or rum.

DEFINITION

Brown rice syrup is a liquid sweetener made by fermenting brown rice with special enzymes until its natural starches begin to break down. The mixture is strained and cooked down until it reaches a syrupy consistency. It's mildly sweet with a light caramel flavor and color, and is available in gluten-free as well as several flavored varieties in most grocery and natural foods stores.

Hot Fudge Sauce

True chocoholics will love the ultra-rich dark chocolate flavor of this hot fudge sauce, which is a triple combination of chocolate: chocolate soy milk, chopped dark chocolate, and *raw cacao powder*.

Yield:	Prep time:	Cook time:	Serving size:
3 cups	5 minutes	1½ to 2 hours	¼ cup

¾ cup raw cacao powder or cocoa powder

1½ cups chocolate soy or other nondairy milk

3 (3-oz.) vegan dark chocolate bars, roughly chopped

⅔ cup brown rice syrup

2 tsp. vanilla extract

Pinch sea salt

3 TB. cornstarch

3 TB. water

1. In a small slow cooker, place raw cacao powder. Slowly whisk in ½ cup chocolate soy milk. Slowly whisk in remaining 1 cup chocolate soy milk. Add dark chocolate, brown rice syrup, vanilla extract, and sea salt, and stir well to combine.

2. Cover and cook on high for 1½ to 2 hours, on low for 3 or 4 hours, or until sauce is hot and bubbling around edges.

3. In a small bowl, stir together cornstarch and water. Add to the slow cooker, and cook for 5 to 10 more minutes or until sauce thickens slightly.

4. Serve hot, warm, or cold as a topping for nondairy ice cream, cakes, and your other favorite desserts. Store hot fudge sauce in an airtight container in the refrigerator for up to 7 to 10 days.

Variation: For a milder chocolate flavor, replace the dark chocolate with 1⅓ cups vegan chocolate chips. For **Mocha-Almond Fudge Sauce,** use ½ cup chocolate almond milk, and add ¾ cup freshly brewed coffee, ⅓ cup coffee liqueur, and ½ teaspoon almond extract.

DEFINITION

Raw cacao powder is a powder made from raw cacao beans that have gone through a cold-pressing process to remove the fat (cacao butter) and are then finely ground into a powder, much like cocoa powder (made from roasted cacao beans). It has a deep, dark, almost coffeelike flavor. Raw foodists often use it as a replacement for cocoa powder in recipes.

Smoky-Sweet Barbecue Sauce

The rich sweetness of brown sugar nicely plays off the zesty tang of apple cider vinegar and garlic. Small doses of smoked paprika, chipotle chile powder, and *smoked sea salt* impart a slight smokiness to this lip-smackin'-good sauce.

Yield:	Prep time:	Cook time:	Serving size:
4 cups	5 to 7 minutes	2 to 2½ hours	⅓ to ½ cup

1 cup yellow onion, finely diced	1 TB. spicy brown mustard
½ TB. olive oil	1 TB. nutritional yeast flakes
1 TB. minced garlic	1 tsp. smoked paprika
1 (28-oz.) can tomato sauce or tomato purée	1 tsp. chipotle chile powder
	½ tsp. ground cumin
½ cup light brown or muscovado sugar, packed	½ tsp. smoked sea salt
¼ cup apple cider vinegar	½ tsp. freshly ground black pepper or garlic pepper

1. In a medium nonstick skillet over medium heat, combine yellow onion and olive oil, and sauté, stirring often, for 3 minutes.

2. Add garlic, and sauté, stirring often, for 1 more minute. Remove the skillet from heat.

3. In a small slow cooker, combine onion mixture, tomato sauce, light brown sugar, apple cider vinegar, spicy brown mustard, nutritional yeast flakes, smoked paprika, chipotle chile powder, cumin, smoked sea salt, and black pepper.

4. Cover and cook on high for 2 to 2½ hours, on low for 4 or 5 hours, or until hot and bubbling around edges. Taste and adjust seasonings as desired.

5. Use hot, warm, or cold as a condiment or sauce for sandwiches, baked beans, tofu, tempeh, seitan, or other dishes. Store barbecue sauce in an airtight container in the refrigerator for up to 2 weeks or in the freezer for up to 3 months.

Variation: For a mild-flavored sauce, replace the chipotle chile powder with regular chili powder.

DEFINITION

Smoked sea salt is sea salt that's been slow-smoked for several hours over various types of wood, such as hickory, mesquite, or alder. It has a full-bodied, very intense, smoky flavor and aroma.

Red Wine Marinara Sauce

Everyone should have a good marinara sauce in their arsenal of recipes. You'll love the flavor of this slow-cooked sauce made with crushed tomatoes, sautéed onions and garlic, robust red wine, fresh basil, and a bit of red pepper flakes for a spicy kick.

Yield:	Prep time:	Cook time:	Serving size:
7 or 8 cups	5 to 7 minutes	3 to 3½ hours	½ to ¾ cup

1½ cups (1 large) yellow onion, diced	1 TB. unbleached cane sugar
1 TB. olive oil	1½ tsp. dried oregano
2 TB. minced garlic	1 tsp. smoked paprika
1½ tsp. crushed red pepper flakes	1 tsp. sea salt
2 (28-oz.) cans crushed tomatoes, with juice	½ tsp. freshly ground black pepper or garlic pepper
½ cup red wine (such as Burgundy, Zinfandel, or Merlot)	⅓ cup fresh basil, cut chiffonade
2 TB. nutritional yeast flakes	⅓ cup chopped fresh Italian flat-leaf parsley

1. In a medium nonstick skillet over medium heat, combine yellow onion and olive oil, and sauté, stirring often, for 3 minutes.

2. Add garlic and crushed red pepper flakes, and sauté, stirring often, for 1 minute. Remove the skillet from heat.

3. In a medium slow cooker, combine onion mixture, crushed tomatoes, red wine, nutritional yeast flakes, unbleached cane sugar, oregano, smoked paprika, sea salt, and black pepper.

4. Cover and cook on high for 3 to 3½ hours, on low for 6 or 7 hours, or until hot and bubbling around edges. Stir in basil and Italian flat-leaf parsley. Taste and adjust seasonings as desired.

5. Use hot or warm as a condiment or sauce for sandwiches, pasta, lasagna, or other dishes. Store marinara sauce in an airtight container in the refrigerator for up to 7 days or in the freezer for up to 4 months.

Variation: For **Mushroom Marinara Sauce,** sauté 1½ cups (8 ounces) crimini or white button mushrooms, cut in half and thinly sliced, or roughly chopped, along with the onions.

> **LOW AND SLOW**
>
> This recipe makes enough marinara sauce for several meals. You can refrigerate it for later use for up to 1 week, or you can divide the cooled sauce into 2- to 4-cup portions, place each in a zipper-lock bag or airtight container, and freeze for up to 4 months.

Golden Onion and Garlic Gravy

Briefly sautéing the onions and garlic heightens the flavor of savory herbs in the poultry seasoning blend, which is used to enhance this quick-and-easy, gold-toned gravy.

Yield:	Prep time:	Cook time:	Serving size:
4 cups	7 to 10 minutes	1½ to 2 hours	¼ cup

¾ cup yellow onion, finely diced

½ TB. olive oil

2 TB. minced garlic

3 cups Homemade Vegetable Broth (recipe in Chapter 8)

½ cup nutritional yeast flakes

2 TB. tamari, shoyu, or Bragg Liquid Aminos

½ TB. poultry seasoning blend

½ tsp. sea salt

¼ tsp. freshly ground black pepper or garlic pepper

¼ cup whole-wheat flour

¼ cup water

1. In a medium nonstick skillet over medium heat, combine yellow onion and olive oil, and sauté, stirring often, for 3 minutes.

2. Add garlic, and sauté, stirring often, for 1 minute. Remove the skillet from heat.

3. In a medium slow cooker, combine onion mixture, Homemade Vegetable Broth, nutritional yeast flakes, tamari, poultry seasoning blend, sea salt, and black pepper.

4. Cover and cook on high for 1½ to 2 hours, on low for 3 or 4 hours, or until hot and bubbling around edges.

5. In a small bowl, stir together whole-wheat flour and water. Add to the slow cooker, and cook for 5 to 10 more minutes or until gravy thickens. Taste and adjust seasonings as desired.

6. Serve hot on biscuits, mashed potatoes, or your other favorite vegetables, grains, or main dishes.

Variations: For **Gluten-Free Onion and Garlic Gravy,** replace the whole-wheat flour with 3 tablespoons cornstarch. For **Roasted Garlic and Onion Gravy,** skip step 1, replace the onion and garlic with ¾ cup Caramelized Onions (recipe in Chapter 7), finely diced, and ¼ cup Roasted Garlic (recipe in Chapter 7), puréed or finely diced.

LOW AND SLOW

If you don't have any poultry seasoning blend, you can prepare this gravy using 1 tablespoon chopped fresh thyme (or 1 teaspoon dried thyme) and 1 tablespoon chopped fresh sage (or ½ teaspoon rubbed/dried sage).

Amazing Accompaniments

In This Chapter

- Unbelievable fruit butters
- Perfect veggie purées
- Sweet and spicy chutney
- Slow-roasted onions and garlic

At times, we all can use a little help making things better, and often it only takes a little extra effort to make things a whole lot better. This same logic applies to food. For instance, a plain slice of freshly baked bread (like the ones in Chapter 17) tastes great, but undoubtedly, it tastes even better with a flavorful topping, like Spiced Apple Butter spread on top. Simply by adding a sweet or savory embellishment, you can easily elevate the flavors and visual appeal of your dishes.

The accompaniments in this chapter take the flavor levels of food from lackluster to spectacular. Think of these flavorful butters, purées, and condiments as your handy assistants in the kitchen, ready and waiting to help you add tons of flavor and aroma to your meals.

I've included many variation ideas, but feel free to play around with the suggested ingredients and seasonings to create your own versions of these handy helpers.

Spiced Apple Butter

Apple butter is synonymous with *autumn*. For decades, cooks have painstakingly cooked down basketfuls of apples with plenty of sugar and spices to create a thick and fragrant spread for their breads and for use in their baked goods.

Yield:	Prep time:	Cook time:	Serving size:
4 cups	15 to 20 minutes	8 to 10 hours or overnight	2 or 3 tablespoons

4 or 5 large apples of choice, cored and sliced (about 6 cups)

1 cup light brown or muscovado sugar, packed

1 cup water

1 tsp. ground cinnamon

¼ tsp. ground allspice

¼ tsp. ground cloves

¼ tsp. freshly grated nutmeg

1. In a medium slow cooker, combine apples, light brown sugar, water, cinnamon, allspice, cloves, and nutmeg.

2. Cover and cook on low for 8 to 10 hours or overnight, stirring occasionally, or until mixture is very thick and dark brown in color.

3. Uncover, and using a potato masher, roughly mash apple mixture. Cook uncovered for 30 more minutes.

4. Turn off slow cooker, and allow apple mixture to cool for 30 minutes.

5. Using an immersion blender, blend apple mixture for 1 or 2 minutes or until smooth. (Alternatively, use a blender or food processor fitted with an S blade to blend apple mixture.)

6. Serve hot, warm, or cold as a topping for bread, English muffins, or waffles, or as an ingredient in baked goods, cakes, and your other favorite desserts. Store apple butter in airtight containers in the refrigerator for up to 2 weeks or in the freezer for up to 4 months.

Variations: For **Sugar-Free Apple Butter,** omit the light brown sugar and replace the water with 1 cup apple juice or apple cider. For **Spiced Pear Butter,** use 2 pounds Anjou or Bosc pears, peeled, cored, and cut into 1-inch chunks, instead of the apples. Replace the water with 1 cup pear nectar, and swap out the nutmeg with ¼ teaspoon ground ginger.

COOKER CAVEAT

The Environmental Working Group's Shopper's Guide to Pesticides in Produce lists apples as the produce that contains the highest amount of pesticide residues. When you can, purchase organically grown apples over conventionally grown. Because this recipe calls for unpeeled apples, I strongly urge you to use organic apples.

Pumpkin Patch Butter

Muscovado sugar, with its undertones of molasses, along with sweet maple syrup, fragrant spices, and vanilla, perfectly complement the flavor of pumpkin in this velvety-smooth spread.

Yield:	Prep time:	Cook time:	Serving size:
4 cups	15 to 20 minutes	8 to 10 hours or overnight	2 or 3 tablespoons

2 (15-oz.) cans pumpkin purée

½ cup maple syrup

½ cup light or dark muscovado sugar, packed

1½ tsp. vanilla extract

¾ tsp. ground cinnamon

¼ tsp. ground allspice

¼ tsp. ground cloves

¼ tsp. freshly grated nutmeg

1. In a medium cooker, combine pumpkin purée, maple syrup, muscovado sugar, vanilla extract, cinnamon, allspice, cloves, and nutmeg.

2. Cover and cook on low for 8 to 10 hours or overnight, stirring occasionally, or until mixture is very thick and dark brown in color.

3. Uncover and cook for 30 more minutes. Turn off slow cooker and allow pumpkin mixture to cool for 30 minutes.

4. Serve hot, warm, or cold as a topping for slices of bread, English muffins, or waffles, or as an ingredient in baked goods, cakes, and your other favorite desserts. Store pumpkin butter in airtight containers in the refrigerator for up to 2 weeks or in the freezer for up to 4 months.

Variation: Instead of canned pumpkin purée, you can use 4 cups Pumpkin Purée (variation later in this chapter). Or feel free to replace Pumpkin Purée with Wonderful Winter Squash Purée (recipe later in this chapter) or Sweet Potato Purée (variation later in this chapter). You can also replace all the spices with 1½ teaspoons pumpkin pie spice instead. For **Sugar-Free Pumpkin Butter,** replace muscovado sugar with ½ cup apple or spiced cider.

LOW AND SLOW

Rich in vitamins A and C, pumpkins, winter squashes, and sweet potatoes are all readily available in the fall and winter months and can often be used interchangeably in both sweet and savory recipes.

Wonderful Winter Squash Purée

With the help of your slow cooker, you can easily cook a winter squash soft enough to blend it into a sweet and creamy purée you can use in baked goods or, with some dressing up, as a tasty side dish.

Yield:	Prep time:	Cook time:	Serving size:
3 cups	25 to 30 minutes	4 to 6 hours	½ cup

1 large or 2 medium butternut, delicata, turban, or acorn squash (about 3 lb.)

1. Lightly coat a medium or large slow cooker's ceramic crock insert with vegetable cooking spray or oil of choice.

2. Cut off and discard squash stems. Cut squash in ½ lengthwise, and using a spoon, remove and discard seeds. Cut squash into large pieces, and place in the slow cooker.

3. Cover and cook on low for 4 to 6 hours or until squash skin and flesh are very soft and easily pierced with a knife. Turn off slow cooker, and allow squash to cool for 15 minutes.

4. Using a knife, remove skin from squash. Transfer cooked squash to a food processor fitted with an S blade, and process for 2 minutes. Scrape down the sides of the container with a spatula, and process for 1 or 2 more minutes or until mixture reaches a very smooth purée.

5. Use winter squash purée as a side dish or in baked goods and your other favorite recipes as desired. Store in airtight containers or zipper-lock bags in the refrigerator for up to 5 days, or make in large batches and freeze for up to 6 months.

Variations: To make **Sweetened Winter Squash Purée,** add ⅓ cup (or more as desired) maple syrup, unbleached cane sugar, or brown sugar when processing the winter squash. For 4 to 4½ cups **Pumpkin Purée,** cut off stem, scoop out seeds, and cut a 5-pound sugar pie pumpkin in half, as needed, to fit into a medium or large slow cooker. Cover and cook on low for 6 to 8 hours or until pumpkin is very soft. Let cool, scoop out pumpkin flesh, and mash with a potato masher or process in a food processor fitted with an S blade until smooth. For **Sweet Potato Purée,** replace the winter squash with 6 large sweet potatoes, whole and unpeeled.

COOKER CAVEAT

Winter squashes and pumpkins both have rather tough skins. Be sure to use a sharp chef's knife or cleaver to cut off the stem and slice through the outer layer of skin.

Mango Chutney

A sweet and savory condiment made with juicy mangoes, plump raisins, garlic, ginger, tangy apple cider vinegar, and spicy jalapeño pepper, chutney is typically served alongside Indian dishes, especially with curries.

Yield:	Prep time:	Cook time:	Serving size:
4 cups	15 to 20 minutes	3½ to 4 hours	3 or 4 tablespoons

5 large mangoes, peeled, pitted, and cut into ½-in. cubes

½ cup raisins

½ cup red onion, finely diced

½ cup light brown or muscovado sugar, packed

⅓ cup water

¼ cup apple cider vinegar

1 medium jalapeño pepper, ribs and seeds removed, and finely diced

½ TB. peeled and minced fresh ginger

½ TB. minced garlic

1 tsp. *garam masala* or curry powder

1. In a medium slow cooker, combine mangoes, raisins, red onion, light brown sugar, water, apple cider vinegar, jalapeño pepper, ginger, garlic, and garam masala.

2. Cover and cook on high for 3½ to 4 hours, on low for 7 or 8 hours, or until mixture is thickened and mangoes are very soft.

3. Serve hot, warm, or cold as desired. Store chutney in airtight containers in the refrigerator for up to 2 weeks.

Variation: You can replace the fresh mangoes with 5 cups frozen mango chunks, thawed and cut into ½-inch cubes. For **Mango, Apricot, and Date Chutney,** replace the raisins with ¼ cup dried apricots cut into ½-inch-long strips and ¼ cup date pieces coated with oat flour or pitted dates cut into ½-inch-long strips.

DEFINITION

Garam masala literally means "hot spice" in Hindi. This flavorful seasoning blend is made with a combination of pungent and warming spices and doesn't necessarily have a hot flavor like cayenne or chipotle chile powder. It's commonly used in Indian and Southern Asian cuisines as an alternative to curry powder, and although blends vary by brand, most contain cardamom, cinnamon, coriander, cumin, cloves, and black pepper.

Caramelized Onions

Cooking down sweet Walla Walla or Vidalia onions until they're caramelized and dark golden brown in color further enhances their already sweet flavor.

Yield:	Prep time:	Cook time:	Serving size:
4 cups	15 to 20 minutes	3 to 3½ hours	¼ cup

¼ cup nonhydrogenated margarine

¼ cup olive oil

¼ cup Homemade Vegetable Broth (recipe in Chapter 8)

2 TB. unbleached cane sugar

4 or 5 large sweet Walla Walla, Vidalia, or Maui onions, peeled and thinly sliced

Sea salt

Freshly ground black pepper

1. In a medium slow cooker, combine nonhydrogenated margarine, olive oil, Homemade Vegetable Broth, and unbleached cane sugar. Cook on high for 5 to 10 minutes or until margarine melts. Add sweet onions, and stir to coat.

2. Cover and cook on high for 3 to 3½ hours, on low for 6 or 7 hours, or until onions are very soft and golden brown. Taste and season with sea salt and black pepper as desired.

3. Use hot, warm, or cold as a condiment on toast, crackers, or sandwiches or use to flavor sauces, mashed potatoes, grains, pasta, or other dishes as desired. Store caramelized onions in an airtight container or zipper-lock bag in the refrigerator for up to 1 week, or in the freezer for several months.

Variation: For added flavor, add 1 tablespoon chopped fresh thyme or 1 teaspoon dried thyme to the onion mixture. For **Caramelized Onions with Vermouth,** use 2 tablespoons olive oil and 2 tablespoons nonhydrogenated margarine, and add ¼ cup dry vermouth, 2 tablespoons nutritional yeast flakes, and 1 tablespoon chopped fresh thyme or 1 teaspoon dried thyme to the onion mixture.

LOW AND SLOW

Typically, chefs and home cooks caramelize sliced onions by cooking them down on the stovetop, using a large skillet with some oil, butter, or margarine over low heat, stirring occasionally, for close to an hour or until they're very soft and golden brown. Using a slow cooker easily achieves the same result without much effort from the cook.

Roasted Garlic

Roasting garlic transforms the bitey pungency associated with fresh cloves into savory little morsels that have a sweet, mellow, and somewhat nutty flavor.

Yield:	Prep time:	Cook time:	Serving size:
1½ to 2 cups	5 minutes	2½ to 3 hours	3 or 4 whole cloves or 1 tablespoon mashed or puréed roasted garlic

8 large heads garlic

1. Cut off pointy top of each head of garlic, about ½ inch down, to partially expose garlic cloves. Place garlic in a medium slow cooker.

2. Cover and cook on high for 2½ to 3 hours, on low for 5 or 6 hours, or until garlic is very soft. Uncover, turn off the slow cooker, and allow garlic to cool completely.

3. Using tongs or a slotted spoon, remove garlic, squeeze cloves out of garlic heads, and discard skins. (Alternatively, you can mash the cloves with a fork or potato masher, or process them in a food processor fitted with an S blade for a very smooth purée.)

4. Use roasted garlic as a condiment on toast, crackers, or sandwiches as well as to flavor sauces, dips, mashed potatoes, grains, pasta, or other dishes as desired. Store whole cloves of roasted garlic in an airtight container or zipper-lock bag in the refrigerator for up to 1 week or in the freezer for several months.

Variation: For added flavor, sprinkle 1 tablespoon chopped fresh rosemary or thyme, or 1 teaspoon dried, over top of garlic heads.

LOW AND SLOW

Here's another great way to store your roasted garlic for later use. Place tablespoonfuls of roasted garlic purée on a parchment paper–lined cookie sheet. Freeze until solid, transfer to an airtight or zipper-lock bag, label and date the bag, and store in the freezer for up to 6 months.

Soups, Chilies, and Chowders

Move over stockpots and Dutch ovens! You've got some serious competition when it comes to making soups, chilies, and chowders. Actually, in terms of ease and convenience, the slow cooker wins this contest hands down. When you make a pot of soup or chili on the stovetop, you must stir it every now and again or it can burn on the bottom. Or if it's cooking at a too-high temperature with the lid on, the trapped heat could cause it to boil over.

You have no such worries when you use a slow cooker to create these by-the-bowlful meals. You'll truly marvel at how ideal this appliance is for making both big and small batches of thick, thin, and veggie-filled soups, as well as hearty chilies and chowders. And once the cooker is filled and gets going, its low, slow, and steady cooking style tackles this task easily and effortlessly.

So relax. Your worries about how you're going to get a home-cooked meal on the table on a busy weeknight are over, thanks to your super-duper slow cooker!

Bold and Brothy Soups

In This Chapter

- Delicious DIY vegetable broth
- Wholesome grain-enhanced soups
- Veggie-packed soups
- Warming soups with European flair

Soups are the ultimate comfort food, both nourishing and nurturing, and a mainstay of daily diets across the world. I think perhaps Louis P. De Gouy fully understood and expressed this sentiment best in *The Soup Book* (1949), when he wrote, "There is nothing like a plate or a bowl of hot soup, its wisp of aromatic steam making the nostrils quiver with anticipation, to dispel the depressing effects of a grueling day at the office or the shop, rain or snow in the streets, or bad news in the papers."

To get you off to a great start with your soup-making, this chapter begins with a recipe for Homemade Vegetable Broth. Sure, you can buy cartons of vegetable broth in most stores, but it's so easy to make your own, especially with the slow cooker. This lightly seasoned broth makes an appearance in many of the recipes in this book and is a key ingredient for the broth-based soups in this chapter, which are loaded with vegetables, rice, and even pasta.

Homemade Vegetable Broth

This simple, cut-and-cook recipe produces a mild-flavored vegetable broth suitable not only for making soups, but also for adding extra flavor to all your favorite recipes.

Yield:	Prep time:	Cook time:	Serving size:
8 cups	10 to 15 minutes	4 or 5 hours	1 cup

4 large carrots, cut into 1-in. pieces

4 large stalks celery, cut into 1-in. pieces

2 medium yellow onions, cut into 8 wedges

4 cloves garlic, sliced

4 sprigs Italian flat-leaf parsley

2 bay leaves

1 tsp. sea salt

8 whole black peppercorns

8 cups water

1. In a medium slow cooker, combine carrots, celery, yellow onions, garlic, Italian flat-leaf parsley, bay leaves, sea salt, and black peppercorns. Pour in water.

2. Cover and cook on high for 4 or 5 hours, on low for 8 to 10 hours, or until vegetables are very soft.

3. Uncover, and using a slotted spoon, remove and discard bay leaf. Also, remove vegetables, save vegetables for another use (season with herbs, sea salt, and freshly ground black pepper and eat as a side dish) or discard as desired.

4. Allow vegetable broth to cool slightly, strain through a fine-mesh sieve into a large pot, and let broth cool completely. Store portions of vegetable broth in air-tight containers in the refrigerator for up to 5 days, or freeze for up to 6 months.

Variation: For **Roasted Vegetable Broth,** on a large cookie sheet, combine carrots, celery, onions, and garlic. Drizzle 1 tablespoon olive oil over the top, and toss well to combine. Roast vegetables in a 425°F oven for 20 to 30 minutes, stirring every 10 minutes, or until lightly browned. Transfer roasted vegetables to slow cooker, add remaining ingredients, and proceed with recipe.

LOW AND SLOW

Most sauce recipes call for at least 1 or 2 cups vegetable broth, so I suggest dividing the finished vegetable broth into 2-cup portions. However, for those times when you only need a small amount of vegetable broth, try this: fill your ice-cube trays with vegetable broth (1 cube = 2 tablespoons), freeze until solid, transfer to a zipper-lock bag, label and date it, and store in the freezer.

Butter Bean and Barley Soup

The subtle flavor of the herbed tomato broth of this chunky soup is enhanced by the creaminess of plump butter beans and wholesome hulled barley.

Yield:	Prep time:	Cook time:	Serving size:
3 quarts	15 to 20 minutes	3 to 3½ hours	1 cup

3 cups (1 or 2 large) turnips, peeled, and cut into 1-in. cubes

1½ cups cooked butter beans or 1 (15-oz.) can butter beans, drained and rinsed

1½ cups (2 or 3 large) carrots, diced

1 cup celery (including inner leaves and tops), diced

1 medium leek, washed well, cut in ½ lengthwise, and white and green parts thinly sliced

1 cup yellow onion, diced

⅓ cup hulled or pearled barley, rinsed

3 TB. tomato paste

1½ TB. minced garlic

1½ TB. nutritional yeast flakes

1½ tsp. dried basil

1½ tsp. dried thyme

1 tsp. chili powder

¾ tsp. dried marjoram

1 tsp. sea salt

½ tsp. freshly ground black pepper

5 cups Homemade Vegetable Broth (recipe earlier in this chapter)

⅓ cup chopped fresh parsley

1. In a medium or large slow cooker, combine turnips, butter beans, carrots, celery, leek, yellow onion, barley, tomato paste, garlic, nutritional yeast flakes, basil, thyme, chili powder, marjoram, sea salt, and black pepper. Pour in Homemade Vegetable Broth.

2. Cover and cook on high for 3 to 3½ hours, on low for 6 or 7 hours, or until vegetables and barley are tender.

3. Stir in parsley. Taste and adjust seasonings as desired, and serve hot.

Variation: If you're not a fan of turnips, feel free to replace them with an equal amount of Yukon Gold potatoes.

LOW AND SLOW

I prefer the flavor and texture of hulled barley, which has the outer inedible hull removed, but the nutritious grain's germ and bran are still intact. However, if you can't find it, you can use pearl (or pearled) barley, which is barley that's been further processed to remove the beneficial bran and polished (better known as pearling).

Mama Mia Minestrone

Italians are famous for many pasta-based dishes, including minestrone soup, and the zesty, full flavor of this version is made by combining fresh and frozen veggies, fire-roasted tomatoes, and beans with your favorite pasta variety.

Yield:	Prep time:	Cook time:	Serving size:
3 quarts	20 to 25 minutes	3 to 3½ hours	1 cup

1 cup yellow onion, diced

1 cup carrots, diced

1 cup celery (including inner leaves and tops), diced

1 TB. olive oil

2 TB. minced garlic

1 (1- to 1½-lb.) head *escarole,* roughly chopped

1 (16-oz.) pkg. frozen California blend vegetables (broccoli, cauliflower, and carrots), thawed and roughly chopped

1 large zucchini, cut into quarters lengthwise and thinly sliced

1 (15-oz.) can mixed beans, drained and rinsed

2 TB. nutritional yeast flakes

1 bay leaf

1½ TB. Italian seasoning blend

1 tsp. crushed red pepper flakes

1 tsp. sea salt

½ tsp. freshly ground black pepper

1 (28-oz.) can crushed fire-roasted tomatoes

3 cups Homemade Vegetable Broth (recipe earlier in this chapter)

¼ cup red wine (such as Burgundy, Merlot, or Zinfandel)

¾ cup whole-grain shells, orzo, elbow macaroni, ditalini, or other small shape pasta

⅓ cup fresh basil, cut chiffonade

⅓ cup chopped fresh Italian flat-leaf parsley

1. In a medium nonstick skillet over medium heat, combine yellow onion, carrots, celery, and olive oil, and sauté over medium heat, stirring often, for 5 minutes.

2. Add garlic, and sauté, stirring often, for 1 more minute. Remove the skillet from heat.

3. In a medium or large slow cooker, combine onion mixture, escarole, California blend vegetables, zucchini, mixed beans, nutritional yeast flakes, bay leaf, Italian seasoning blend, crushed red pepper flakes, sea salt, and black pepper. Stir in crushed fire-roasted tomatoes, Homemade Vegetable Broth, and red wine.

4. Cover and cook on high for 3 to 3½ hours, on low for 6 or 7 hours, or until vegetables are tender.

5. Stir in whole-grain pasta, basil, and Italian flat-leaf parsley during last 30 minutes of cooking time.

6. Remove and discard bay leaf. Taste and adjust seasonings as desired, and serve hot.

Variation: Feel free to omit or substitute other fresh or frozen vegetables, as well as other canned beans, as desired. For a nonalcoholic version, omit the red wine. If you don't have Italian seasoning blend, you can use 1 teaspoon dried basil, 1 teaspoon dried oregano, 1 teaspoon dried thyme, and 1 teaspoon dried marjoram or rosemary instead. For **Hearty Minestrone with Sausage,** use a large-size pasta such as penne or ziti, and add 4 Seitan Chorizo Sausages or Beer Brats (recipes in Chapter 11), thinly sliced.

DEFINITION

Escarole is a variety of endive that has very broad, bitter-tasting leaves. A medium head of escarole usually yields about 7 cups torn leaves. It can be eaten raw in salads, blanched or boiled in water, or sautéed.

Basque Potato Soup

Seitan Chorizo Sausage adds both to the spicy and smoky flavor of the tomato-based broth as well as the bulk of this hearty soup made with chunks of red-skinned potatoes, onions, and celery.

Yield:	Prep time:	Cook time:	Serving size:
3 quarts	10 to 15 minutes	2½ to 3 hours	1 cup

4 cups (5 or 6 medium) red-skinned potatoes, cut into 1-in. cubes

2 cups (2 medium) yellow onion, diced

1½ cups (2 or 3 large stalks) celery (including inner leaves and tops), diced

1½ TB. minced garlic

1 bay leaf

2 tsp. dried thyme

2 tsp. smoked paprika

1½ tsp. sea salt

½ tsp. freshly ground black pepper

¼ tsp. cayenne or chipotle chile powder

3 cups Homemade Vegetable Broth (recipe earlier in this chapter)

1 (28-oz.) can crushed fire-roasted tomatoes

3 Seitan Chorizo Sausages (recipe in Chapter 11), thinly sliced

⅓ cup chopped fresh Italian flat-leaf parsley

1 TB. fresh lemon juice

1. In a medium or large slow cooker, combine red-skinned potatoes, yellow onion, celery, garlic, bay leaf, thyme, smoked paprika, sea salt, black pepper, and cayenne. Stir in Homemade Vegetable Broth and crushed fire-roasted tomatoes.

2. Cover and cook on high for 2½ to 3 hours, on low for 5 or 6 hours, or until vegetables are tender.

3. Stir in Seitan Chorizo Sausages, Italian flat-leaf parsley, and lemon juice during the last 30 minutes of cooking time.

4. Remove and discard bay leaf. Taste and adjust seasonings as desired, and serve hot.

Variation: For an even chunkier soup, add 2 cups green cabbage, shredded. For **Basque Bean Soup,** add 1½ cups cooked Great Northern beans or 1 (15-ounce) can Great Northern beans, drained and rinsed.

SLOW INTERESTING

This soup originates from the Basque people, who live along the Bay of Biscay and the Western Pyrenees Mountains, near the border of northeastern Spain and southwestern France. Vegetables and legumes grow abundantly in this region's fertile soil, and as a result, have greatly influenced the Basque-style cuisine.

Caldo Verde

Caldo verde means "green soup," and the subtle flavors of this beloved Portuguese potato and kale soup will easily win you over.

Yield:	Prep time:	Cook time:	Serving size:
3 quarts	20 to 25 minutes	2½ to 3 hours	1 cup

4 cups (5 or 6 medium) Yukon Gold or red-skinned potatoes, cut into 1-in. cubes

1½ cups (1 large) yellow onion, diced

1½ cups (2 or 3 large stalks) celery (including inner leaves and tops), cut in ½ lengthwise and thinly sliced

1 bunch green or lacinato kale, stems removed and cut *chiffonade* (about 7 or 8 cups)

2 TB. minced garlic

1 bay leaf

1½ tsp. sea salt

½ tsp. freshly ground black pepper

¼ tsp. cayenne or chipotle chile powder

6 cups Homemade Vegetable Broth (recipe earlier in this chapter)

⅓ cup chopped fresh Italian flat-leaf parsley

¼ cup nutritional yeast flakes

1. In a medium or large slow cooker, layer, in order, Yukon Gold potatoes, yellow onion, celery, lacinato kale, garlic, bay leaf, sea salt, and black pepper. Pour in Homemade Vegetable Broth.

2. Cover and cook on high for 2½ to 3 hours, on low for 5 or 6 hours, or until vegetables are tender.

3. Stir in Italian flat-leaf parsley and nutritional yeast flakes during the last 15 minutes of cooking time.

4. Remove and discard bay leaf. Taste and adjust seasonings as desired, and serve hot.

Variation: For an even chunkier soup, add 1½ cups cooked kidney beans or 1 (15-ounce) can kidney beans, drained and rinsed. For **Ligurian-Style Caldo Verde,** add 3 Seitan Chorizo Sausages (recipe in Chapter 11), thinly sliced, 2 teaspoons smoked paprika, and 1½ teaspoons crushed red pepper flakes.

DEFINITION

Chiffonade is French for "made from rags," a technique for slicing herbs and vegetables into long, thin, ribbonlike strips. This reference usually applies to leaves of basil, mint, or leafy green vegetables. To chiffonade something, stack and roll a small pile of leaves; slice the roll crosswise into fine, thin strips; and gently toss the strips with your fingers to separate them.

Borscht

Fresh beets give this Eastern and Central European comfort food its ruby-red color, while cabbage and potatoes give it some heft. A little tomato, apple, and citrus juice impart a slight tang and sweetness to the soup.

Yield:	Prep time:	Cook time:	Serving size:
3 quarts	20 to 25 minutes	3 to 3½ hours	1 cup

3 cups (2 large or 3 medium) red beets, peeled, and julienned

2 cups (½ medium head) green cabbage, shredded

1½ cups (3 or 4 medium) red-skinned potatoes, julienned

2 large Gala or other apples, cored and diced

1 cup red or yellow onion, diced

¾ cup tomato, diced

½ cup chopped fresh dill or 2 TB. dried dill weed

2 TB. chopped fresh thyme or 2 tsp. dried

5 cups Homemade Vegetable Broth (recipe earlier in this chapter)

¼ cup fresh orange juice

2 TB. fresh lemon juice

Sea salt

Freshly ground black pepper

Vegan sour cream

Chopped fresh dill

1. In a medium or large slow cooker, layer, in order, red beets, green cabbage, red-skinned potatoes, Gala apples, red onion, tomato, dill, and thyme. Pour in Homemade Vegetable Broth.

2. Cover and cook on high for 3 to 3½ hours, on low for 6 or 7 hours, or until vegetables are tender.

3. Stir in orange juice and lemon juice during the last 15 minutes of cooking time.

4. Taste, season with sea salt and black pepper, and adjust seasonings as desired. Serve hot, garnishing individual servings with 1 dollop vegan sour cream and a little chopped fresh dill as desired.

Variation: For **Golden Borscht,** replace red beets with an equal amount of golden beets, peeled and julienned.

LOW AND SLOW

While cutting red beets, be sure to wear a pair of vinyl food handler's gloves to avoid staining your hands. If you own a dark-colored cutting board, use it as well. If you don't, rub a cut lemon on your cutting board after you're done to help remove any beet stains.

Thick and Creamy Soups

In This Chapter

- Velvety smooth soups
- Thick potato-rich soups
- Creamy grain-thickened soups
- Hearty bean-based soups

The soup recipes in the previous chapter relied heavily on vegetable broth and other liquidy ingredients, which is what puts them on the lighter side of the soup spectrum. However, when the summer sun starts to fade and the autumn winds begin to blow, we often seek out heartier soups, something thick and creamy.

Get ready to learn the slow-cook and blend technique for making velvety-smooth vegetable purées and luscious, creamy-textured soups without having to add a speck of dairy or tons of oil or margarine. Yes, you can have filling and great-tasting soups that aren't overly fattening.

I round out the chapter with a trio of thick, bean- and veggie-based soups sure to satisfy even the hungriest of diners.

Butternut Bisque

Puréeing cubes of slow-roasted butternut squash and coconut milk gives this golden soup a velvety smooth texture, and adding a bit of fresh ginger gives it a nice zing.

Yield:	Prep time:	Cook time:	Serving size:
3 quarts	10 to 15 minutes	3 to 3½ hours	1 cup

1 cup (2 or 3 large) shallots, diced

2 large stalks celery (including inner leaves and tops), diced

½ TB. olive oil

2 TB. peeled and minced fresh ginger

1 large butternut squash, peeled, stem and seeds removed, and cut into 1-in. cubes

5 cups water

2 tsp. dried thyme or marjoram

¾ tsp. sea salt

2 cups coconut milk beverage or other nondairy milk

1. In a medium nonstick skillet over medium heat, combine shallots, celery, and olive oil, and sauté, stirring often, for 3 minutes.

2. Add ginger, and sauté, stirring often, for 1 minute. Remove the skillet from heat.

3. In a medium or large slow cooker, combine butternut squash, shallot mixture, water, thyme, and sea salt, and stir well.

4. Cover and cook on high for 3 to 3½ hours, on low for 6 or 7 hours, or until vegetables are tender.

5. Stir in coconut milk beverage during the last 30 minutes of cooking time.

6. In a food processor fitted with an S blade or a blender, process soup in small batches for 1 or 2 minutes or until a smooth purée. Scrape down the sides of the container with a spatula, and process for 30 more seconds. Transfer puréed mixture to a large bowl, and repeat procedure. Carefully return puréed soup mixture to the slow cooker. (Alternatively, allow soup to cool for several minutes, and then use an immersion blender to purée mixture directly in the slow cooker.)

7. Taste and adjust seasonings as desired, and serve hot.

Variation: You can also prepare this soup with other varieties of winter squash, such as delicata, turban, or acorn. For **Mapley Butternut Bisque,** add ⅓ cup maple syrup.

SLOW INTERESTING

All winter squashes are rich in beta-carotene, vitamins A and C (and even some B), potassium, and manganese, as well as excellent sources of dietary fiber. Try to work winter squashes into more of your meals during the fall and winter months when they're most plentiful.

Roasted Garlic, Potato, and Leek Potage

Potage is a French culinary term used to describe a thick or creamy soup, and although this soup contains only a few ingredients, roasted garlic and soy creamer give it a full flavor and rich mouthfeel—and without any additional oil or margarine.

Yield:	Prep time:	Cook time:	Serving size:
3 quarts	10 to 15 minutes	3 to 3½ hours	1 cup

12 cloves Roasted Garlic (recipe in Chapter 7)

3 lb. (8 or 9 large) Yukon Gold potatoes, quartered lengthwise and thinly sliced

1 medium leek, washed well, cut in ½ lengthwise, and thinly sliced

1½ TB. chopped fresh thyme or 1½ tsp. dried

1½ tsp. sea salt

¾ tsp. *lemon pepper*

4 cups water or Homemade Vegetable Broth (recipe in Chapter 8)

1½ cups plain soy or coconut creamer

⅓ cup chopped fresh parsley

1. In a small bowl, mash Roasted Garlic with a fork or potato masher. (Alternatively, process them in a food processor fitted with an S blade until a smooth purée.)

2. In a medium or large slow cooker, layer, in order, Yukon Gold potatoes, leek, garlic mixture, thyme, sea salt, and lemon pepper. Pour in water.

3. Cover and cook on high for 3 to 3½ hours, on low for 6 or 7 hours, or until vegetables are tender.

4. Stir in soy creamer during the last 15 minutes of cooking time.

5. In a food processor fitted with an S blade or a blender, process soup in small batches for 1 or 2 minutes or until a smooth purée. Scrape down the sides of the container with a spatula, and process for 30 more seconds. Transfer puréed mixture to a large bowl, and repeat procedure. Carefully return puréed soup mixture to the slow cooker. (Alternatively, allow soup to cool for several minutes, and use an immersion blender to purée mixture directly in the slow cooker.)

6. Stir in parsley. Taste and adjust seasonings as desired, and serve hot.

Variation: For a chunkier soup, only purée half of it, rather than the entire amount.

> **DEFINITION**
>
> **Lemon pepper** is a seasoning made from grinding together dried lemon zest and cracked black peppercorns. This process infuses the black pepper with the flavorful and extremely fragrant essential oil contained within the lemon zest. Try using lemon pepper instead of black pepper to season your favorite soups, vegetables, grains, and pasta dishes.

Creamy Tomato Soup

This slow-cooker version of the childhood favorite—cream of tomato soup—is made with canned tomatoes, onions, garlic, and vegan creamer and has the same silky richness you fondly remember. Serve it with vegan grilled cheese sandwiches for a nostalgic lunch treat.

Yield:	Prep time:	Cook time:	Serving size:
3 quarts	10 to 15 minutes	3 to 3½ hours	1 cup

1½ cups (1 large) yellow onion, diced
1 TB. olive oil
1 TB. minced garlic
2 (28-oz.) cans crushed tomatoes, with juice
4 cups water
1 (6-oz.) can tomato paste

4 sprigs Italian flat-leaf parsley
1 bay leaf
1 TB. unbleached cane sugar
1 tsp. sea salt
1 tsp. smoked paprika
1 pt. plain soy or coconut creamer
2 TB. nutritional yeast flakes

1. In a medium nonstick skillet over medium heat, combine yellow onion and olive oil, and sauté, stirring often, for 3 minutes.

2. Add garlic, and sauté, stirring often, for 1 minute. Remove the skillet from heat.

3. In a medium or large slow cooker, combine onion mixture, crushed tomatoes, water, tomato paste, Italian flat-leaf parsley, bay leaf, unbleached cane sugar, sea salt, and smoked paprika.

4. Cover and cook on high for 3 to 3½ hours, on low for 6 or 7 hours, or until vegetables are tender. Remove and discard parsley sprigs and bay leaf.

5. Stir in soy creamer and nutritional yeast flakes during the last 15 minutes of cook time.

6. In a food processor fitted with an S blade or a blender, process soup in small batches for 1 or 2 minutes or until a smooth purée. Scrape down the sides of the container with a spatula, and process for 30 more seconds. Transfer puréed mixture to a large bowl, and repeat procedure. Carefully, return puréed soup mixture to the slow cooker. (Alternatively, allow soup to cool for several minutes, and then use an immersion blender to purée mixture directly in the slow cooker.)

7. Taste and adjust seasonings as desired, and serve hot.

Variation: For **Creamy Fire-Roasted Tomato and Basil Soup,** use fire-roasted crushed tomatoes; omit the parsley; and after blending the soup, stir in ½ cup fresh basil, cut chiffonade.

> **SLOW INTERESTING**
>
> This soup calls for several sprigs fresh parsley. A sprig is a cluster of leaves that is still attached to the central stem. The stem is roughly 3 or 4 inches in length.

Cream of Broccoli and Cauliflower Soup

Broccoli and cauliflower go hand in hand in this creamy and versatile soup that can be served either chunky-style or puréed if you want to sneak these often maligned vegetables past your kids.

Yield:	Prep time:	Cook time:	Serving size:
3 quarts	10 to 15 minutes	3 to 3½ hours	1 cup

2 cups (2 or 3 medium) Yukon Gold potatoes, peeled, and cut into 1-in. cubes

2 (16-oz.) pkg. frozen broccoli and cauliflower florets, thawed

1½ cups (1 large) yellow onion, diced

1½ TB. minced garlic

1 bay leaf

1½ TB. chopped fresh thyme or 1½ tsp. dried

1 tsp. sea salt

¾ tsp. white or lemon pepper

3 cups Homemade Vegetable Broth (recipe in Chapter 8)

2 cups soy or other nondairy milk

2 TB. cornstarch or *arrowroot*

2 TB. nutritional yeast flakes

1 TB. Dijon mustard

⅓ cup chopped fresh parsley

1. In a medium or large slow cooker, layer, in order, Yukon Gold potatoes, broccoli and cauliflower florets, yellow onion, garlic, bay leaf, thyme, sea salt, and white pepper. Pour in Homemade Vegetable Broth.

2. Cover and cook on high for 3 to 3½ hours, on low for 6 or 7 hours, or until vegetables are tender.

3. In a medium bowl, whisk together soy milk, cornstarch, nutritional yeast flakes, and Dijon mustard. Stir in soy milk mixture during the last 30 minutes of cooking time.

4. Stir in parsley. Remove and discard bay leaf. Taste and adjust seasonings as desired, and serve hot.

Variation: You can also prepare this soup using 3 cups each fresh broccoli and cauliflower, roughly chopped. For **Cheesy Broccoli-Cauliflower Soup,** add 1½ cups Wine Is Fine Fondue (recipe in Chapter 5) or Mellow Cheese Fondue (variation in Chapter 5) or 1½ cups shredded vegan cheddar cheese.

DEFINITION

Arrowroot is a gluten-free binder and thickening agent that has a neutral taste. It can be used in place of flour or cornstarch in baking as well as to thicken gravies, sauces, soups, stews, and dessert recipes.

Creamy Vegetable and Mixed Rice Soup

Adding a few tablespoons sherry and toasted sesame oil gives this soup's creamy base a slightly smoky-nuttiness that nicely complements the earthy flavors of the mixed rice blend, *lacinato kale*, and aromatic vegetables.

Yield:	Prep time:	Cook time:	Serving size:
3 quarts	20 to 25 minutes	3 to 3½ hours	1 cup

4 cups (½ a bunch) lacinato kale, stems removed, and cut chiffonade

1¼ cups (2 large) carrots, cut in ½ lengthwise, and thinly sliced

1¼ cups (2 or 3 large stalks) celery (including inner leaves and tops), cut in ½ lengthwise, and thinly sliced

8 oz. crimini or white button mushrooms, cut in ½ and thinly sliced

¾ cup green onions, white and green parts, thinly sliced

1 TB. minced garlic

1 bay leaf

1 TB. onion powder

1 tsp. dried basil

1 tsp. dried thyme or marjoram

1 tsp. sea salt

½ tsp. lemon or garlic pepper

½ tsp. freshly ground black pepper

4 cups Homemade Vegetable Broth (recipe in Chapter 8)

¾ cup mixed rice and wild rice blend, rinsed

2 cups soy or other nondairy milk

1 cup white whole-wheat or other flour

3 TB. dry sherry, or white wine (such as Chardonnay or Riesling)

2 TB. nutritional yeast flakes

1½ TB. toasted sesame oil

⅓ cup chopped fresh parsley

1. In a medium or large slow cooker, layer, in order, lacinato kale, carrots, celery, crimini mushrooms, green onions, garlic, bay leaf, onion powder, basil, thyme, sea salt, lemon pepper, and black pepper. Pour in Homemade Vegetable Broth.

2. Cover and cook on high for 3 to 3½ hours, on low for 6 or 7 hours, or until vegetables are tender.

3. Stir in mixed rice and wild rice blend during the last hour of cooking time.

4. In a medium bowl, whisk together soy milk, white whole-wheat flour, sherry, nutritional yeast flakes, and toasted sesame oil. Stir in soy milk mixture during the last 15 minutes of cooking time.

5. When rice is tender and soup has thickened, stir in parsley. Remove and discard bay leaf. Taste and adjust seasonings as desired, and serve hot.

Variation: If you don't have any mixed rice and wild rice blend on hand, you can substitute an equal amount of long-grain brown rice.

DEFINITION

Lacinato kale is an heirloom variety of kale with tender, dark blue-green leaves that have a slightly sweeter and more delicate taste than curly green kale. It's also referred to as Tuscan, Italian, or dinosaur kale—the latter because its extremely wrinkled leaves have a somewhat prehistoric look.

Smoky Chipotle Black Bean Soup

Smoked sea salt and chipotle chile powder give this thick black bean soup a smoky and spicy kick. Some smart garnishes add not only a delightful contrast of color and texture, but a cooling effect as well.

Yield:	Prep time:	Cook time:	Serving size:
10 or 11 cups	20 to 25 minutes, plus 1 hour soak time	5 or 6 hours	1 cup

1 lb. dried black beans, sorted and rinsed

1½ cups (1 large) red onion, diced

1½ cups (1 large) green bell pepper, ribs and seeds removed, and diced

1 cup celery (including inner leaves and tops), diced

½ TB. olive oil

1½ TB. minced garlic

2 tsp. chili powder

2 tsp. ground cumin

1 tsp. chipotle chile powder or ½ tsp. cayenne

1 tsp. dried oregano

7 cups water

⅓ cup chopped fresh cilantro

2 TB. nutritional yeast flakes

2 TB. fresh lime juice

¾ tsp. smoked sea salt or sea salt

½ tsp. freshly ground black pepper

Vegan sour cream or yogurt

Store-bought salsa or diced tomato

Diced avocado

1. Place black beans in a large pot, and cover with water. Bring to a boil over high heat, and boil for 2 minutes. Cover, remove from heat, and set aside to soak for 1 hour. Drain black beans in a colander, and discard soaking liquid.

2. In a large, nonstick skillet over medium heat, combine red onion, green bell pepper, celery, and olive oil, and sauté, stirring often, for 3 minutes.

3. Add garlic, chili powder, cumin, chipotle chile powder, and oregano, and sauté, stirring often, for 1 minute. Remove the skillet from heat.

4. In a medium or large slow cooker, combine presoaked black beans and onion mixture. Pour in water.

5. Cover and cook on high for 5 or 6 hours, on low for 7 or 8 hours, or until black beans are tender.

6. Transfer 2 cups black bean mixture to a blender, and process for 1 or 2 minutes or until a smooth purée. Return purée to the slow cooker.

7. Stir in cilantro, nutritional yeast flakes, lime juice, smoked sea salt, and black pepper, and cook for 10 minutes.

8. Taste and adjust seasonings as desired, and serve hot, garnishing individual servings with vegan sour cream, salsa, and diced avocado as desired.

Variation: For a milder version, omit the chipotle chile powder.

LOW AND SLOW

Chipotle chile powder is a convenient way to add a bit of heat and smoky flavor to dishes. However, if you can't find any at your local store, check the Mexican foods aisle for canned chipotles in adobo sauce (a sauce made of tomatoes, vinegar, and spices). Finely chop the canned chipotle chiles or purée them along with the adobo sauce for use in recipes. One tablespoon canned chipotle can be used as a substitute for 1 teaspoon chipotle chile powder.

Navy Bean and Sausage Soup

As this soup cooks, the navy beans release their natural starch, which helps slightly thicken the soup's herby broth. Slices of Seitan Chorizo Sausage are added to give the soup a slightly smoky flavor.

Yield:	Prep time:	Cook time:	Serving size:
10 or 11 cups	10 to 15 minutes	5 or 6 hours, plus 1 hour soak time	1 cup

1 lb. dried navy beans, sorted and rinsed

1¼ cups (1 large) yellow onion, diced

1¼ cups (2 large) carrots, diced

1¼ cups (2 or 3 large stalks) celery (including inner leaves and tops), diced

1½ TB. minced garlic

1 bay leaf

1½ tsp. dried thyme

1 tsp. dried oregano

1 tsp. rubbed sage

7 cups water

2 Seitan Chorizo Sausages (recipe in Chapter 11), cut into quarters lengthwise and thinly sliced

⅓ cup chopped fresh parsley

2 TB. nutritional yeast flakes

¾ tsp. smoked sea salt or sea salt

½ tsp. freshly ground black pepper

1. Place navy beans in a large pot, and cover with water. Bring to a boil over high heat, and boil for 2 minutes. Cover, remove from heat, and set aside to soak for 1 hour. Drain navy beans in a colander, and discard soaking liquid.

2. In a medium or large slow cooker, combine presoaked navy beans, yellow onion, carrots, celery, garlic, bay leaf, thyme, oregano, and rubbed sage. Pour in water.

3. Cover and cook on high for 5 or 6 hours, on low for 7 or 8 hours, or until navy beans are tender.

4. Stir in Seitan Chorizo Sausages, parsley, nutritional yeast flakes, smoked sea salt, and black pepper, and cook for 15 minutes.

5. Remove and discard bay leaf. Taste and adjust seasonings as desired, and serve hot.

Variation: You can also make this soup using other white beans, such as Great Northern, cannellini, or butter beans, as well as use an equal amount Beer Brats (recipe in Chapter 11) in place of the Seitan Chorizo Sausages.

> **SLOW INTERESTING**
>
> According to legend, navy beans got their nautical moniker due to the fact that they've long been a staple of the British and U.S. Navy diet. The dried beans travel well and are easy to use to make many filling, protein-rich meals for the hard-working sailors.

Split Pea Soup

Split peas cook down with pieces of potato and aromatic vegetables to create a thick and hearty, stick-to-your-ribs soup that's excellent served with saltine crackers or slices of bread.

Yield:	Prep time:	Cook time:	Serving size:
10 or 11 cups	10 to 15 minutes	5 or 6 hours	1 cup

1 lb. dried split peas, sorted and rinsed

3 cups (4 or 5 medium) red-skinned potatoes, cut into 1-in. cubes

1½ cups (1 large) yellow onion, diced

1½ cups (2 large) carrots, diced

1½ cups (2 or 3 large stalks) celery (including inner leaves and tops), diced

1 TB. minced garlic

1 bay leaf

1 tsp. dried basil

1 tsp. dried oregano

1 tsp. dried thyme

1 tsp. chili powder

9 cups water

⅓ cup chopped fresh parsley

2 TB. nutritional yeast flakes

1 TB. fresh lemon juice

1 tsp. sea salt

½ tsp. lemon pepper

½ tsp. freshly ground black pepper

1. In a medium or large slow cooker, combine split peas, red-skinned potatoes, yellow onion, carrots, celery, garlic, bay leaf, basil, oregano, thyme, and chili powder. Pour in water.

2. Cover and cook on high for 5 or 6 hours, on low for 7 or 8 hours, or until split peas are tender and broken down. Stir soup after 3 hours cooking time to prevent split peas from sticking to the bottom of the slow cooker.

3. Stir in parsley, nutritional yeast flakes, lemon juice, sea salt, lemon pepper, and black pepper, and cook for 15 minutes.

4. Remove and discard bay leaf. Taste and adjust seasonings as desired, and serve hot.

Variation: For **Curried Split Pea and Parsnip Soup,** replace the red-skinned potatoes with 3 cups (3 or 4 large) parsnips, peeled and cut into 1-inch cubes, and replace the basil, oregano, and chili powder with 1 tablespoon curry powder.

SLOW INTERESTING

Green split peas are rich in protein, complex carbohydrates, several vitamins and minerals, and beneficial dietary fiber, all while being extremely low in fat and sodium. This makes them a great choice if you're trying to eat more healthy and nutritious meals.

Chunky Chilies and Chowders

In This Chapter

- Meat-free chilies
- Bold and beany chilies
- Rich and creamy chowders
- Very vegan chowders

Although they may have originated in other lands, chilies and chowders have become standard American fare from coast to coast—in the kitchens of our homes, cafeterias, diners, and even upscale bistros. Luckily for all of us who like to experiment in the kitchen, when it comes to making chili, anything goes! Does your man think chili isn't chili without some kind of meat in it? If so, slip one past him with this chapter's Chili Sin Carne. Hate tomatoes? Give the White Chili a try.

Perhaps you want to increase your family's daily vegetable consumption. Easily get more veggies into them by throwing together a batch of Chunky Veggie Chili, or for something a bit richer, move on to the creamy chowder recipes, which include both all-veg, as well as two seafood-free varieties. Cut a generous slice of bread (check out the recipes in Chapter 17) or bust out the tortilla chips and saltines for the perfect pairing to your big bowlful of chili or chowder.

Chili Sin Carne

Crumbled and browned bits of tempeh provide a chewy, meatlike texture to this spicy chili that tastes great with a little shredded vegan cheese on top.

Yield:	Prep time:	Cook time:	Serving size:
10 or 11 cups	20 to 25 minutes	4 or 5 hours	1½ cups

1 (8-oz.) pkg. tempeh

1 TB. tamari, shoyu, or Bragg Liquid Aminos

1 TB. olive oil

1½ cups (1 large) yellow onion, diced

1½ cups (1 large) green bell pepper, ribs and seeds removed, and diced

1 medium jalapeño pepper, ribs and seeds removed, and finely diced

2 TB. minced garlic

1 TB. chili powder

½ TB. ground cumin

½ TB. dried oregano

1 tsp. smoked paprika

½ tsp. chipotle chile powder or cayenne

¾ tsp. sea salt

½ tsp. freshly ground black pepper

3 cups cooked kidney beans or pinto beans, or 2 (15-oz.) cans kidney or pinto beans, drained and rinsed

1 (28-oz.) can crushed fire-roasted tomatoes, with juice

1 (14-oz.) can diced fire-roasted tomatoes with green chiles, with juice

⅓ cup chopped fresh cilantro

2 TB. nutritional yeast flakes

Shredded vegan cheddar cheese or other variety

1. Using your fingers, crumble tempeh into a small bowl. Drizzle tamari over the top, and toss gently to coat.

2. In a large, nonstick skillet over medium heat, combine tempeh and olive oil, and sauté, stirring often, for 3 minutes.

3. Add yellow onion, green bell pepper, and jalapeño pepper, and sauté, stirring often, for 3 minutes.

4. Add garlic, chili powder, cumin, oregano, smoked paprika, chipotle chile powder, sea salt, and black pepper, and sauté, stirring often, for 1 minute. Remove the skillet from heat.

5. In a medium or large slow cooker, combine tempeh mixture, kidney beans, crushed fire-roasted tomatoes, and diced fire-roasted tomatoes with green chiles.

6. Cover and cook on high for 4 or 5 hours, on low for 7 or 8 hours, or until vegetables are tender.

7. Stir in cilantro and nutritional yeast flakes, and cook for 15 minutes.

8. Taste and adjust seasonings as desired, and serve hot, garnishing individual servings with shredded vegan cheddar cheese as desired.

Variation: If you prefer your chili with a mild heat level, omit the chipotle chile powder. If you want it to be spicier, add some hot pepper sauce to the finished chili.

SLOW INTERESTING

In Spanish, *chile con carne* (or *chili con carne* as it's more commonly known) refers to a stewlike dish made of chile peppers and meat. In contrast, *chili sin carne* is made without meat.

Chunky Veggie Chili

Nearly every color in the rainbow is represented in this thick and chunky chili that's loaded with a wide assortment of savory, spicy, and even sweet-tasting vegetables, as well as several types of beans and smoky, fire-roasted tomatoes.

Yield:	Prep time:	Cook time:	Serving size:
11 or 12 cups	20 to 25 minutes	4 or 5 hours	1½ cups

2 (15-oz.) cans mixed beans, drained and rinsed

2 cups (2 large) garnet yams or sweet potatoes, peeled, and cut into 1-in. cubes

1 cup red or yellow onion, diced

1 cup green bell pepper, ribs and seeds removed, and diced

1 cup red or yellow bell pepper, ribs and seeds removed, and diced

1 medium Anaheim or jalapeño pepper, ribs and seeds removed, and finely diced

1½ TB. minced garlic

2 TB. chili powder

1 TB. smoked paprika

½ TB. ground cumin

½ TB. dried oregano

1 tsp. sea salt

½ tsp. freshly ground black pepper

1 (28-oz.) can crushed fire-roasted tomatoes

1 (28-oz.) can diced fire-roasted tomatoes with green chiles, with juice

1 medium yellow summer squash, cut into quarters lengthwise, and thinly sliced

1 medium zucchini, cut into quarters lengthwise, and thinly sliced

1 cup fresh or frozen cut corn

⅓ cup chopped fresh cilantro or Italian flat-leaf parsley

Vegan sour cream or yogurt

Shredded vegan cheddar cheese or other variety

Diced avocado

1. In a medium or large slow cooker, combine mixed beans, garnet yams, red onion, green bell pepper, red bell pepper, Anaheim pepper, garlic, chili powder, smoked paprika, cumin, oregano, sea salt, and black pepper. Pour in crushed fire-roasted tomatoes and diced fire-roasted tomatoes with green chiles.

2. Cover and cook on high for 4 or 5 hours, on low for 7 or 8 hours, or until vegetables are tender.

3. Stir in yellow summer squash, zucchini, and corn during the last 30 minutes of cooking time.

4. When vegetables are tender, stir in cilantro. Taste and adjust seasonings as desired, and serve hot, garnishing individual servings with vegan sour cream, shredded vegan cheddar cheese, and diced avocado as desired.

Variation: If you can't find cans of mixed beans, you can replace them with black, kidney, pinto, or other bean variety of choice.

SLOW INTERESTING

Many farmers' markets and natural foods stores sell heirloom vegetable varieties like purple beauty peppers or cocozelle summer squash. I highly recommend swapping them out for their more commonly available cousins in recipes much like this one whenever you want to broaden your vegetable horizons and culinary creativity and palate.

White Chili

Not all chilies are red. For a change of pace, try this medium-hot chili that's tomato free and loaded with chewy pieces of seitan, Great Northern beans, corn, bell peppers, green chiles, and plenty of spices.

Yield:	Prep time:	Cook time:	Serving size:
10 or 11 cups	20 to 25 minutes	4 or 5 hours	1½ cups

3 cups cooked Great Northern beans, or 2 (15-oz.) cans Great Northern beans, drained and rinsed

1½ cups Chick'n-Style Simmered Seitan (variation in Chapter 11), roughly chopped

1½ cups fresh or frozen cut corn

1½ cups (1 large) yellow onion, diced

1½ cups (1 large) green bell pepper, ribs and seeds removed, and diced

1 medium jalapeño pepper, ribs and seeds removed, and finely diced

1 (4-oz.) can diced mild green chiles, with liquid

1½ TB. minced garlic

1 tsp. ground cumin

1 tsp. dried oregano

½ tsp. ground *coriander*

½ tsp. sea salt

½ tsp. lemon pepper

½ tsp. freshly ground black pepper

6 cups Homemade Vegetable Broth (recipe in Chapter 8)

⅓ cup chopped fresh *cilantro*

2 TB. nutritional yeast flakes

Baked tortilla chips

Vegan sour cream or yogurt

Shredded vegan cheddar cheese or other variety

Diced avocado

1. In a medium or large slow cooker, layer, in order, Great Northern beans, Chick'n-Style Simmered Seitan, corn, yellow onion, green bell pepper, jalapeño pepper, green chiles, garlic, cumin, oregano, coriander, sea salt, lemon pepper, and black pepper. Pour in Homemade Vegetable Broth.

2. Cover and cook on high for 4 or 5 hours, on low for 7 or 8 hours, or until vegetables are tender.

3. Stir in cilantro and nutritional yeast flakes, and cook for 15 minutes.

4. Taste and adjust seasonings as desired, and serve hot, garnishing individual servings with baked tortilla chips, vegan sour cream, shredded vegan cheddar cheese, and diced avocado as desired.

Variation: For added flavor, in a large, nonstick skillet over medium heat, sauté yellow onion, green bell pepper, jalapeño pepper, and garlic in ½ tablespoon olive oil for 5 minutes, and add to the slow cooker.

> **DEFINITION**
>
> **Cilantro** is a member of the parsley family and is used in Mexican cooking, especially salsa, as well as in some Indian and Asian dishes. Use cilantro in moderation, as some find the flavor overwhelming. **Coriander** is the rich, warm, spicy seed of the cilantro plant. It's used in all types of cuisines, from African to South American, and dishes from entrées to desserts.

Roasted Corn Chowder

Pan-roasting corn in a dry cast-iron skillet is a quick and easy way to caramelize the natural sugars contained within the corn kernels, and gives them a similar smoky flavor to grilled corn. This added step really boosts this chowder's lush flavor.

Yield:	Prep time:	Cook time:	Serving size:
2½ quarts	20 to 25 minutes	2½ to 3 hours	1½ cups

6½ cups fresh or 2 (16-oz.) pkg. frozen cut corn, thawed

4 cups water

3 TB. nutritional yeast flakes

3 cloves garlic, sliced

1 tsp. smoked paprika

1 tsp. chili powder

1 tsp. sea salt

½ tsp. garlic pepper

¼ tsp. freshly ground black pepper

1 large green bell pepper, ribs and seeds removed, and diced

1 large red bell pepper, ribs and seeds removed, and diced

1 medium yellow onion, diced

2 cups soy or other nondairy milk

⅓ cup chopped fresh Italian flat-leaf parsley

1. Place a large cast-iron skillet over medium heat, and heat for 1 or 2 minutes or until really hot. (Alternatively, use a large nonstick skillet, but do not preheat skillet.) Add 3 cups corn, and dry-sauté, stirring occasionally, for 5 to 7 minutes or until corn is lightly browned around the edges. Remove the skillet from heat.

2. In a blender or food processor fitted with an S blade, process remaining 3½ cups corn, water, nutritional yeast flakes, garlic, smoked paprika, chili powder, sea salt, garlic pepper, and black pepper for 1 or 2 minutes or until smooth.

3. In a medium or large slow cooker, combine blended corn mixture, pan-roasted corn, green bell pepper, red bell pepper, and yellow onion.

4. Cover and cook on high for 2½ to 3 hours, on low for 5 or 6 hours, or until vegetables are tender.

5. Stir in soy milk and Italian flat-leaf parsley during last 30 minutes of cooking time.

6. Taste and adjust seasonings as desired, and serve hot.

COOKER CAVEAT

The four major crops that are genetically modified are soybeans, corn, cottonseed, and canola oil, and much controversy surrounds the safety of consuming these altered foods. You can avoid them by looking for "non-GMO" or "made without genetically modified ingredients" on product labels and buying certified organic whenever possible. These standards and regulations prohibit the use of altered seeds.

Manhattan Seitan and Sea Vegetable Chowder

Chopped pieces of seitan are the visual stand-in for clams, and *sea vegetables* do their part by providing a fresh-from-the-sea flavor to this veganized version of the tomato-based chowder that hails from New York State.

Yield:	Prep time:	Cook time:	Serving size:
11 or 12 cups	20 to 25 minutes	3½ to 4 hours	1½ cups

3 (6-in.) pieces kombu

2 cups hot water

3 cups (4 or 5 medium) red-skinned potatoes, cut into 1-in. cubes

1 cup yellow onion, diced

1 cup carrots, diced

1 cup celery (including inner leaves and tops), diced

1 cup green bell pepper, ribs and seeds removed, and diced

1½ TB. minced garlic

1½ cups Chick'n-Style Simmered Seitan (variation in Chapter 11), roughly chopped

3 TB. dulse flakes or nori flakes

1 bay leaf

1½ TB. Old Bay Seasoning

1½ tsp. dried basil

1 tsp. dried oregano

1 tsp. smoked or sweet paprika

½ tsp. sea salt

½ tsp. freshly ground black pepper

½ tsp. crushed red pepper flakes

2½ cups Homemade Vegetable Broth (recipe in Chapter 8)

1 (28-oz.) can crushed fire-roasted tomatoes

⅓ cup chopped fresh Italian flat-leaf parsley

1. Place kombu in a small bowl. Pour in hot water, and set aside for 30 minutes to allow kombu to rehydrate and soften. Remove kombu from soaking liquid, set soaking liquid aside, and finely chop kombu into small strips.

2. In a medium or large slow cooker, layer, in order, red-skinned potatoes, yellow onion, carrots, celery, green bell pepper, garlic, Chick'n-Style Simmered Seitan, dulse flakes, kombu strips, bay leaf, Old Bay Seasoning, basil, oregano, smoked paprika, sea salt, black pepper, and crushed red pepper flakes. Pour in reserved kombu soaking liquid, Homemade Vegetable Broth, and crushed fire-roasted tomatoes.

3. Cover and cook on high for 3½ to 4 hours, on low for 7 or 8 hours, or until vegetables are tender.

4. Stir in Italian flat-leaf parsley. Remove and discard bay leaf. Taste and adjust seasonings as desired, and serve hot.

Variation: If you really enjoy the flavor and texture of sea vegetables, you can also add a handful of hijiki or arame. For **Manhattan Chickpea Chowder,** replace the chopped Chick'n-Style Simmered Seitan with 1½ cups cooked chickpeas or 1 (15-ounce) can chickpeas, drained and rinsed.

DEFINITION

Sea vegetables are edible plants that grow in the ocean. Some commonly used varieties include arame, dulse, kelp, kombu, hijiki, nori, and wakame. They provide beneficial dietary sources of iodine, iron, magnesium, calcium, vitamin K, and several B vitamins.

New England Oyster Mushroom Chowder

Vegan creamer provides the creamy backdrop to this chowder that's studded with vegetables. However, it's the last-minute addition of *oyster mushrooms* coated in Old Bay Seasoning that gives it a chewy, faux-clam texture and seafoodlike flavor.

Yield:	Prep time:	Cook time:	Serving size:
11 or 12 cups	20 to 25 minutes	3½ to 4 hours	1½ cups

3 cups (4 or 5 medium) Yukon Gold potatoes, quartered lengthwise, and thinly sliced

1½ cups (1 large) yellow onion, diced

1 cup celery (including inner leaves and tops), diced

1½ TB. minced garlic

3 TB. dulse flakes or nori flakes

1 bay leaf

1 TB. herbes de Provence

1 tsp. vegetarian Worcestershire sauce

½ tsp. sea salt

½ tsp. freshly ground black pepper

4½ cups Homemade Vegetable Broth (recipe in Chapter 8)

1½ cups plain soy or coconut creamer

3 TB. arrowroot, cornstarch, or flour of choice

2 TB. nutritional yeast flakes

12 oz. oyster mushrooms

1½ TB. Old Bay Seasoning

½ TB. olive oil

⅓ cup chopped fresh Italian flat-leaf parsley

1. In a medium or large slow cooker, layer, in order, Yukon Gold potatoes, yellow onion, celery, garlic, dulse flakes, bay leaf, herbes de Provence, vegetarian Worcestershire sauce, sea salt, and black pepper. Pour in Homemade Vegetable Broth.

2. Cover and cook on high for 3½ to 4 hours, on low for 7 or 8 hours, or until vegetables are tender.

3. In a medium bowl, whisk together soy creamer, arrowroot, and nutritional yeast flakes. Stir in soy creamer mixture during last 30 minutes of cooking time.

4. To prepare oyster mushrooms, leave very small ones whole, and halve or quarter larger ones as desired. In a medium nonstick skillet over medium heat, combine oyster mushrooms, Old Bay Seasoning, and olive oil, and sauté, stirring often, for 3 minutes. Remove the skillet from heat.

5. Stir in oyster mushrooms and Italian flat-leaf parsley. Remove and discard bay leaf. Taste and adjust seasonings as desired, and serve hot.

Variation: For a creamier version, blend 2 cups chowder in a blender or food processor fitted with an S blade until a smooth purée and then stir back into the slow cooker. (Alternatively, use an immersion blender directly in the slow cooker, and pulse several times to purée some of the chowder.)

DEFINITION

Oyster mushrooms are a variety of mushroom with a slightly puffy, oyster-shape cap, and practically no stem. They grow on dead logs in clusters. Many people claim the oyster mushrooms have a similar taste and smell to their namesake.

Main Attractions

Get ready for recipes that take center stage on your plate! In Part 5, I show you how to use several different cooking techniques, all of which will really help expand your culinary repertoire.

We start off making meatless meats like seitan, sausages, and teriyaki-style tofu. Then, we learn how to use some of them to make fabulously filling sandwiches and other handheld dinner options.

Feel like you stepped back into your grandmother's kitchen by slow cooking one of the international stews or one-pot meals in Chapters 12 and 13. These chapters contain many stellar recipes ideal for taking to potlucks, family dinners, or holiday get-togethers, like Veggie Lasagna, Biscuit-Topped Veggie Potpie, and even an impressive Stuffed Seitan Roast.

Meatless Meats and Super Sandwiches

In This Chapter

- Homemade seitan and boldly flavored sausages
- Terrific teriyaki tofu
- Sensational and saucy sandwiches
- Seitan sausage-filled selections
- Meaty mushroom fajitas

Most grocery and natural foods stores carry a wide selection of vegan meat replacement products. These convenience foods do come in handy at certain times, but at a price, as many contain overly processed ingredients as well as excessive sodium and fat. But there is good news! It's really easy to make your own homemade meatless meats. Plus, when you make them yourself, you call the shots when it comes to the ingredients.

The slow cooker is a natural for making seitan. Whether you simmer it for long hours in a flavorful broth or steam it, the end results are fantastic. You can make another excellent meat alternative by browning slices of tofu or tempeh and then slow-cooking them in a homemade teriyaki sauce. These glazed slices are terrific as an entrée, on sandwiches or salads, or in your favorite slow cooker recipes.

Speaking of sandwiches, you'll love the steaming hot offerings in this chapter. You also learn how to use lentils in place of ground beef to make meatless sloppy joes, as well as transform portobello mushrooms, onions, and bell peppers into a fantastic fajita filling. Each sandwich recipe makes either 4 or 6 servings, or enough for the average family of 4 to enjoy at one meal or to supply a single person or couple with enough for several days' worth of lunches.

Beef-Style Simmered Seitan

Tamari plays a major role in developing the deep brown color of both the base and simmering broth used to create this amazing beefy-flavored *seitan*, which you can use as a meat replacement in other recipes.

Yield:	Prep time:	Cook time:	Serving size:
2 pounds seitan, plus 3 or 4 cups cooking liquid	15 to 20 minutes	5 to 7 minutes, plus 6 hours	½ to ¾ cup

4⅓ cups water

3 cups Homemade Vegetable Broth (recipe in Chapter 8)

½ cup tamari, shoyu, or Bragg Liquid Aminos

4 TB. tomato paste

1 bay leaf

⅔ cup crimini or white button mushrooms, roughly chopped

⅓ cup shallots or red onions, finely diced

2 TB. minced garlic

2 TB. Italian seasoning blend or 2 tsp. each dried basil, oregano, and marjoram

1 TB. onion powder

1 TB. garlic powder or garlic granules

1 TB. vegetarian Worcestershire sauce

½ tsp. garlic pepper

¼ tsp. freshly ground black pepper

¼ cup chopped fresh parsley

1½ cups vital wheat gluten

¼ cup chickpea/garbanzo bean flour

¼ cup nutritional yeast flakes

1. In a large, oval slow cooker, combine 4 cups water, 2 cups Homemade Vegetable Broth, ¼ cup tamari, 2 tablespoons tomato paste, and bay leaf. Cover and cook on high for 20 minutes.

2. Meanwhile, in a small nonstick skillet over medium heat, combine crimini mushrooms, remaining ⅓ cup water, shallots, and garlic. Cook for 5 to 7 minutes or until vegetables are tender. Remove the skillet from heat.

3. Transfer mushroom mixture to a blender or a food processor fitted with an S blade. Add remaining 1 cup Homemade Vegetable Broth, remaining ¼ cup tamari, remaining 2 tablespoons tomato paste, Italian seasoning blend, onion powder, garlic powder, vegetarian Worcestershire sauce, garlic pepper, and black pepper, and process for 1 minute. Scrape down the sides of the container with a spatula, add parsley, and process for 1 more minute or until very smooth.

4. In a large bowl, combine vital wheat gluten, chickpea/garbanzo bean flour, and nutritional yeast flakes, and stir well. Add wet ingredients to dry ingredients, and stir well to combine.

5. Transfer seitan mixture to a clean counter or work surface. Using your hands, knead mixture for 3 to 5 minutes or until a smooth and pliable ball of dough forms. Divide dough into 4 pieces, and flatten each slightly. Let rest for 5 minutes.

6. Carefully add seitan pieces to hot broth mixture. Cover and cook on high for 6 hours, on low for 8 to 10 hours, or until seitan is firm to the touch.

7. Using a slotted spoon, remove seitan from cooking liquid and immerse in a bowl of ice water to "shock" it and make the final texture much firmer. Slice seitan for use as a sandwich filling, or cube or chop for use in soups, stews, and sides and main dishes. If you aren't using the seitan right away, store submerged in the cooled cooking liquid in an airtight container in the refrigerator for up to 5 days. Or freeze seitan in an airtight container or zipper-lock bags and use the cooking liquid in place of vegetable broth to flavor sauces, soups, and pasta and grain dishes.

Variation: For **Chick'n-Style Simmered Seitan,** omit the tomato paste, and replace the Italian seasoning blend with 1½ tablespoons poultry seasoning blend, and ½ tablespoon dried thyme. Replace the mushrooms with ⅓ cup finely diced carrots, and ⅓ cup finely diced celery. And add an additional 2 tablespoons nutritional yeast flakes with the dry ingredients.

DEFINITION

Seitan (a.k.a. wheat meat or gluten) is a meat replacement originally made by rinsing and kneading whole-wheat flour under water to help remove its starch and leave only the protein-rich gluten behind. For a faster preparation, vital wheat gluten is used.

Seitan Chorizo Sausages

If you like hot and spicy foods, you'll eagerly gobble up this smoky and spicy vegan chorizo sausage.

Yield:	Prep time:	Cook time:	Serving size:
8 (5-inch) sausages	15 to 20 minutes	1½ to 2 hours, plus 20 minutes rest time	1 sausage

1¼ cups vital wheat gluten

½ cup chickpea/garbanzo bean flour

¼ cup nutritional yeast flakes

2½ TB. minced garlic

1 TB. smoked paprika

1 TB. chili powder

1 TB. crushed red pepper flakes

2 tsp. dried oregano

1 tsp. ground cumin

1 tsp. ground coriander

1 tsp. smoked sea salt

¾ tsp. chipotle chile powder

½ tsp. garlic pepper or freshly ground black pepper

1 cup Homemade Vegetable Broth (recipe in Chapter 8)

⅓ cup tomato paste

¼ cup red wine vinegar or red wine (such as Burgundy or Merlot)

2 TB. olive oil

1. Place a trivet or foil ring in the bottom of a medium or large slow cooker. Place a medium bowl (or whatever size fits your slow cooker) on top of the trivet, add 2 inches water, and preheat the slow cooker to high.

2. In a large bowl, combine vital wheat gluten, chickpea/garbanzo bean flour, nutritional yeast flakes, garlic, smoked paprika, chili powder, crushed red pepper flakes, oregano, cumin, coriander, smoked sea salt, chipotle chile powder, and garlic pepper.

3. In a medium bowl, combine Homemade Vegetable Broth, tomato paste, red wine vinegar, and olive oil. Add wet ingredients to dry ingredients, and stir well to combine. Using your hands, knead mixture in the bowl for 2 or 3 minutes or until a smooth and pliable ball of dough forms.

4. Cut 8 (6×8-inch) pieces of parchment paper and aluminum foil. Place parchment paper on top of pieces of aluminum foil on a work surface in an assembly line fashion.

5. Place ⅓ cup chorizo sausage mixture lengthwise in the center of the parchment paper. Using your hands, shape each portion into a 5-inch log. Fold over edges of the parchment paper to enclose chorizo sausage log. Roll up aluminum foil to enclose chorizo sausage log, and twist ends to secure.

6. Place chorizo sausages in the bowl inside the slow cooker. Cover and cook on high for 1½ to 2 hours, on low for 3 or 4 hours, or until chorizo sausages are firm to the touch. Remove chorizo sausages from the slow cooker, place on a large plate, and set aside to cool for 20 minutes.

7. Serve immediately or refrigerate until ready to eat. Serve as a sandwich filling or side dish, or slice or chop for use in recipes. Store in an airtight container or zipper-lock bag in the refrigerator for up to 5 days, or freeze for up to 3 months.

Variation: To make **Chorizo-Style Luncheon Meat,** shape the chorizo sausage mixture into 1 (9-inch) log, and roll it up in a 12×12-inch piece of parchment paper and aluminum foil.

SLOW INTERESTING

Due to concerns about the possible ties between aluminum foil usage and Alzheimer's disease, I avoid letting aluminum foil come into direct contact with my food while it cooks or bakes. This is the reasoning behind layering parchment paper between the food items and the aluminum foil.

Beer Brats

When making your own vegan sausages from scratch, you're not limited to just using water or vegetable broth in your wet ingredients. Beer lovers will flip for the heady hops-infused flavor of these seitan-based, brat-style sausages.

Yield:	Prep time:	Cook time:	Serving size:
6 (5-inch) sausages	15 to 20 minutes	1½ to 2 hours, plus 20 minutes rest time	1 sausage

½ cup cooked navy or Great Northern beans or canned beans, drained and rinsed

1 TB. unbleached cane sugar

½ TB. smoked paprika

½ TB. chili powder

1 tsp. onion powder

1 tsp. garlic powder or garlic granules

1 tsp. dried marjoram or oregano

1 tsp. rubbed (or dried) sage

1 tsp. smoked sea salt

½ tsp. ground allspice

½ tsp. white pepper

½ tsp. freshly ground black pepper

1½ cups *vital wheat gluten*

1 (12-oz.) bottle pale ale or amber brown beer

1. Place a trivet or foil ring in the bottom of a medium or large slow cooker. Place a medium bowl (or whatever size fits your slow cooker) on top of the trivet. Add 2 inches water, and preheat the slow cooker to high.

2. In a large bowl, using a fork or potato masher, mash navy beans until smooth. Add unbleached cane sugar, smoked paprika, chili powder, onion powder, garlic powder, marjoram, rubbed sage, smoked sea salt, allspice, white pepper, and black pepper, and stir well.

3. Add vital wheat gluten and pale ale, and stir well to combine. Using your hands, knead mixture in the bowl for 2 or 3 minutes or until a smooth and pliable ball of dough forms.

4. Cut 6 (6×8-inch) pieces of parchment paper and aluminum foil. Place parchment paper on top of pieces of aluminum foil on a work surface in assembly line fashion.

5. Place ⅓ cup brat sausage mixture lengthwise in the center of the parchment paper. Using your hands, shape each portion into a 5-inch log. Fold over edges of the parchment paper to enclose brat sausage log. Roll up aluminum foil to enclose brat sausage log, and twist ends to secure.

6. Place brat sausages in the bowl inside the slow cooker. Cover and cook on high for 1½ to 2 hours, on low for 3 or 4 hours, or until brat sausages are firm to the touch. Remove brat sausages from the slow cooker, place on a large plate, and set aside to cool for 20 minutes.

7. Serve immediately or refrigerate until ready to eat. Serve as a sandwich filling or side dish, or slice or chop for use in recipes. Store in an airtight container or zipper-lock bag in the refrigerator for up to 5 days, or freeze for up to 3 months.

Variation: For a nonalcoholic version, use nonalcoholic beer or replace beer with 1½ cups Homemade Vegetable Broth (recipe in Chapter 8).

DEFINITION

Vital wheat gluten (a.k.a. instant gluten flour or gluten flour) is a powdered form of dehydrated pure wheat gluten. It's often mixed with liquid and seasonings to make seitan and its many meat analog variations, in addition to being added to breads and other baked goods. Find it in bulk bins or packaged in most grocery and natural foods stores.

Teriyaki-Glazed Tofu

Slices of tofu are seared and then combined with a homemade teriyaki sauce, which is transformed in the slow cooker into a sweet and tangy glaze coating.

Yield:	Prep time:	Cook time:	Serving size:
8 slices	5 to 10 minutes	10 to 15 minutes, plus 2 to 2½ hours	2 slices

1 lb. extra-firm or super-firm tofu

1 TB. peanut oil or other oil

⅓ cup tamari, shoyu, or Bragg Liquid Aminos

¼ cup brown rice vinegar

1½ TB. toasted sesame oil

1½ TB. minced garlic

1½ TB. peeled and minced fresh ginger

½ TB. vegetarian Worcestershire sauce

½ tsp. dry mustard

½ tsp. crushed red pepper flakes

2 TB. water

1 TB. cornstarch

1. If using extra-firm tofu, squeeze block of tofu over the sink to remove excess water. Place tofu in a colander in the sink, cover with a plate, place a 28-ounce can on top of the plate, and leave tofu to press for 20 minutes.

2. Cut tofu block in half lengthwise, turn each half cut side down, and cut each half into 4 slices for a total of 8 slices. If using super-firm tofu, skip pressing procedure, and cut block lengthwise into 8 slices.

3. In a medium nonstick skillet over medium heat, heat ½ tablespoon peanut oil. Add 4 tofu slices, and cook for 2 or 3 minutes or until golden brown. Flip over tofu with a spatula, and cook for 2 or 3 more minutes or until golden brown and crisp around the edges. Transfer tofu to a plate, and repeat cooking procedure with remaining ½ tablespoon peanut oil and 4 tofu slices.

4. In a medium slow cooker, combine tamari, brown rice vinegar, toasted sesame oil, garlic, ginger, vegetarian Worcestershire sauce, dry mustard, and crushed red pepper flakes. Layer tofu slices diagonally in the slow cooker, and spoon teriyaki sauce mixture over top of each slice.

5. Cover and cook on high for 2 to 2½ hours, on low for 4 or 5 hours, or until teriyaki sauce mixture is hot and bubbling. After 1 hour, carefully flip over tofu slices, and again spoon teriyaki sauce mixture over top of each slice.

6. In a small bowl, stir together water and cornstarch. Add cornstarch mixture to the slow cooker, and cook for 5 more minutes or until slightly thickened. Serve hot, warm, or at room temperature as a side dish or sandwich filling, or cut into smaller slices or cubes and use to add flavor to sauces, pasta or grain-based dishes, soups, stews, or main dishes.

Variation: For **Teriyaki-Glazed Tempeh,** replace tofu with 2 (8-ounce) packages tempeh, cut each block lengthwise into 3 pieces, and cook tempeh pieces in peanut oil until lightly browned on both sides.

COOKER CAVEAT

Don't skip the initial step of cooking the tofu slices in oil. Searing the outer surface of the tofu slices until they're golden brown not only adds to the flavor of the final dish, but also helps the tofu slices keep their firm texture when slow cooked in the tangy sauce.

Open-Faced Seitan Sandwiches with Gravy

This recipe utilizes both the Beef-Style Simmered Seitan and its leftover cooking liquid to re-create a diner classic with these hot seitan sandwiches served open-faced and topped with gravy.

Yield:	Prep time:	Cook time:	Serving size:
4 sandwiches	5 to 7 minutes	5 to 7 minutes	1 sandwich

1 lb. Beef-Style Simmered Seitan or Chick'n-Style Simmered Seitan (recipe and variation earlier in this chapter), thinly sliced

1½ cups Beef-Style or Chick'n-Style Simmered Seitan cooking liquid

2 TB. water

1 TB. cornstarch

4 slices Hearty Herb Bread or Wheat Bread (recipe and variation in Chapter 17)

1. In a medium saucepan over medium heat, combine Beef-Style Simmered Seitan and Beef-Style Simmered Seitan cooking liquid. Heat for 2 or 3 minutes or until seitan slices are hot. Using a slotted spoon, remove seitan slices from cooking liquid, place on a large plate, and set aside.

2. In a small bowl, stir together water and cornstarch. Stir cornstarch mixture into hot cooking liquid, and cook for 2 or 3 more minutes or until mixture has thickened to a gravylike consistency.

3. To assemble each sandwich, place 1 slice Hearty Herb Bread on a plate, top with 4 ounces seitan slices, and top with gravy as desired. Serve immediately.

Variation: This sandwich is also great with the bread toasted. And for a diner-style meal, serve sandwiches with a side of Marvelous Mashed Potatoes (recipe in Chapter 14). For **French Dip Sandwiches,** prepare recipe using Beef-Style Simmered Seitan, and assemble sandwiches on 4 (4-inch-long) pieces French baguette or submarine rolls, split. Also, don't thicken the cooking liquid with cornstarch; place ½-cup portions into small bowls, and serve *au jus* on the side for dipping the sandwiches into.

LOW AND SLOW

For a hot mock roast beef sandwich, use Beef-Style Simmered Seitan. If you're more in the mood for a mock turkey sandwich, use the Chick'n-Style Simmered Seitan.

BBQ Tempeh and Slaw Sandwiches

Creamy coleslaw is commonly served alongside barbecue or layered on top when eaten sandwich-style. In this recipe, browned tempeh slices are slow cooked in barbecue sauce and then layered with cool and crisp coleslaw on hamburger buns.

Yield:	Prep time:	Cook time:	Serving size:
6 sandwiches	10 minutes	20 minutes, plus 1½ to 2 hours	1 sandwich

1½ TB. tamari, shoyu, or Bragg Liquid Aminos

1½ TB. olive oil

2 (8-oz.) pkg. tempeh

1½ cups Smoky-Sweet Barbecue Sauce (recipe in Chapter 6)

2 cups bagged coleslaw mix

¼ cup vegan mayonnaise

1 TB. apple cider vinegar

1 tsp. spicy brown mustard

¼ tsp. celery seed

Sea salt

Freshly ground black pepper

6 whole-grain hamburger buns or rolls, split

1. Preheat the oven to 425°F. Lightly coat an 8×10-inch baking pan with vegetable cooking spray or oil of choice.

2. In the prepared baking pan, stir together tamari and olive oil.

3. Cut each block of tempeh into 3 slices. Place in a single layer in the baking pan, and flip over each slice to evenly coat on all sides with tamari mixture.

4. Bake for 10 minutes or until lightly browned. Flip over tempeh slices with a spatula, and bake for 10 more minutes. Remove from the oven.

5. Diagonally layer tempeh slices in a medium slow cooker, and spoon Smoky-Sweet Barbecue Sauce over top of each slice.

6. Cover and cook on high for 1½ to 2 hours, on low for 3 or 4 hours, or until barbecue sauce is hot and bubbling. After 1 hour, carefully flip over tempeh slices, and spoon barbecue sauce over top of each slice again.

7. Meanwhile, in a medium bowl, combine coleslaw mix, mayonnaise, apple cider vinegar, spicy brown mustard, and celery seed. Taste and season with sea salt and black pepper as desired. Chill coleslaw for at least 30 minutes to allow flavors to blend.

8. To assemble each sandwich, on bottom half of 1 whole-grain hamburger bun, layer 1 tempeh slice and ¼ cup coleslaw. Add top half of bun, and serve immediately.

Variation: For **BBQ Tofu and Slaw Sandwiches,** replace the tempeh with 1 pound super-firm tofu, cut lengthwise into 8 slices.

> **SLOW INTERESTING**
>
> Vegenaise, Organicville Non-Dairy, and Nasoya Nayonaise are all good options when it comes to vegan mayonnaise. Look for jars in the refrigerated condiment section of your local grocery or natural foods store.

Lentil Sloppy Joes

A childhood favorite gets a vegan makeover in this meatless version of sloppy joes that features a rich and spicy tomato sauce filled with onions, bell peppers, and brown lentils.

Yield:	Prep time:	Cook time:	Serving size:
6 sandwiches	7 to 10 minutes	5 minutes, plus 3 to 3½ hours	1 sandwich

1 TB. olive oil

¾ cup yellow onion, diced

¾ cup green bell pepper, ribs and seeds removed, and diced

1 medium jalapeño pepper, ribs and seeds removed, and finely diced

1 TB. minced garlic

¾ cup brown lentils, sorted and rinsed

1 TB. tamari, shoyu, or Bragg Liquid Aminos

1 TB. brown sugar, packed

1 TB. nutritional yeast flakes

1 TB. chili powder

½ TB. vegetarian Worcestershire sauce

1 tsp. smoked paprika

1 tsp. dried basil

1 tsp. dried oregano

¼ tsp. chipotle chile powder

¼ tsp. freshly ground black pepper

1½ cups water

1 (15-oz.) can tomato sauce

Sea salt

6 whole-grain hamburger buns or rolls, split

1. In a medium nonstick skillet over medium heat, heat olive oil. Add yellow onion and green bell pepper, and sauté, stirring often, for 3 minutes.

2. Add jalapeño pepper and garlic, and sauté, stirring often, for 2 minutes. Remove from heat.

3. In a medium slow cooker, combine brown lentils, onion mixture, tamari, brown sugar, nutritional yeast flakes, chili powder, vegetarian Worcestershire sauce, smoked paprika, basil, oregano, chipotle chile powder, and black pepper. Pour in water and tomato sauce, and stir well to combine.

4. Cover and cook on high for 3 to 3½ hours, on low for 6 or 7 hours, or until lentils are tender and sauce is very thick. Taste and season with sea salt and additional black pepper as desired.

5. To assemble sandwiches, divide sloppy joe mixture evenly among whole-grain buns, and serve hot.

Variation: For **Seitan Sloppy Joes,** omit the water, and replace the lentils with 1 pound Beef-Style Simmered Seitan (recipe earlier in this chapter), roughly chopped.

SLOW INTERESTING

Traditionally, Worcestershire sauce contains anchovies. Fortunately for vegetarians and vegans, several companies sell vegetarian Worcestershire sauce made with a combination of tamari, apple cider vinegar, spices, and tamarind to create a condiment with a similar full-body flavor and pungent tang reminiscent of the classic Worcestershire sauce.

Sausage Subs with Peppers and Onions

Seitan Chorizo Sausages are quickly browned in a skillet and then slow cooked with yellow onions; red, orange, and green bell peppers; and jalapeños for a spicy, Spanish version of this popular street food.

Yield:	Prep time:	Cook time:	Serving size:
6 sandwiches	10 to 15 minutes	5 minutes, plus 2½ to 3 hours	1 sandwich

6 Seitan Chorizo Sausages (recipe earlier in this chapter)

½ TB. olive oil

1 large yellow onion, cut into ½-in.-thick slices

1 large green bell pepper, ribs and seeds removed, and cut into ½-in.-thick slices

1 large red bell pepper, ribs and seeds removed, and cut into ½-in.-thick slices

1 large orange or yellow bell pepper, ribs and seeds removed, and cut into ½-in.-thick slices

1 medium jalapeño pepper, ribs and seeds removed, and thinly sliced

3 cloves garlic, thinly sliced

1 tsp. crushed red pepper flakes

Sea salt

Freshly ground black pepper

½ cup Homemade Vegetable Broth (recipe in Chapter 8)

6 (6-in.) submarine rolls or hot dog buns

1. In a medium nonstick skillet over medium heat, combine Seitan Chorizo Sausages and olive oil. Cook, stirring often, for 3 to 5 minutes or until sausages are lightly browned. Remove the skillet from heat.

2. In a medium or large slow cooker, combine yellow onion, green bell pepper, red bell pepper, orange bell pepper, jalapeño pepper, garlic, and crushed red pepper flakes. Season with sea salt and black pepper, and stir well to combine. Place chorizo sausages on top of vegetable mixture, and pour in Homemade Vegetable Broth.

3. Cover and cook on high for 2½ to 3 hours, on low for 5 or 6 hours, or until vegetables are tender.

4. Partially split open each submarine roll. Place 1 chorizo sausage inside, top with some onion and peppers mixture, and serve hot.

Variation: For a less-spicy version, omit the jalapeño pepper and red pepper flakes. For **Beer Brats with Peppers and Onions,** replace the Seitan Chorizo Sausages with 6 Beer Brats (recipe earlier in this chapter).

LOW AND SLOW

For a delicious main dish, instead of using these components to make submarine sandwiches, cut the Seitan Chorizo Sausages into 2-inch-thick slices and serve the sausage, onion, and peppers mixture over cooked pasta or Creamy Polenta (recipe in Chapter 16).

Portobello Mushroom Fajitas

In these fusion fajitas, meaty *portobello mushrooms* are simmered in a tangy broth with red onions and bell peppers and then rolled in flour tortillas with slices of creamy avocado and shredded pepper Jack cheese.

Yield:	Prep time:	Cook time:	Serving size:
8 fajitas	15 to 20 minutes	3 to 3½ hours	1 fajita

3 large (or 4 medium) portobello mushrooms, cut into ½-in.-thick slices

2 large red onions, cut into ½-in.-thick slices

2 large green bell peppers, ribs and seeds removed, and cut into ½-in.-thick slices

1 large red bell pepper, ribs and seeds removed, and cut into ½-in.-thick slices

1 large orange or yellow bell pepper, ribs and seeds removed, and cut into ½-in.-thick slices

2 medium jalapeño peppers, ribs and seeds removed, and thinly sliced

Sea salt

Freshly ground black pepper

⅓ cup water

2 TB. olive oil

2 TB. tamari, shoyu, or Bragg Liquid Aminos

2 TB. balsamic vinegar

2 TB. minced garlic

1 tsp. dried oregano

1 tsp. chili powder

1 tsp. smoked paprika

½ tsp. crushed red pepper flakes

¼ tsp. chipotle chile powder or cayenne

⅓ cup chopped fresh cilantro

2 TB. fresh lime juice

2 TB. nutritional yeast flakes

8 (8-in.) whole-wheat or sprouted grain flour tortillas

2 large Hass avocadoes, pitted and sliced

Shredded vegan pepper Jack cheese or other variety

1. In a medium or large slow cooker, combine portobello mushrooms, red onions, green bell peppers, red bell pepper, orange bell pepper, and jalapeño peppers. Season with sea salt and black pepper as desired, and stir well to combine.

2. In a small bowl, combine water, olive oil, tamari, balsamic vinegar, garlic, oregano, chili powder, smoked paprika, crushed red pepper flakes, and chipotle chile powder. Pour tamari mixture over vegetable mixture in slow cooker.

3. Cover and cook on high for 3 to 3½ hours, on low for 6 or 7 hours, or until vegetables are tender.

4. Stir in cilantro, lime juice, and nutritional yeast flakes.

5. In a large skillet over medium heat, warm each whole-wheat tortilla for 30 seconds per side, or heat in the microwave for 20 to 30 seconds.

6. Place 1 warmed tortilla on a large plate. Spoon ¾ cup vegetable mixture horizontally in the center of tortilla. Top with a few slices Hass avocado and 2 tablespoons shredded pepper Jack cheese. Fold left side of tortilla toward the center to enclose filling and then fold right side of tortilla over left. Serve immediately.

Variation: For **Portobello Mushroom Cheese Steak Sandwiches,** omit the cilantro, lime juice, and avocado slices, and sprinkle 1 cup shredded vegan mozzarella or Monterey Jack cheese over the vegetable mixture 5 minutes prior to serving. Instead of flour tortillas, divide vegetable mixture among 6 submarine rolls, partially split open, and serve hot.

DEFINITION

Portobello mushrooms, a mature and larger form of the smaller crimini mushroom, are brownish, chewy, and flavorful and often served as whole caps, grilled, and as thin sautéed slices.

Stupendous Supper Stews

In This Chapter

- Hearty, dumpling-topped stews
- European-style savory stews
- Marvelous meatless stews
- Vegetable stews with an Asian flair

If you're looking for something to warm and fill you up, you've come to the right place. For many, stew is the quintessential comfort food, and the aroma given off as it simmers will have you eagerly awaiting your first bowlful.

The words *soup* and *stew* are often used interchangeably, but the two do differ. In general, stews are more full flavored than soups and have a thicker and heartier consistency because they often contain larger-size pieces of vegetables and other ingredients. Typically, a stew is cooked on the stove top in a Dutch oven or large pot, but you can achieve comparable results with your slow cooker without having to hang around and keep a watchful eye on your simmering stew.

Chick'n and Vegetable Stew with Dumplings

Dumplings are a lot like drop biscuits but are cooked on top of a simmering broth, soup, or stew. In this hearty stew, dumplings are set afloat on top of a mouthwatering blend of vegetables and pieces of Chick'n-Style Simmered Seitan.

Yield:	Prep time:	Cook time:	Serving size:
9 cups and 6 dumplings	20 to 25 minutes	3 to 3½ hours	1½ cups and 1 dumpling

3 cups (4 or 5 medium) red-skinned potatoes, cut into 1-in. cubes

2½ cups (1 lb.) whole baby carrots

1½ cups fresh or frozen pearl onions, peeled

1½ cups (2 or 3 large stalks) celery (including inner leaves and tops), cut into ½-in.-thick slices

2 TB. nutritional yeast flakes

1 TB. minced garlic

1 bay leaf

2 tsp. herbes de Provence or poultry seasoning blend

1 tsp. seasoning salt (such as Herbamare)

½ tsp. freshly ground black pepper

2½ cups Homemade Vegetable Broth (recipe in Chapter 8)

1½ cups Chick'n-Style Simmered Seitan cooking liquid (variation in Chapter 11) or water

1 lb. (about 3 cups) Chick'n-Style Simmered Seitan (variation in Chapter 11), cut into 1-in. cubes

⅓ cup chopped fresh parsley

⅔ cup white whole-wheat or whole-wheat pastry flour

½ tsp. aluminum-free baking powder

¼ tsp. sea salt

6 TB. soy or other nondairy milk

1½ TB. sunflower or other oil

1. In a medium or large slow cooker, layer, in order, red-skinned potatoes, baby carrots, pearl onions, celery, nutritional yeast flakes, garlic, bay leaf, herbes de Provence, seasoning salt, and black pepper. Pour in Homemade Vegetable Broth and Chick'n-Style Simmered Seitan cooking liquid.

2. Cover and cook on high for 3 to 3½ hours, on low for 6 or 7 hours, or until vegetables are tender.

3. Stir in Chick'n-Style Simmered Seitan and parsley during the last 35 minutes of cook time. Taste and adjust seasonings as desired.

4. Meanwhile, in a small bowl, combine white whole-wheat flour, aluminum-free baking powder, and sea salt. Stir in soy milk and sunflower oil, and mix until a soft dough forms.

5. Remove and discard bay leaf. Drop dumpling mixture by heaping tablespoonfuls on top of stew. Cook on high for 25 to 30 more minutes or until a toothpick inserted in center of dumpling comes out clean. Serve hot.

Variations: For **Herbed Dumplings,** stir in 2 or 3 tablespoons chopped fresh parsley, basil, thyme, or dill and/or chives when making the dumpling dough after combining the wet and dry ingredients. For **Beefy Seitan and Veggie Stew with Dumplings,** replace Chick'n-Style Simmered Seitan with an equal amount of Beef-Style Simmered Seitan (recipe in Chapter 11), cut into 1-inch cubes, and prepare the stew using 2 cups vegetable broth and 2 cups leftover cooking liquid from preparing Beef-Style Simmered Seitan.

COOKER CAVEAT

For fluffy dumplings, first be sure the stew or broth is piping hot. Then drop the dumpling dough on top of something that can support it within the stew, like a chunky piece of vegetable, rather than placing directly into the cooking liquid. This way, the dumplings will begin to instantly steam-cook, and they'll float on top of the stew instead of settling down into the cooking liquid, which will make them soggy.

Southwestern Posole with Cornmeal Dumplings

For Mexicans, Native Americans, and many in the Southwest, posole is a traditional dish eaten on Christmas Eve to celebrate life's blessings. This fiery stew utilizes the favorite culinary staples of those regions: beans, squashes, chiles, and hominy.

Yield:	Prep time:	Cook time:	Serving size:
9 or 10 cups and 6 dumplings	20 to 25 minutes	3 to 3½ hours	1½ cups and 1 dumpling

1½ cups (1 large) yellow onion, diced

1 large green bell pepper, ribs and seeds removed, and diced

1 large red or orange bell pepper, ribs and seeds removed, and diced

2 (15-oz.) cans white hominy, drained and rinsed

1½ cups cooked *anasazi*, kidney, or pinto beans, or 1 (15-oz.) can anasazi, kidney, or pinto beans, drained and rinsed

1 medium yellow summer squash, cut in ½ lengthwise, and sliced

1 medium zucchini, cut in ½ lengthwise, and sliced

2 medium jalapeño peppers, ribs and seeds removed, and finely diced

2 TB. minced garlic

1½ TB. chili powder

1 TB. ground cumin

1 TB. dried oregano

1½ tsp. smoked paprika

1 tsp. chipotle chile powder or ½ tsp. cayenne

1 tsp. sea salt

½ tsp. freshly ground black pepper

1 (28-oz.) can diced fire-roasted tomatoes with green chiles

2 cups Homemade Vegetable Broth (recipe in Chapter 8)

⅓ cup chopped fresh cilantro

3 TB. nutritional yeast flakes

6 TB. white whole-wheat or whole-wheat pastry flour

4 TB. cornmeal (preferably medium-grind)

1 tsp. aluminum-free baking powder

2 TB. water

1 TB. Ener-G Egg Replacer

2 TB. soy or other nondairy milk

1 TB. sunflower or other oil

1. In a medium or large slow cooker, layer, in order, yellow onion, green bell pepper, red bell pepper, hominy, anasazi beans, yellow summer squash, zucchini, jalapeño peppers, garlic, chili powder, cumin, oregano, smoked paprika, chipotle chile powder, sea salt, and black pepper. Pour in fire-roasted tomatoes with green chiles and Homemade Vegetable Broth.

2. Cover and cook on high for 3 to 3½ hours, on low for 6 or 7 hours, or until vegetables are tender.

3. During the last 35 minutes of cook time, stir in cilantro and 2 tablespoons nutritional yeast flakes. Taste and adjust seasonings as desired.

4. Meanwhile, in a small bowl, combine white whole-wheat flour, cornmeal, remaining 1 tablespoon nutritional yeast flakes, and aluminum-free baking powder.

5. In another small bowl, whisk together water and Ener-G Egg Replacer vigorously for 1 minute or until very frothy (like beaten egg whites). Stir egg replacer mixture, soy milk, and sunflower oil into flour mixture until a soft dough forms.

6. Drop dumpling mixture by heaping tablespoonfuls on top of stew. Cook on high for 25 to 30 more minutes or until a toothpick inserted in center of dumpling comes out clean. Serve hot.

Variation: For **Cheesy Cornmeal Dumplings,** stir in ½ cup shredded vegan cheddar cheese or other variety when making the dumpling dough, after combining the wet and dry ingredients.

> **DEFINITION**
>
> **Anasazi beans,** small, kidney-shape relatives of pinto beans, have a unique deep-red and white swirled appearance. This heirloom bean is also called Aztec bean, Cave bean, New Mexico Appaloosa bean, or Jacob's Cattle beans. The cooked bean has a mild, sweet flavor and a slightly mealy texture.

Moroccan Chickpea Stew with Couscous

Ground cumin and smoked paprika impart a warm, earthy, and somewhat nutty quality to this stew, full of chunks of winter squash, cabbage, chickpeas, and assorted vegetables.

Yield:	Prep time:	Cook time:	Serving size:
9 cups stew and 4 cups couscous	20 to 25 minutes	3½ to 4 hours	1½ cups stew and ⅔ cup couscous

1½ cups (1 large) yellow onion, diced

½ TB. olive oil

1½ TB. ground cumin

2 tsp. smoked paprika

1 TB. tomato paste

2 cups (½ medium acorn or 1 medium delicata) acorn or delicata squash, peeled, seeded, and cut into 1-in. cubes

2 cups (¼ medium) butternut squash, peeled, seeded, and cut into 1-in. cubes

2 cups (1 large or 2 medium) turnips, peeled and cut into 1-in. cubes

1½ cups (2 or 3 large) carrots, cut in ½ lengthwise and then into 1-in. pieces

1½ cups (2 or 3 large stalks) celery (including inner leaves and tops), cut into 1-in. pieces

2 cups (¼ small head) green cabbage, cut into 1-in. pieces

1 tsp. sea salt

½ tsp. freshly ground black pepper

3 cups Homemade Vegetable Broth (recipe in Chapter 8)

1½ cups (2 medium) zucchini, cut in ½ lengthwise and then into 1-in. pieces

1½ cups cooked chickpeas, or 1 (15-oz.) can chickpeas, drained and rinsed

⅓ cup chopped fresh Italian flat-leaf parsley

3 cups water

1½ cups whole-wheat couscous

1. In a medium nonstick skillet over medium heat, combine yellow onion and olive oil. Sauté, stirring often, for 5 minutes.

2. Add cumin and smoked paprika, and sauté, stirring often, for 1 minute.

3. Add tomato paste, and sauté, stirring often, for 1 minute. Remove the skillet from heat.

4. In a medium or large slow cooker, layer, in order, acorn squash, butternut squash, turnips, carrots, celery, green cabbage, onion mixture, sea salt, and black pepper. Pour in Homemade Vegetable Broth.

5. Cover and cook on high for 3½ to 4 hours, on low for 7 or 8 hours, or until vegetables are tender.

6. During the last 30 minutes of cook time, stir in zucchini, chickpeas, and Italian flat-leaf parsley. Taste and adjust seasonings as desired.

7. Meanwhile, in a medium saucepan over high heat, bring water to a boil. Stir in couscous, cover, remove from heat, and set aside for 5 minutes to allow couscous to cook. Fluff couscous with a fork to loosen grains.

8. Serve hot, spooning stew over couscous for each serving.

Variation: Feel free to replace the turnips with potatoes and the acorn and butternut squash with other varieties of winter squash, such as turban, buttercup, kabocha, or even pumpkin.

LOW AND SLOW

I try to use whole-wheat couscous and other whole grains as much as possible, but you can use the light, white variety if you want, or substitute millet or quinoa for a gluten-free option.

Provençal Vegetable Stew with Pistou

Hailing from the Provence region of France, this hearty bean-and-vegetable stew has a wonderful savoriness on its own, but it's the fragrant freshness of the basil and garlic pistou that brings all the flavors together.

Yield:	Prep time:	Cook time:	Serving size:
9 or 10 cups	20 to 25 minutes	3 to 3½ hours	1½ cups and 1½ tablespoons pistou

1 medium leek, washed well, cut in ½ lengthwise, and thinly sliced

2 cups (4 or 5 large) carrots, cut into ½-in.-thick slices

1 cup yellow onion, diced

3½ TB. olive oil

1 TB. minced garlic

1½ cups cooked Great Northern or cannellini beans, or 1 (15-oz.) can Great Northern or cannellini beans, drained and rinsed

1 lb. fresh green beans, cut into 3-in. pieces, or 1 (16-oz.) pkg. frozen green beans, thawed

2 medium zucchini, cut into 1-in.-thick slices

2 cups (2 medium) tomatoes, diced, or 1 (14-oz.) can diced tomatoes, with juice

3 TB. nutritional yeast flakes

1 bay leaf

1½ tsp. herbes de Provence

1½ tsp. sea salt

½ tsp. freshly ground black pepper

4 cups Homemade Vegetable Broth (recipe in Chapter 8)

2 large cloves garlic

3 cups fresh basil leaves, packed

1. In a medium nonstick skillet over medium heat, combine leek, carrots, yellow onion, and ½ tablespoon olive oil. Sauté, stirring often, for 5 minutes.

2. Add minced garlic, and sauté, stirring often, for 1 minute. Remove the skillet from heat.

3. In a medium or large slow cooker, layer, in order, Great Northern beans, green beans, zucchini, leek mixture, tomatoes, 2 tablespoons nutritional yeast flakes, bay leaf, herbes de Provence, 1 teaspoon sea salt, and black pepper. Pour in Homemade Vegetable Broth.

4. Cover and cook on high for 3 to 3½ hours, on low for 6 or 7 hours, or until vegetables are tender.

5. Meanwhile, in a food processor fitted with an S blade, process garlic cloves, remaining ½ teaspoon sea salt, and basil for 1 or 2 minutes or until basil and garlic are finely chopped. Scrape down the sides of the container with a spatula. With the machine running, slowly add remaining 3 tablespoons olive oil and 1 tablespoon nutritional yeast flakes through the feed tube, and process for 1 minute or until smooth.

6. Remove and discard bay leaf. Taste stew and adjust seasonings as desired. Serve hot, garnishing individual servings with 1½ tablespoons pistou. (Alternatively, stir all pistou into stew before serving.)

Variation: Feel free to add other fresh vegetables to this stew, such as 3 cups red-skinned potatoes, cut into 1-inch cubes, or 3 cups spinach or Swiss chard, roughly chopped. For added flavor, stir ¼ cup tomato, finely diced, into the prepared pistou. You can also prepare the pistou using equal parts of fresh basil and parsley.

SLOW INTERESTING

The French call the flavorful paste of basil, garlic, and olive oil *pistou*. Coincidentally, it contains many of the same ingredients found in an Italian pesto, but pesto also typically contains pine nuts or other varieties of nuts, too.

Ratatouille

This classic French comfort food is best made in the summer, when garden-fresh produce is abundant. Slow cooking helps meld all the flavors of the assorted vegetables and herbs, and crushed red pepper flakes give it a nice little kick.

Yield:	Prep time:	Cook time:	Serving size:
9 or 10 cups	20 to 25 minutes	3 to 3½ hours	1½ cups

1 large eggplant (about 1½ lb.), cut into 2-in. cubes

1 large green bell pepper, ribs and seeds removed, and cut into 2-in. strips

1 large red or orange bell pepper, ribs and seeds removed, cut into 2-in. strips

1 large orange or yellow bell pepper, ribs and seeds removed, cut into 2-in. strips

1 medium red or yellow onion, cut into 1-in. strips

2 medium zucchini, cut into 1-in.-thick slices

1 lb. (2 large or 3 medium) tomatoes, cut into 1-in. cubes or 1 pint cherry tomatoes, cut in half

¼ cup Roasted Garlic (recipe in Chapter 7), thinly sliced, or 2 TB. minced garlic

2 TB. tomato paste

2 TB. nutritional yeast flakes

2 TB. balsamic or red wine vinegar

½ TB. *herbes de Provence* or Italian seasoning blend

1 tsp. crushed red pepper flakes

1 tsp. sea salt

½ tsp. freshly ground black pepper

2 cups Homemade Vegetable Broth (recipe in Chapter 8)

½ cup fresh basil, cut chiffonade

¼ cup chopped fresh parsley

1. In a medium or large slow cooker, combine eggplant, green bell pepper, red bell pepper, orange bell pepper, red onion, zucchini, tomatoes, Roasted Garlic, tomato paste, nutritional yeast flakes, balsamic vinegar, herbes de Provence, crushed red pepper flakes, sea salt, and black pepper. Pour in Homemade Vegetable Broth.

2. Cover and cook on high for 3 to 3½ hours, on low for 6 or 7 hours, or until vegetables are tender.

3. Stir in basil and parsley. Taste and adjust seasonings as desired. Serve hot, cold, or at room temperature with slices of bread. To stretch this ratatouille recipe to feed a large crowd, serve individual servings on top of Creamy Polenta (recipe in Chapter 16).

Variation: For added color, replace 1 zucchini with 1 yellow summer squash. For **Ratatouille Niçoise,** add ¾ cup Niçoise olives or other black olives, pitted and cut in ½ lengthwise, and 2 tablespoons capers.

> **DEFINITION**
>
> **Herbes de Provence** is a seasoning mix commonly used in the south of France that includes basil, fennel, marjoram, rosemary, sage, and thyme. American versions also often include lavender.

Seitan Cacciatore

Cacciatore is Italian for "hunter's style," and this vegan version is filled with chunks of bell peppers, onions, mushrooms, and pieces of Chick'n-Style Simmered Seitan covered in a robust, red wine and fire-roasted tomato sauce.

Yield:	Prep time:	Cook time:	Serving size:
8 cups	20 to 25 minutes	3 to 3½ hours	1½ cups

1½ cups (1 large) yellow onion, cut into 1-in. strips

1½ cups (8 oz.) crimini or white button mushrooms, cut in ½ and sliced

1 large green bell pepper, ribs and seeds removed, and cut into 1-in. pieces

1 large red bell pepper, ribs and seeds removed, and cut into 1-in. pieces

1½ TB. minced garlic

1 bay leaf

1 TB. Italian seasoning blend or 1 tsp. each dried basil, oregano, and thyme

½ TB. smoked paprika

1 tsp. crushed red pepper flakes

1 tsp. sea salt

½ tsp. freshly ground black pepper

1 (28-oz.) can crushed fire-roasted tomatoes, with juice

1 (14-oz.) can diced fire-roasted tomatoes, with juice

1 cup red wine (such as Burgundy, Merlot, or Zinfandel)

1 lb. (about 3 cups) Chick'n-Style Simmered Seitan (variation in Chapter 11), cut into 1-in. cubes

1½ TB. nutritional yeast flakes

⅓ cup chopped fresh basil or Italian flat-leaf parsley

1. In a medium or large slow cooker, layer, in order, yellow onion, crimini mushrooms, green bell pepper, red bell pepper, garlic, bay leaf, Italian seasoning blend, smoked paprika, crushed red pepper flakes, sea salt, and black pepper. Pour in crushed fire-roasted tomatoes with juice, diced fire-roasted tomatoes with juice, and red wine.

2. Cover and cook on high for 3 to 3½ hours, on low for 6 or 7 hours, or until vegetables are tender.

3. Stir in Chick'n-Style Simmered Seitan, nutritional yeast flakes, and basil, and cook for 10 minutes. Remove and discard bay leaf. Taste and adjust seasonings as desired. Serve hot over cooked pasta (such as fettuccine or penne).

Variation: For a gluten-free **Tempeh Cacciatore,** replace the Chick'n-Style Simmered Seitan with an 8-ounce package tempeh, cut into 1-inch cubes, but add them during the last 30 minutes of cooking time.

LOW AND SLOW

For a one-pot meal, instead of serving the finished Seitan Cacciatore on top of cooked pasta, add 8 ounces dry pasta (use a large-size variety like rigatoni, penne, or ziti) directly to the slow cooker, and slow cook on high for an additional 15 to 20 minutes or until pasta is al dente.

Rainbow Vegetable Curry

A colorful assortment of vegetables are cloaked in a rich sauce made by combining coconut milk and *red curry paste*, resulting in a full-flavored mildly hot curry dish.

Yield:	Prep time:	Cook time:	Serving size:
9 to 10 cups	20 to 25 minutes	3 to 3½ hours	1½ cups

3 cups (3 large) sweet potatoes, peeled and cut into 2-in. cubes

2½ cups (1 lb.) broccoli, cut into small florets

2½ cups (1 lb.) cauliflower, cut into small florets

2 large carrots, thinly sliced diagonally

1 large green bell pepper, ribs and seeds removed, and cut into 1-in. pieces

1 large red bell pepper, ribs and seeds removed, and cut into 1-in. pieces

1 cup yellow onion, diced

1 medium Thai red chile pepper or jalapeño pepper, ribs and seeds removed, and finely diced

2 cups coconut milk beverage or 1 (14-oz.) can lite coconut milk

1½ cups Homemade Vegetable Broth (recipe in Chapter 8)

1½ TB. red curry or panang curry paste

¼ cup chopped fresh mint or basil, cut chiffonade

Sea salt

Freshly ground black pepper

Toasted cashews

1. In a medium or large slow cooker, layer, in order, sweet potatoes, broccoli, cauliflower, carrots, green bell pepper, red bell pepper, yellow onion, and Thai red chile pepper.

2. In a medium bowl, whisk together coconut milk, Homemade Vegetable Broth, and red curry paste. Pour coconut milk mixture over vegetable mixture.

3. Cover and cook on high for 2 to 2½ hours, on low for 4 or 5 hours, or until vegetables are tender.

4. Stir in mint. Taste and season with sea salt and black pepper as desired. Serve hot over cooked jasmine or brown rice, garnishing individual servings with toasted cashews.

Variation: For a hot-and-spicy vegetable curry, replace the red curry paste with green curry paste. For a lightly spiced curry, use yellow curry paste.

> **DEFINITION**
>
> **Red curry paste** is a spicy, thick paste made by grinding together red chiles, lemongrass, shallots, garlic, ginger, kaffir lime, oil, salt, and several spices. It's used as a condiment and flavoring for curries, soups, stews, stir-fries, and noodle dishes.

Sweet-and-Sour Tempeh

A take-out favorite gets a slow cooker makeover in this tempeh and veggie combo covered in a sweet, sour, and slightly tangy sauce made of ketchup, *brown rice vinegar*, pineapple juice, brown sugar, fresh ginger, and garlic.

Yield:	Prep time:	Cook time:	Serving size:
8 cups	20 to 25 minutes	2 to 2½ hours	1½ cups

2 cups (1 lb.) broccoli, cut into small florets

2 large carrots, thinly sliced diagonally

2 large stalks celery, thinly sliced diagonally

1 large green bell pepper, ribs and seeds removed, and cut into 1-in. pieces

1 large red bell pepper, ribs and seeds removed, and cut into 1-in. pieces

1 small red onion, cut into ½ moons

1 (28-oz.) can pineapple chunks in juice

¼ cup tamari, shoyu, Bragg Liquid Aminos

¼ cup ketchup

¼ cup light brown sugar, packed

¼ cup brown rice vinegar

1½ TB. peeled and minced fresh ginger

1½ TB. minced garlic

12 oz. tempeh, cut into 1-in. cubes

4½ TB. cornstarch

1 TB. olive or other oil

6 TB. water

1. In a medium or large slow cooker, layer, in order, broccoli, carrots, celery, green bell pepper, red bell pepper, and red onion.

2. Drain pineapple juice into a medium bowl. Place pineapple chunks in a small bowl, and set aside. Add tamari, ketchup, light brown sugar, brown rice vinegar, ginger, and garlic to pineapple juice, and whisk well to combine. Pour pineapple juice mixture into the slow cooker.

3. Cover and cook on high for 2 to 2½ hours, on low for 4 or 5 hours, or until vegetables are tender.

4. During the last 20 minutes of cook time, place tempeh cubes on a large plate, sprinkle 1½ tablespoons cornstarch over top, and toss to coat.

5. In a large nonstick skillet over medium heat, sauté tempeh in olive oil, stirring occasionally, for 10 to 15 minutes or until browned on all sides. Remove the skillet from heat.

6. In a small bowl, stir together remaining 3 tablespoons cornstarch and water. When vegetables are tender, stir cornstarch mixture and reserved pineapple chunks into the slow cooker, and cook for 5 to 10 minutes or until sauce is thickened.

7. Stir in tempeh cubes. Taste and adjust seasonings as desired, and serve hot over cooked brown rice or noodles.

Variation: For extra color and texture, add 2 cups shredded red cabbage during the last 30 minutes of cook time. For **Sweet-and-Sour Tofu,** replace the tempeh cubes with 1 pound firm or extra-firm tofu, cut into 1-inch cubes.

DEFINITION

Brown rice vinegar is produced from fermented brown rice, water, and koji (a beneficial type of mold), or from unrefined rice wine (sake) and water. It's often used in Asian-style dishes.

Family-Style Favorites

In This Chapter

- Saucy and cheesy pasta dishes
- Comforting casseroles
- Warming potpies
- Savory seitan roasts

Trying to get dinner on the table after a hectic day can be overwhelming at times. But with the help of your slow cooker and the family-style main dish recipes in this chapter, you can tackle this task with ease. These one-pot wonders are perfect for feeding your spouse or family a warm and filling weeknight meal, and they can be equally impressive when served as an entrée when entertaining.

With many of these recipes, you can load up your slow cooker before going to bed or work. Then, you can either cook them slowly on low while you're away, or quickly on high when you get home, and you'll still have enough time to make a salad or relax a bit with a glass of wine before eating dinner.

You'll also love the fact that several of these recipes make use of recipes from other chapters. This is a great way of transforming a simple rice or bean dish into something totally new and different, and no one will ever know they're actually eating leftovers!

Grown-Up Mac-n-Cheese with Breadcrumb Topping

Mac-n-cheese is beloved by young and old alike, but this version was developed to appeal to the adult crowd, as it uses the booze-boosted Wine Is Fine Fondue for the macaroni's cheesy coating. Just before serving, it's gilded with a savory breadcrumb topping.

Yield:	Prep time:	Cook time:	Serving size:
8 or 9 cups	15 minutes	20 to 25 minutes, plus 1½ to 2 hours	1½ cups

12 oz. elbow macaroni

1 batch Wine Is Fine Fondue (recipe in Chapter 5)

1½ cups water

Sea salt

Freshly ground black pepper

1 cup dry breadcrumbs

1½ TB. nonhydrogenated margarine

½ tsp. garlic powder or garlic granules

½ tsp. smoked paprika

1. Fill a large saucepan ⅔ full of water, and bring to a boil over medium-high heat. Add elbow macaroni, and cook, stirring occasionally, according to the package directions or until *al dente*. Remove the saucepan from heat. Drain macaroni in a colander, but do not rinse.

2. Lightly coat a medium or large slow cooker's ceramic crock insert with vegetable cooking spray or oil of choice.

3. Add cooked macaroni, Wine Is Fine Fondue, and water to the slow cooker, and stir gently. Taste and season with sea salt and black pepper as desired.

4. Cover and cook on high for 1½ to 2 hours, on low for 3 or 4 hours, or until hot and bubbling.

5. Meanwhile, in a small nonstick skillet over medium heat, combine breadcrumbs, nonhydrogenated margarine, garlic powder, and smoked paprika, and cook, stirring often, for 3 to 5 minutes or until golden brown. Remove the skillet from heat.

6. Before serving hot, spoon breadcrumb topping evenly over top of mac-n-cheese.

Variation: For a nonalcoholic, kid-friendly **Creamy Mac-n-Cheese,** replace the Wine Is Fine Fondue with Mellow Cheese Fondue (variation in Chapter 5).

> **LOW AND SLOW**
>
> If you're a gluten-free vegan, you can prepare this tasty mac-n-cheese with corn and quinoa elbow macaroni or other gluten-free shaped pasta. Swap out the breadcrumb topping with rice breadcrumbs or breadcrumbs made from your favorite gluten-free bread, too.

Veggie Lasagna

Yes, you can make lasagna in your slow cooker! This Italian family favorite features alternating layers of lasagna noodles, a homemade tofu ricotta studded with chopped veggies, fresh spinach, vegan mozzarella, and a robust marinara sauce.

Yield:	Prep time:	Cook time:	Serving size:
12 cups	22 to 25 minutes	3 to 3½ hours	1½ cups

1 lb. firm or extra-firm tofu

⅓ cup soy or other nondairy milk

⅓ cup nutritional yeast flakes

¼ cup fresh lemon juice

¼ cup fresh basil, cut chiffonade

¼ cup chopped Italian flat-leaf parsley

2 TB. minced garlic

1 TB. onion powder

1 tsp. dried oregano

1 tsp. sea salt

½ tsp. freshly ground black pepper

½ tsp. crushed red pepper flakes

¼ tsp. freshly grated nutmeg

1 (10-oz.) pkg. frozen California blend vegetables (broccoli, cauliflower, and carrots), thawed and roughly chopped

½ cup red onion, diced

½ cup red bell pepper, ribs and seeds removed, and diced

4 cups Red Wine Marinara Sauce (recipe in Chapter 6)

12 uncooked lasagna noodles

1 (6-oz.) pkg. baby spinach or 4 cups packed spinach, triple washed

1¼ cups shredded vegan mozzarella cheese

1. Lightly coat a medium or large slow cooker's ceramic crock insert with vegetable cooking spray or oil of choice.

2. Using your fingers, crumble tofu into a medium bowl. Add soy milk, nutritional yeast flakes, lemon juice, basil, Italian flat-leaf parsley, garlic, onion powder, oregano, sea salt, black pepper, crushed red pepper flakes, and nutmeg, and mash with a fork or potato masher until smooth.

3. Add California blend vegetables, red onion, and red bell pepper, and stir well to combine.

4. In the slow cooker, spoon ¾ cup Red Wine Marinara Sauce. Place 3 uncooked lasagna noodles side by side on top of marinara sauce, breaking them in half and overlapping as needed to fit. Top with ⅓ of tofu ricotta mixture, ⅓ of baby spinach, and ¼ cup mozzarella cheese. Repeat layering procedure 2 more times. Finish with a final layer of 2 broken lasagna noodles and remaining marinara sauce.

5. Cover and cook on high for 3 to 3½ hours, on low for 5 or 6 hours, or until hot and bubbling.

6. During the last 15 minutes of cook time, sprinkle remaining ½ cup mozzarella cheese over top. Serve hot.

Variation: For added flavor, replace the Red Wine Marinara Sauce with Mushroom Marinara Sauce (variation in Chapter 6).

LOW AND SLOW

The tofu ricotta featured in this recipe is quite versatile and can also be used as a filling when making stuffed shells or manicotti, a topping for pizza or toasted bread slices, or tossed together with other varieties of cooked pasta and vegetables when making tasty casseroles.

Deconstructed Enchiladas

These unrolled enchiladas are made of stacked layers of savory refried beans, a sautéed vegetable medley, fiery red chile sauce, and shredded cheddar cheese.

Yield:	Prep time:	Cook time:	Serving size:
10 or 11 cups	15 to 20 minutes	5 minutes, plus 1½ to 2 hours	1½ cups

¾ cup yellow onion, diced

¾ cup green bell pepper, ribs and seeds removed, and diced

¾ cup red bell pepper, ribs and seeds removed, and diced

½ TB. olive oil

1 medium jalapeño pepper, ribs and seeds removed, and finely diced

1½ TB. minced garlic

1 TB. nutritional yeast flakes

1 tsp. dried oregano

1 tsp. chili powder

½ tsp. *smoked paprika*

½ tsp. ground cumin

½ tsp. sea salt

½ tsp. freshly ground black pepper

¼ cup chopped fresh cilantro

6 (6-in.) corn tortillas

2 cups Refried Pinto Bean Dip (recipe in Chapter 5)

1 (19-oz.) can red chile enchilada sauce

2 cups shredded vegan cheddar cheese or other variety

1. Lightly coat a medium slow cooker's ceramic crock insert with vegetable cooking spray or oil of choice.

2. In a medium nonstick skillet over medium heat, combine yellow onion, green bell pepper, red bell pepper, and olive oil. Sauté, stirring often, for 3 minutes.

3. Add jalapeño pepper, garlic, nutritional yeast flakes, oregano, chili powder, smoked paprika, cumin, sea salt, and black pepper, and sauté, stirring often, for 1 minute.

4. Stir in cilantro. Remove the skillet from heat.

5. On a work surface or large cutting board, place 5 corn tortillas. Spread a heaping ⅓ cup Refried Pinto Bean Dip on top of each corn tortilla.

6. Spoon ⅓ cup red chile enchilada sauce into the slow cooker. Place 1 refried bean–covered tortilla on top of enchilada sauce. Top with ⅓ of vegetable mixture and ¼ cup cheddar cheese. Repeat layering procedure 4 more times. Finish with remaining plain corn tortilla and remaining enchilada sauce.

7. Cover and cook on high for 1½ to 2 hours, on low for 3 or 4 hours, or until hot and bubbling.

8. During the last 15 minutes of cook time, sprinkle remaining ⅓ cup cheddar cheese over top. Serve hot.

Variation: For **Deconstructed Green Chile Enchiladas,** replace the jalapeño pepper with 1 (4-ounce) can diced mild green chiles, with liquid, and swap out the red chile enchilada sauce with an equal amount of green chile enchilada sauce or 2½ cups salsa verde.

DEFINITION

Smoked paprika is a variety of Spanish paprika made from mature pimento peppers that are dried, naturally smoked over oak wood fires, and stone-ground to a fine, powdery consistency. It has a deep red color with a slightly smoky and bittersweet flavor.

Tempeh and Bean Tamale Pie

This tasty tamale pie is fast and easy and includes a spicy *tempeh* and bean chili–like filling that's covered in a cornbread topping.

Yield:	Prep time:	Cook time:	Serving size:
9 or 10 cups	15 to 20 minutes	10 minutes, plus 3½ to 4 hours	1½ cups

1 TB. olive oil

1 (8-oz.) pkg. tempeh

1 cup yellow onion, diced

¾ cup green bell pepper, ribs and seeds removed, and diced

¾ cup red bell pepper, ribs and seeds removed, and diced

1 medium jalapeño pepper, ribs and seeds removed, and finely diced

1½ TB. minced garlic

1 TB. nutritional yeast flakes

1 TB. chili powder

½ TB. dried oregano

½ tsp. ground cumin

½ tsp. sea salt

½ tsp. freshly ground black pepper

1½ cups cooked kidney beans, or 1 (15-oz.) can kidney beans, drained and rinsed

1½ cups cooked black beans or 1 (15-oz.) can black beans, drained and rinsed

1 (28-oz.) can crushed fire-roasted tomatoes with green chiles, with juice

¼ cup chopped fresh cilantro

1 cup soy or other nondairy milk

1 TB. apple cider vinegar

2 TB. water

1 TB. Ener-G Egg Replacer

1 cup white whole-wheat or whole-wheat pastry flour

1 cup cornmeal (preferably medium-grind)

¼ cup unbleached cane sugar

½ TB. aluminum-free baking powder

½ tsp. baking soda

2 TB. sunflower or other oil

1. Lightly coat a medium slow cooker's ceramic crock insert with vegetable cooking spray or oil of choice.

2. In a large nonstick skillet over medium heat, heat olive oil. Using your fingers, crumble tempeh into the skillet, and sauté, stirring often, for 5 minutes.

3. Add yellow onion, green bell pepper, and red bell pepper, and sauté, stirring often, for 3 minutes.

4. Add jalapeño pepper, garlic, nutritional yeast flakes, chili powder, oregano, cumin, sea salt, and black pepper, and sauté, stirring often, for 2 minutes. Remove the skillet from heat.

5. In the slow cooker, combine tempeh mixture, kidney beans, black beans, and crushed fire-roasted tomatoes with green chiles with juice.

6. Cover and cook on high for 2 hours.

7. Stir in cilantro. Taste and adjust seasonings as desired.

8. During the last 5 minutes of cook time, in a small bowl, stir together soy milk and apple cider vinegar, and set aside for 5 minutes to thicken.

9. In another small bowl, combine water and Ener-G Egg Replacer, and whisk vigorously for 1 minute or until very frothy (like beaten egg whites).

10. In a medium bowl, whisk together white whole-wheat flour, cornmeal, unbleached cane sugar, aluminum-free baking powder, and baking soda. Add soy milk mixture, egg replacer mixture, and sunflower oil, and whisk well to combine.

11. Evenly spread cornbread topping on top of tempeh filling. Cover; slightly vent lid with a toothpick, chopstick, or wooden spoon; and cook on high for 1½ to 2 hours or until a toothpick inserted into cornbread topping comes out clean. Serve hot.

Variation: For **Cheesy Tamale Pie,** sprinkle ½ cup shredded cheddar or pepper Jack cheese over the top of the cornbread topping during last 15 minutes of cook time.

DEFINITION

Tempeh is a cultured food product made by mixing partially cooked soybeans with a beneficial mold (*Rhizosporus oligosporus*) and fermenting it. This results in a firm soybean cake with a marbled appearance, which is why tempeh is often classified as the bleu cheese version of tofu.

Biscuit-Topped Veggie Potpie

Forget about those processed little potpies in your grocer's freezer. This slow cooker version is filled with chunks of fresh and frozen veggies floating in a luscious herbed gravy, and instead of pastry, it's topped with cut biscuits.

Yield:	Prep time:	Cook time:	Serving size:
9 cups and 6 biscuits	20 to 25 minutes	3 to 3½ hours	1½ cups and 1 biscuit

5 cups (7 or 8 medium) red-skinned potatoes, cut into 1-in. cubes

1½ cups (1 large) yellow onion, diced

1½ cups (2 or 3 large stalks) celery (including inner leaves and tops), cut into ½-in.-thick slices

1½ cups (8 oz.) crimini or white button mushrooms, cut in ½ and thinly sliced

1 (16-oz.) pkg. frozen mixed vegetable blend (carrots, cut corn, green beans, and peas), thawed

4 cups Homemade Vegetable Broth (recipe in Chapter 8)

⅔ cup chickpea/garbanzo bean flour or other flour

¼ cup nutritional yeast flakes

2 tsp. poultry seasoning blend

1½ tsp. dried thyme

1½ tsp. dried dill weed

1 tsp. seasoning salt (such as Herbamare)

½ tsp. freshly ground black pepper

⅓ cup chopped fresh parsley

1½ cups whole-wheat pastry flour

1 TB. aluminum-free baking powder

½ tsp. sea salt

6 TB. soy or other nondairy milk

3 TB. sunflower or other oil

1. In a large oval slow cooker, layer, in order, red-skinned potatoes, yellow onion, celery, crimini mushrooms, and mixed vegetable blend.

2. In a medium bowl, whisk together Homemade Vegetable Broth, chickpea/ garbanzo bean flour, nutritional yeast flakes, poultry seasoning blend, thyme, dill weed, seasoning salt, and black pepper. Stir mixture into the slow cooker.

3. Cover and cook on high for 2½ to 3 hours, on low for 5 or 6 hours, or until vegetables are tender.

4. Stir in parsley. Taste and adjust seasonings as desired.

5. Meanwhile, in a medium bowl, stir together whole-wheat pastry flour, aluminum-free baking powder, and sea salt. Add soy milk and sunflower oil, and stir until well combined and a ball of dough forms.

6. Transfer dough to a floured work surface. Using your hands, knead dough for 1 minute. Pat dough into a ½-inch-thick 5×7½-inch rectangle. Cut into 6 (2½-inch) squares.

7. Gently place biscuits on top of veggie potpie mixture in an even layer. Cover; slightly vent lid with a toothpick, chopstick, or wooden spoon; and cook on high for 30 to 40 minutes or until biscuits are tender. Serve hot.

Variations: Feel free to use other fresh and frozen vegetables in the filling, such as turnips, parsnips, sweet potatoes, leafy greens, or California blend vegetables. For **Gluten-Free Biscuit-Topped Veggie Potpie,** replace the whole-wheat pastry flour in the biscuit topping with an equal amount of Bob's Red Mill Gluten-Free All-Purpose Baking Flour and also add ½ teaspoon xanthan gum. For **Biscuit-Topped Chick'n and Veggie Potpie,** before topping with biscuit mixture, add 1 pound (about 3 cups) Chick'n-Style Simmered Seitan (variation in Chapter 11), cut into 1-inch cubes.

COOKER CAVEAT

Just as when placing dumplings onto a stew, be sure the veggie potpie filling is really hot and bubbling before you place the biscuits on top. This ensures the biscuits float on the surface as they cook, which prevents them from being soggy on the bottom.

Beefy Seitan Pot Roast with Vegetables

Rather than simmering the beef-flavored seitan in broth (as in Chapter 11's Beef-Style Simmered Seitan), in this dish, the seitan is cooked on top of chunks of vegetables, which are bathed in a savory broth that's later thickened into a scrumptious gravy.

Yield:	Prep time:	Cook time:	Serving size:
1½ pounds seitan roast, 6 cups vegetables, and 2 cups gravy	15 to 20 minutes	2½ to 3 hours	4 ounces seitan, 1 cup vegetables, and ⅓ cup gravy

1 lb. (10 or 12) small new potatoes, cut in ½, or red-skinned potatoes, cut in ¼s

¾ lb. (1½ cups) baby carrots or 3 or 4 large carrots, cut into 3-in. pieces

1 medium yellow onion, cut into 8 wedges

3 large stalks celery (including inner leaves and tops), cut into 2-in. pieces

2½ tsp. dried basil

2½ tsp. dried thyme

Sea salt

Freshly ground black pepper

3⅔ cups Homemade Vegetable Broth (recipe in Chapter 8)

1¾ cups vital wheat gluten

½ cup chickpea/garbanzo bean flour

¼ cup nutritional yeast flakes

1 TB. onion powder

1 TB. garlic powder or garlic granules

⅓ cup tamari, shoyu, or Bragg Liquid Aminos

¼ cup red wine

¼ tsp. freshly ground black pepper

2 TB. tomato paste

1 TB. vegetarian Worcestershire sauce

3 TB. water

1½ TB. cornstarch

1. Lightly coat a medium or large slow cooker's ceramic crock insert with vegetable cooking spray or oil of choice.

2. In the slow cooker, combine new potatoes, carrots, yellow onion, celery, 1½ teaspoons basil, and 1½ teaspoons thyme. Season with sea salt and black pepper, and stir well to combine. Pour in 3 cups Homemade Vegetable Broth.

3. Cover and start cooking on high (or low).

4. Meanwhile, in a large bowl, combine vital wheat gluten, chickpea/garbanzo bean flour, nutritional yeast flakes, onion powder, garlic powder, remaining 1 teaspoon basil, and remaining 1 teaspoon thyme, and ¼ teaspoon black pepper. Add remaining ⅔ cup Homemade Vegetable Broth, tamari, red wine, tomato paste, and vegetarian Worcestershire sauce, and stir well.

5. Transfer seitan mixture to a clean counter or work surface. Using your hands, knead mixture for 3 to 5 minutes or until a smooth and pliable dough forms. Form dough into an oval- or loaf-shape roast that will fit inside your slow cooker. Carefully place seitan pot roast on top of vegetables.

6. Cover and cook on high for 2½ to 3 hours, on low for 5 or 6 hours, or until vegetables are tender and seitan pot roast is very firm to the touch.

7. Using 2 spatulas or slotted spoons, carefully remove seitan pot roast from the slow cooker and place on a cutting board. Remove vegetables and place on a large platter.

8. In a small bowl, stir together water and cornstarch. Stir cornstarch mixture into the slow cooker, and cook for 5 to 10 minutes or until mixture is thickened. Transfer gravy to a gravy boat or small bowl.

9. Thinly slice seitan pot roast and arrange on a platter. Surround with cooked vegetables, and serve hot with gravy.

Variation: Feel free to replace the yellow onion with red onion or small shallots, and the new potatoes with an equal amount of parsnips or turnips, cut into 3-inch pieces.

COOKER CAVEAT

When making seitan, be sure to only use vital wheat gluten (instant gluten flour), not high-gluten wheat flour, which is often used in bread baking as well. These two flour products are quite different, and using the latter when making seitan could have disastrous results.

Stuffed Seitan Roast

Here's your answer as to what to serve for your vegan Thanksgiving entrée. You'll win rave reviews with this succulent seitan roast that's filled with the Savory Bread Stuffing (recipe in Chapter 16).

Yield:	Prep time:	Cook time:	Serving size:
3- to 3½-pound roast	25 to 30 minutes	3 to 3½ hours	2 slices

1½ cups vital wheat gluten

¾ cup chickpea/garbanzo bean flour

3 TB. nutritional yeast flakes

1 TB. onion powder

1 TB. garlic powder or garlic granules

2 tsp. poultry seasoning blend

½ tsp. garlic pepper or freshly ground black pepper

2 cups Homemade Vegetable Broth (recipe in Chapter 8)

4 TB. tamari, shoyu, or Bragg Liquid Aminos

6 cups uncooked Savory Bread Stuffing (recipe in Chapter 16)

1 batch Golden Onion and Garlic Gravy (recipe in Chapter 6)

1. Lightly coat a large oval slow cooker's ceramic crock insert with vegetable cooking spray or oil of choice.

2. In a large bowl, combine vital wheat gluten, chickpea/garbanzo bean flour, nutritional yeast flakes, onion powder, garlic powder, poultry seasoning blend, and garlic pepper. Add 1¼ cups Homemade Vegetable Broth and 3 tablespoons tamari, and stir well.

3. Transfer seitan mixture to a work surface. Using your hands, knead mixture for 3 to 5 minutes or until a smooth and pliable dough forms. Let seitan mixture rest for 10 minutes.

4. Place a large piece of plastic wrap or parchment paper on a work surface, and place seitan mixture on top. Using a rolling pin, roll out seitan mixture into a ¼-inch-thick 8×10-inch rectangle, with the shorter side nearest you. Leaving a 1-inch margin on the sides, place Savory Bread Stuffing horizontally in center of seitan rectangle, and flatten it slightly to pack it down on seitan rectangle. Fold bottom half of seitan rectangle over stuffing mixture, and roll up tightly like a jelly roll cake to enclose stuffing mixture. Firmly pinch seam to seal.

5. Slide a 3-foot piece of unbleached cotton kitchen twine underneath seitan roast. Starting 1 inch in from outer edge of roast, working with one end of the twine, wrap twine around seitan roast at the left end, and tightly tie in a knot to secure. While keeping twine taut, working in 3-inch intervals, wrap twine around roast, slip long end of twine underneath, and cinch and pull on twine like a belt. Repeat procedure 2 more times, and tie twine end into a knot at the other end of seitan roast. Place stuffed seitan roast seam side down in the slow cooker. Using a fork, pierce stuffed seitan roast in several places.

6. In a small bowl, stir together remaining ¾ cup Homemade Vegetable Broth and remaining 1 tablespoon tamari. Pour evenly over top of stuffed seitan roast.

7. Cover and cook on high for 3 to 3½ hours, on low for 6 or 7 hours, or until stuffed seitan roast is very firm to the touch.

8. After 3 hours, baste stuffed seitan roast with cooking liquid, and continue to baste once every hour after that as needed.

9. Uncover and allow stuffed seitan roast to cool inside the slow cooker for 15 minutes. Using 2 spatulas or slotted spoons, carefully remove stuffed seitan roast and place on a cutting board. Place whole or thinly sliced stuffed seitan roast on a platter, and serve hot with Golden Onion and Garlic Gravy.

Variation: You can also prepare the stuffed seitan roast with Savory Mushroom Bread Stuffing or Apple-Nut Bread Stuffing (variations in Chapter 16).

> **LOW AND SLOW**
>
> You can find unbleached cotton kitchen twine in kitchen specialty stores, as well as most grocery and natural foods stores, in the same aisle that stocks parchment paper, plastic wrap, and aluminum foil.

Santa Fe–Style Stuffed Peppers

The classic combination of beans and rice gets a little help from some staples commonly used in Southwestern cuisine—corn, salsa, and cilantro—to achieve a lively, piquant filling for these stuffed bell peppers.

Yield:	Prep time:	Cook time:	Serving size:
6 stuffed peppers	10 minutes	1½ to 2 hours	1 stuffed pepper

6 large bell peppers

2 cups cooked brown rice or other variety

1½ cups cooked black beans, or 1 (15-oz.) can black beans, drained and rinsed

⅔ cup fresh or frozen cut corn, thawed

⅔ cup salsa

¼ cup black olives, pitted, and thinly sliced

¼ cup green onions, white and green parts, thinly sliced

¼ cup chopped fresh cilantro

1 tsp. chili powder

1 tsp. dried oregano

½ tsp. ground coriander or ground cumin

Sea salt

Freshly ground black pepper

⅔ cup shredded vegan pepper Jack or cheddar cheese

½ cup water

1. Lightly coat a large oval slow cooker's ceramic crock insert with vegetable cooking spray or oil of choice.

2. Cut off tops of bell peppers, and remove and discard ribs and seeds.

3. In a large bowl, combine brown rice, black beans, corn, salsa, black olives, green onions, cilantro, chili powder, oregano, and coriander. Taste and season with sea salt and black pepper as desired. Stir in pepper Jack cheese.

4. Fill each bell pepper with rice-and-bean mixture, and lightly pack it down with the back of a spoon. Place bell peppers upright, side by side in a single layer, in the slow cooker. Do not stack. Pour water around outside of bell peppers.

5. Cover and cook on high for 1½ to 2 hours, on low for 3 or 4 hours, or until bell peppers are tender. Serve hot.

Variation: For **Spicy Quinoa-Stuffed Peppers,** replace the rice and bean mixture in the filling with 3½ cups Spanish-Style Quinoa (variation in Chapter 16), and stir together with cheese before filling bell peppers.

> **LOW AND SLOW**
>
> For an eye-catching batch of stuffed peppers, prepare this recipe using a combination of differently colored bell peppers—red, green, orange, or yellow.

Creole Collard Rolls

You'll love how well collard greens, black-eyed peas, and brown rice come together in creating these tasty, filled and rolled morsels for a soul food–inspired supper.

Yield:	Prep time:	Cook time:	Serving size:
12 collard rolls	20 to 25 minutes	1½ to 2 hours	2 collard rolls

13 large collard greens (about 2 bunches), stems removed and leaves intact

Boiling water

3 cups Black-Eyed Peas with Collards and Yams (recipe in Chapter 15)

3 cups cooked brown rice or other grain

Sea salt

Freshly ground black pepper

Hot pepper sauce

1½ cups Homemade Vegetable Broth (recipe in Chapter 8)

1. In a medium or large slow cooker, place collard greens. Pour in enough boiling water to fully cover collard greens. Cover and let sit for 8 to 10 minutes to slightly wilt collard greens. Transfer collard greens to a cutting board to cool.

2. Dump out water from the slow cooker, and dry it well. Lightly coat the ceramic crock insert with vegetable cooking spray or oil of choice.

3. Place 1 collard green in the bottom of the slow cooker.

4. In a large bowl, combine Black-Eyed Peas with Collards and Yams and brown rice. Season with sea salt, black pepper, and hot pepper sauce, and stir well.

5. Place 1 collard green on a large plate or work surface. Place ½ cup black-eyed pea and rice mixture at stem end of collard green, fold in each side of collard green toward the center over filling, and roll from stem end to enclose filling.

6. Place filled collard green seam side down on top of the collard green inside the slow cooker. Repeat filling and rolling procedure for remaining collard greens and filling mixture, and stack collard rolls in layers as needed. Pour in Homemade Vegetable Broth.

7. Cover and cook on high for 1½ to 2 hours, on low for 3 or 4 hours, or until collard greens are tender. Serve hot.

Variation: For added flavor, add 1 cup shredded vegan pepper Jack or other variety of cheese to the filling mixture. You can also prepare this recipe using Swiss chard or cabbage leaves.

LOW AND SLOW

Use collard greens that are quite large and firm, have a deep green color, and aren't wilted or yellowed around the edges. If you can only find small collard greens, you may need to overlap two smaller leaves for making each collard roll instead.

Sensational Sides

From time to time, we all can use a little bit of help, and the main attractions in Part 6 will shine even more with the help of a great supporting cast. The following chapters contain a crowd-pleasing collection of veggie-, bean-, and grain-based side dish recipes that complement the main dishes they're served alongside. Or you can skip the main attraction and build a delicious meal by combining a few of Part 6's sensational side dish selections.

Also in this part, I give you a whole chapter dedicated entirely to making wholesome, slow-baked breads inside the warm confines of your slow cooker. I've included recipes for sweet quick breads, biscuits, cornbread, and even yeast-risen breads and rolls.

Versatile Veggies

In This Chapter

- Home-style veggie sides
- Playing with your potatoes
- Creamed and stewed selections
- Braised and glazed roots and cabbages

We vegans just love our vegetables, and rightfully so, as they are jam-packed with vitamins, minerals, antioxidants, protein, and of course, plenty of beneficial dietary fiber. If you want to stay healthy, eat your veggies—and plenty of them!

The recipes in this chapter utilize many commonly used vegetables like onions, potatoes, carrots, corn, tomatoes, and winter and summer squashes, as well as the sometimes-underappreciated cauliflower and cabbages. Hopefully, these recipe ideas will inspire you to play around with slow cooking some of your other favorite vegetable side dishes as well.

If you've been eating vegan for a while, you probably have an arsenal of veggie side dish recipes that are baked, broiled, steamed, sautéed, pan-roasted, simmered, or stewed. You don't have to forgo all these dishes. Many can be adapted to work in the slow cooker, freeing up your oven and stovetop for other items.

Orange-Glazed Baby Carrots

Orange juice, brown sugar, coconut oil, and fresh ginger meld together in the slow cooker to create a sweet and luscious glaze for baby carrots.

Yield:	Prep time:	Cook time:	Serving size:
6 cups	5 to 10 minutes	2 to 2½ hours	¾ cup

2 lb. (4½ cups) baby carrots

⅓ cup light brown or muscovado sugar, packed

1 TB. coconut oil or 2 TB. nonhydrogenated margarine

1½ TB. peeled and minced fresh ginger

Zest of 1 large orange

½ tsp. sea salt

½ cup fresh orange juice

¼ cup water

2 TB. cornstarch or arrowroot

1. In a medium or large slow cooker, layer, in order, baby carrots, brown sugar, coconut oil, ginger, orange zest, and sea salt. Pour in orange juice.

2. Cover and cook on high for 2 to 2½ hours, on low for 4 or 5 hours, or until carrots are tender.

3. Taste and adjust seasonings as desired.

4. In a small bowl, stir together water and cornstarch. Add cornstarch mixture to the slow cooker, and cook for 5 to 10 minutes or until glaze is slightly thickened. Serve hot.

Variation: You can also prepare this recipe using 2 pounds large carrots, cut into 2-inch chunks.

SLOW INTERESTING

Baby carrots is a misnomer, because they're not baby, immature carrots at all. They're actually large carrots that have been whittled down by a machine into 2- or 3-inch pieces with slightly rounded edges.

Coconut Creamed Corn

You'll love this creamed corn, thanks to coconut milk beverage, which not only provides a rich and luscious saucy component to this side dish, but also accentuates the natural sweetness of the corn.

Yield:	Prep time:	Cook time:	Serving size:
6 or 7 cups	5 minutes	2 to 2½ hours	¾ cup

6½ cups fresh or 2 (16-oz.) pkg. frozen cut corn, thawed

3 TB. nutritional yeast flakes

3 TB. chopped fresh thyme or 1 TB. dried thyme

1½ TB. nonhydrogenated margarine

1 tsp. sea salt

½ tsp. garlic pepper

¼ tsp. freshly ground black pepper

2 cups plain coconut milk beverage

¼ cup water

2 TB. *cornstarch* or arrowroot

½ cup green onions, white and green parts, thinly sliced

⅓ cup chopped fresh parsley

1. Lightly coat a medium or large slow cooker's ceramic crock insert with vegetable cooking spray or oil of choice.

2. In the slow cooker, layer, in order, corn, nutritional yeast flakes, thyme, non-hydrogenated margarine, sea salt, garlic pepper, and black pepper. Pour in coconut milk beverage.

3. Cover and cook on high for 2 to 2½ hours, on low for 4 or 5 hours, or until corn is tender.

4. In a small bowl, stir together water and cornstarch. Add cornstarch mixture to the slow cooker, and cook for 5 to 10 minutes or until mixture is slightly thickened.

5. Stir in green onions and parsley, taste and adjust seasonings, and serve hot.

Variation: For a slightly richer version, replace the coconut milk beverage with plain coconut creamer.

DEFINITION

Cornstarch is one of the most commonly used starches in baking and food processing. Essentially, it's the refined starch of the endosperm of the corn kernel. Cornstarch functions as a vegan, gluten-free thickener and is often mixed with cold liquid to make into a paste before adding to a recipe to avoid clumps.

Baked Russet or Sweet Potatoes

It's super easy to load up your slow cooker with some russets in the morning, and when you return home, they're perfectly steamed inside with slightly crisp skin.

Yield:	Prep time:	Cook time:	Serving size:
6 or more baked potatoes	5 minutes	4 or 5 hours	1 baked potato

6 or more large russet, Idaho, or sweet potatoes, scrubbed well

1 or 2 TB. olive oil

Nonhydrogenated margarine

Vegan sour cream or yogurt

Shredded vegan cheddar cheese or other variety

Thinly sliced green onions, white and green parts, or chopped chives

1. Thoroughly dry russet potatoes, and prick each with a fork or a knife in several places. Using your fingers, rub a little olive oil on skin of each potato.

2. Place potatoes in a medium or large slow cooker, either upright or stacked horizontally to fit.

3. Cover and cook on high for 4 or 5 hours, on low for 7 or 8 hours, or until potatoes are tender and easily pierced with a knife.

4. Using a large slotted spoon or tongs, remove potatoes from the slow cooker. Split potatoes open with a knife or fork. Garnish individual servings with non-hydrogenated margarine, vegan sour cream, vegan cheddar cheese, and sliced green onions as desired, and serve hot.

Variation: For added flavor, before cooking the potatoes, season each lightly with sea salt and freshly ground black pepper. For a fat-free version, don't rub olive oil on the potatoes' skins. You can also use the slow cooker to bake garnet yams in the same manner.

COOKER CAVEAT

Be sure to prick the skin of the potatoes, otherwise, they could burst open inside your slow cooker. Don't add any water to the slow cooker because you want the outside skins of the potatoes to be slightly crisp and the insides steamed, and adding liquid would result in potatoes with a texture similar to one that had been boiled or stewed.

Scalloped Potatoes

Humble spud slices are transformed from ho-hum to yum when they're layered with bits of onions and enrobed in a creamy sauce in this classic comfort-food side dish.

Yield:	Prep time:	Cook time:	Serving size:
9 cups	10 to 15 minutes	2 to 2½ hours	1 cup

3 lb. (6 or 7 large) red-skinned potatoes, thinly sliced

1 cup diced red or yellow onion

6 TB. green onions, white and green parts, thinly sliced

6 TB. chopped fresh parsley

3 TB. nutritional yeast flakes

1½ tsp. sea salt or seasoning salt (such as Herbamare)

¾ tsp. freshly ground black pepper

3 cups soy or other nondairy milk

1 TB. olive oil

Smoked or sweet paprika

1. Lightly coat a medium or large slow cooker's ceramic crock insert with vegetable cooking spray or oil of choice.

2. In the slow cooker, layer, in order, ⅓ of red-skinned potatoes, ⅓ cup red onion, 2 tablespoons green onions, 2 tablespoons parsley, 1 tablespoon nutritional yeast flakes, ½ teaspoon sea salt, and ¼ teaspoon black pepper. Repeat layers 2 more times.

3. Pour in soy milk, drizzle with olive oil, and sprinkle with smoked paprika.

4. Cover and cook on high for 2 to 2½ hours, or low for 4 or 5 hours or until potatoes are tender. Serve hot.

Variation: Russets or Yukon Gold potatoes also work in this recipe. For **Au Gratin Potatoes,** add 1½ cups shredded vegan cheddar cheese in the assembly procedure, scattering ½ cup cheddar cheese between each of the layers.

LOW AND SLOW

To quickly and easily cut your potatoes into perfectly thin slices, I recommend using a mandolin or a food processor fitted with a 2-millimeter slicing disc.

Marvelous Mashed Potatoes

Nutritional yeast flakes and margarine impart the perfect buttery cheesiness to Yukon Gold mashed potatoes. With this recipe, you can free up your stovetop for other things by cooking and mashing them directly in the slow cooker, and then use it to keep them hot until ready to serve as well.

Yield:	Prep time:	Cook time:	Serving size:
6 cups	10 to 15 minutes	2 to 2½ hours	1 cup

3 lb. (6 or 7 large) Yukon Gold potatoes, peeled, and cut into 2-in. cubes

2 TB. nonhydrogenated margarine

1½ TB. nutritional yeast flakes

1 tsp. sea salt

½ tsp. freshly ground black pepper or garlic pepper

2 cups water

2 cups plain soy creamer or other nondairy milk

2 TB. chopped chives, or ¼ cup chopped fresh parsley (optional)

1. In a medium or large slow cooker, layer, in order, Yukon Gold potatoes, non-hydrogenated margarine, nutritional yeast flakes, sea salt, and black pepper. Pour in water and soy creamer.

2. Cover and cook on high for 2 to 2½ hours, on low for 4 or 5 hours, or until potatoes are tender. Uncover, turn off slow cooker, and allow potatoes to cool for 15 minutes.

3. Using a potato masher, mash potatoes as smooth or chunky as desired. (Alternatively, use a handheld electric mixer on low speed to whip potato mixture to desired consistency.)

4. Taste and add additional nonhydrogenated margarine or seasonings as desired. For added color and flavor, garnish mashed potatoes with chives or parsley (if using). Serve hot.

Variation: You can also top individual servings with Golden Onion and Garlic Gravy (recipe in Chapter 6). For **Cheezy Mashed Potatoes,** after mashing, add ¾ cup shredded vegan cheddar cheese or other variety.

COOKER CAVEAT

Never use a food processor to prepare mashed potatoes. The fast-moving blade will pulverize the potatoes' cell walls, causing them to release their natural starch. The result is a gummy, gluey, pastey mess.

Indian-Spiced Cauliflower and Potatoes

Cauliflower florets and chunks of potatoes are combined with a blend of earthy spices commonly used in the cuisine of southern India. These spices not only infuse the vegetables with flavor, but also tint them a golden-amber hue.

Yield:	Prep time:	Cook time:	Serving size:
6 or 7 cups	15 to 20 minutes	2 to 2½ hours	1 cup

1 TB. nonhydrogenated margarine or olive oil

1 tsp. black mustard seeds

1 tsp. ground coriander

1 tsp. ground cumin

1 tsp. turmeric

1 tsp. garam masala or curry powder

¼ tsp. cayenne

1 cup yellow onion, diced

1½ TB. minced garlic

1½ TB. peeled and minced fresh ginger

1 large head cauliflower, cut into florets (about 6 cups)

2 cups (1 or 2 medium) Yukon Gold or russet potatoes, cut into 1-in. cubes

1 medium jalapeño pepper or 2 serrano chile peppers, ribs and seeds removed, and finely diced

1 medium tomato, diced

1¼ cups water

¼ cup chopped fresh cilantro

Sea salt

Freshly ground black pepper

1. In a medium nonstick skillet over medium heat, combine nonhydrogenated margarine and black mustard seeds. Cook for 2 or 3 minutes or until mustard seeds begin to pop.

2. Add coriander, cumin, turmeric, garam masala, and cayenne, and sauté, stirring often, for 30 seconds.

3. Add yellow onion, garlic, and ginger, and sauté, stirring often, for 3 minutes. Remove the skillet from heat.

4. In a medium or large slow cooker, layer, in order, cauliflower, Yukon Gold potatoes, onion mixture, jalapeño pepper, and tomato. Pour in water.

5. Cover and cook on high for 2 to 2½ hours, on low for 4 or 5 hours, or until vegetables are tender.

6. Stir in cilantro, taste and season with sea salt and black pepper, and serve hot.

Variation: You can also prepare this dish using orange cauliflower. For **Indian-Spiced Cauliflower, Potatoes, Peas, and Cashews,** add 1 cup fresh or frozen peas, thawed, during the last 30 minutes of cook time and then top individual servings with 2 tablespoons toasted cashews.

LOW AND SLOW

Sautéing the spices in margarine or oil may seem like extra work, but this simple step helps the spices release their essential oils, which in turn boosts their flavor and aroma, and ultimately, really makes a difference in achieving a complex, full-flavored dish.

Sweet Potato–Praline Casserole

This recipe involves several steps, but the final result is well worth it. Slow-cooked sweet potatoes are mashed with soy milk, brown sugar, and spices and then covered with a pralinelike topping during the final cooking phase.

Yield:	Prep time:	Cook time:	Serving size:
7 cups	15 to 20 minutes	2½ to 3 hours	1 cup

3 lb. (6 large) sweet potatoes, peeled, and cut into 2-in. cubes

2 cups water

1 cup soy or other nondairy milk

¾ cup light brown or muscovado sugar, packed

1 tsp. vanilla extract

1 tsp. ground ginger

½ tsp. sea salt

½ cup white whole-wheat flour or other flour

3 TB. nonhydrogenated margarine

¾ tsp. ground cinnamon

⅔ cup toasted pecan pieces or pecans, roughly chopped

1. In a medium or large slow cooker, combine sweet potatoes and water.

2. Cover and cook on high for 2 to 2½ hours, on low for 4 or 5 hours, or until sweet potatoes are tender. Uncover, turn off the slow cooker, and allow sweet potatoes to cool for 15 minutes.

3. Add soy milk, ¼ cup brown sugar, vanilla extract, ginger, and sea salt. Using a potato masher, mash sweet potatoes until smooth and creamy. (Alternatively, use a handheld electric mixer on low speed to whip sweet potatoes until smooth.)

4. In a small bowl, combine remaining ½ cup brown sugar, white whole-wheat flour, nonhydrogenated margarine, and cinnamon, and stir with a fork until it forms a crumbly mixture. Sprinkle over mashed sweet potato mixture. Cover and cook on high for 30 minutes.

5. Uncover and sprinkle toasted pecans over top. Cover and cook for 15 minutes. Serve hot.

Variation: You can also prepare this recipe with garnet yams or winter squash such as butternut, turban, or kabocha.

SLOW INTERESTING

Pecans are commercially available in a variety of sizes, such as mammoth, extra-large, large, medium, and small. The larger their size, the fewer you get per pound. You can purchase these highly prized nuts in several forms, including whole, halves, pieces, and even as a finely ground meal.

Stewed Tomatoes with Summer Squash and Zucchini

This is a great Italian-style side dish to serve during the hot summer months. It features fresh tomatoes, summer squash, zucchini, and herbs and is as visually appealing as it is tasty.

Yield:	Prep time:	Cook time:	Serving size:
6 cups	10 to 15 minutes	2 to 2½ hours	¾ cup

4 cups (2 or 3 large) tomatoes, cut into 2-in. chunks

2 medium yellow summer squash, cut into ½-in.-thick slices

2 medium zucchini, cut into ½-in.-thick slices

2 TB. minced garlic

1½ TB. nutritional yeast flakes

1 tsp. dried oregano or marjoram

½ tsp. sea salt

½ tsp. freshly ground black pepper

½ cup water

⅓ cup chopped fresh basil

¼ cup chopped fresh Italian flat-leaf parsley

1. In a medium slow cooker, layer, in order, tomatoes, yellow summer squash, zucchini, garlic, nutritional yeast flakes, oregano, sea salt, and black pepper. Pour in water.

2. Cover and cook on high for 2 to 2½ hours, on low for 4 or 5 hours, or until vegetables are tender.

3. Stir in basil and Italian flat-leaf parsley, taste and adjust seasonings as desired, and serve hot.

Variation: For added color, use assorted colors of heirloom tomatoes instead of just red tomatoes.

COOKER CAVEAT

Tomatoes, eggplants, potatoes, and other members of the nightshade family contain alkaloid compounds. Most of the alkaloids contained within their flesh provide health benefits; however, some of the alkaloids contained within their leaves can be toxic. Never eat the leaves of these vegetables.

Down-Home Greens

Garlic and onions enhance both the flavor of the leafy greens, as well as the resulting pot liquor of this classic Southern staple. A little molasses and apple cider vinegar give them a hint of sweetness.

Yield:	Prep time:	Cook time:	Serving size:
4 or 5 cups	15 minutes	2 to 2½ hours	¾ to 1 cup

2 large bunches collard greens, turnip greens, kale, Swiss chard, or a combination of greens

1 cup yellow onion, diced

2 TB. minced garlic

1½ TB. nutritional yeast flakes

1½ cups Homemade Vegetable Broth (recipe in Chapter 8)

1 TB. apple cider vinegar

1 TB. blackstrap molasses

Sea salt or seasoning salt (such as Herbamare)

Freshly ground black pepper

Hot pepper sauce or crushed red pepper flakes

1. Remove or trim stems off collard greens, and cut leaves chiffonade into 1-inch strips.

2. In a medium or large slow cooker, layer, in order, collard greens, yellow onion, garlic, and nutritional yeast flakes. Pour in Homemade Vegetable Broth, apple cider vinegar, and blackstrap molasses.

3. Cover and cook on high for 2 to 2½ hours, on low for 4 or 5 hours, or until greens are tender.

4. Taste and season with sea salt, black pepper, and hot pepper sauce, and serve hot.

Variation: For extra flavor, add ¾ cup (1 medium) green bell pepper, ribs and seeds removed, and diced, and 1 medium jalapeño pepper, ribs and seeds removed, and finely diced. For **Savory Greens with Beans,** add 1½ cups cooked black-eyed peas or red beans or 1 (15-ounce) can black-eyed peas or red beans, drained and rinsed, and season with seasoning salt.

SLOW INTERESTING

Blackstrap molasses and leafy greens are both excellent plant-based sources of calcium. In fact, 2 tablespoons blackstrap molasses or 1 cup cooked greens like collard greens provide your body with a greater amount of absorbable calcium than 1 cup cow's milk.

Wine-Braised Cabbage

Braising cabbages and onions in the slow cooker with some white wine and caraway seeds gives them a slightly sweet and piquant flavor you'll love.

Yield:	Prep time:	Cook time:	Serving size:
6 or 7 cups	15 to 20 minutes	2 to 2½ hours	¾ cup

2 cups (2 medium) yellow onion, cut into ½ moons

½ TB. olive oil

½ TB. minced garlic

½ TB. caraway seeds

½ medium head green cabbage, thinly sliced and packed (4 cups)

½ medium head red cabbage, thinly sliced and packed (4 cups)

1 cup white wine (such as Riesling or Chardonnay)

Sea salt

Freshly ground black pepper

1. In a medium nonstick skillet over medium heat, combine yellow onion and olive oil. Sauté, stirring often, for 3 minutes.

2. Add garlic and caraway seeds, and sauté, stirring often, for 1 minute. Remove the skillet from heat.

3. In a medium or large slow cooker, layer, in order, green cabbage, red cabbage, and onion mixture. Pour in white wine.

4. Cover and cook on high for 2 to 2½ hours, on low for 4 or 5 hours, or until vegetables are tender.

5. Taste and season with sea salt and black pepper, and serve hot.

Variation: You can also prepare this recipe using either all green or all red cabbage. For nonalcoholic, vibrant red **Cider-Braised Red Cabbage with Apples,** use only 8 cups red cabbage, replace the yellow onion with red onion, and swap out the white wine with an equal amount of apple cider or apple juice, and add 2 tablespoons maple syrup or brown sugar. I suggest serving this delectable cabbage dish with the Beer Brats (recipe in Chapter 11) and slices of rye or pumpernickel bread for a great German-style meal.

DEFINITION

Braising is a cooking technique in which foods are slowly cooked in a small amount of liquid such as broth, water, or wine in a tightly covered pot, Dutch oven, or slow cooker. This moist-heat method prevents foods from drying during the cooking process.

Bodacious Bean Dishes

In This Chapter

- Sorting, soaking, and slow-cooking beans
- Slow-cooked baked beans
- Saucy and spicy beans
- International bean dishes

Beans are easily cultivated, inexpensive, and with proper handling, have an extremely long shelf life, making them a major component of daily diets throughout the world. Plus, they're so nutritious and are sources of low-fat protein, carbohydrates, dietary fiber, and a long list of vitamins and minerals. There are dozens of bean varieties available in all shapes, sizes, and colors, and each has its own distinct flavor and texture.

Canned beans are a great convenience item to have in your pantry to make your meal preparations easier. A 15-ounce can of beans contains between 1½ to 1¾ cups beans. Before adding them to recipes, drain them in a colander and rinse them with water to remove the canning liquid and any excess salt that may have been added to help them retain their shape.

Although cost-wise canned beans are relatively cheap, they do cost a lot more per pound than dried beans do. So if you're looking for ways to stretch your food dollars, stock up on dried beans and cook them yourself. Remember, the slow cooker was first marketed as a bean cooker, so it's perfect for the task! And unlike cooking beans in a pot on the stove, you don't have to worry about them foaming up or burning in your slow cooker.

Before cooking dried beans, first sort through them to remove any rocks or debris that may have tagged along when they were being packaged. I like to sort my beans on a large plate, in batches, moving small amounts from one side to the other. Then, place them in a colander and give them a good rinse to remove any residual dirt.

To help reduce their cooking time, you'll want to presoak your beans before cooking them in the slow cooker. While your dried beans are slow cooking, be sure to check them from time to time to be sure they're fully covered with water. Presoaking dried beans and cooking them with a bay leaf or a piece of kombu (a sea vegetable) also helps to reduce their gas-producing tendencies. When cooking dried beans, avoid initially adding salt to the cooking liquid because this can toughen their skins. That, in turn, may lengthen the cook time.

LOW AND SLOW

The cook time for dried beans varies depending on where they were grown, how fresh or old they are, and whether you cook them in hard or soft water. They take a slightly longer time to cook at higher altitudes, too. So it's best to give your beans a taste to properly determine when they're done.

Depending on the bean variety, 1 pound dried beans is about 2¼ cups and yields about 6 or 7 cups cooked beans; using ¾ cup dried beans yields approximately the same amount as 1 (15-ounce) can.

For convenience, I like to freeze my cooked beans in 1½- and 3-cup portions because these are the amounts you get from using 1 or 2 (15-ounce) cans.

Simple Slow-Cooked Beans

Save big bucks by cooking large batches of dried beans in your slow cooker and then using them throughout the week or freezing them for later use. Save time by cooking them while you sleep!

Yield:	Prep time:	Cook time:	Serving size:
6 or 7 cups	5 minutes, plus 1 hour or more soak time	3 or 4 hours	½ to 1 cup

1 lb. (about 2¼ cups) dried beans of choice, sorted and rinsed	1 bay leaf or 1 (3-in.) piece kombu Water

1. Presoak beans in a large bowl or pot, cover with several inches cold water, and leave to soak for 6 hours or overnight. Alternatively, to quick-soak beans, place beans in a pot and cover with water. Bring to a boil over high heat, and boil for 2 minutes. Cover, remove from heat, and leave to soak in hot water for 1 hour. Drain beans, and discard soaking liquid.

2. In a medium or large slow cooker, place beans and bay leaf. Add enough water to cover beans by at least 3 inches.

3. Cover and cook on high for 3 or 4 hours, on low for 6 to 8 hours or overnight, or until beans are tender.

4. Allow beans to cool in the slow cooker for 1 hour. Remove and discard bay leaf. Transfer cooked beans to an airtight container, cover with some of the cooking liquid, and store in the refrigerator for up to 1 week. Alternatively, drain beans, portion them into airtight containers or zipper-lock bags, and freeze for up to 6 months.

Variation: You don't need to presoak split peas or lentils because they have very thin skins that easily break down during cooking.

COOKER CAVEAT

Phytohaemagglutnin is a toxic agent found in many varieties of beans, but it's found in highest concentrations in raw red kidney beans. Symptoms of ingesting too much phytohaemagglutnin include abdominal pain, nausea, vomiting, and diarrhea and could even be fatal. If you want to slow cook red kidney beans, health experts recommend you soak them in water for at least 5 hours, boil them in fresh water for at least 10 minutes, and be sure they're fully cooked. Never eat raw or undercooked kidney beans.

Boston Baked Beans

For many, baked beans are a must-have for any picnic or family get-together. In this sure-to-please recipe, tender navy beans are flavored with bits of onions and covered in a rich and tangy sauce enhanced with molasses.

Yield:	Prep time:	Cook time:	Serving size:
8 or 9 cups	10 minutes, plus 1 hour soak time	7 or 8 hours	1 cup

1 lb. (about 2¼ cups) dried navy beans, sorted and rinsed

2 cups (2 medium) yellow onions, diced

¾ cup ketchup

¼ cup blackstrap molasses

¼ cup light brown or muscovado sugar, packed

2 TB. apple cider vinegar

1 TB. chili powder

1 TB. nutritional yeast flakes

2 tsp. dry mustard, or 2 TB. spicy brown or Dijon mustard

4 cups water

Sea salt

Freshly ground black pepper

Hot pepper sauce

1. Place beans in a large pot, and cover with water. Bring to a boil over high heat, and boil for 2 minutes. Cover, remove from heat, and set aside to soak for 1 hour. Drain navy beans in a colander, and discard soaking liquid.

2. In a medium or large slow cooker, combine yellow onions, presoaked navy beans, ketchup, blackstrap molasses, light brown sugar, apple cider vinegar, chili powder, nutritional yeast flakes, and dry mustard. Pour in water.

3. Cover and cook on low for 7 or 8 hours or until navy beans are tender.

4. Taste and season with sea salt, black pepper, and hot pepper sauce. Serve hot, cold, or at room temperature.

Variation: You can also prepare these baked beans with Great Northern beans. For **Creole Baked Beans,** add 2 roughly chopped Seitan Chorizo Sausages (recipe in Chapter 11); 1 large green bell pepper, ribs and seeds removed, and diced; and 1 medium jalapeño pepper, ribs and seeds removed, and finely diced.

SLOW INTERESTING

Traditionally, Boston baked beans are made by slowly cooking the sauce-covered beans in a low-temperature oven for several hours. Low temp … long hours— sound familiar? That's exactly what a slow cooker does!

Savory White Beans

When combined with garlic, sister herbs rosemary and *sage* produce the most savory, yet slightly pungent-flavored broth, which perfectly complements the creamy texture of Great Northern beans.

Yield:	Prep time:	Cook time:	Serving size:
4 or 5 cups	5 to 7 minutes, plus 1 hour or more soak time	3 or 4 hours	1 cup

1 lb. (about 2¼ cups) dried Great Northern beans, sorted and rinsed

2 TB. minced garlic

2 TB. chopped fresh rosemary or 2 tsp. dried rosemary, crushed

2 TB. chopped fresh sage or 2 tsp. rubbed (or dried) sage

1 TB. nutritional yeast flakes (optional)

1 bay leaf

6 cups water

Sea salt

Freshly ground black pepper

1. Presoak Great Northern beans for 6 hours or overnight, or quick-soak for 1 hour. Drain Great Northern beans in a colander, and discard soaking liquid.

2. In a medium or large slow cooker, layer, in order, soaked Great Northern beans, garlic, rosemary, sage, nutritional yeast flakes (if using), and bay leaf. Pour in water.

3. Cover and cook on high for 3 or 4 hours, on low for 6 to 8 hours, or until Great Northern beans are tender.

4. Remove and discard bay leaf. Taste and season with sea salt and black pepper, and serve hot.

Variation: To give these beans some "kick," add 1 teaspoon crushed red pepper flakes. You can use cannellini beans instead, but they may need an additional 1 hour or more cook time.

DEFINITION

Sage is an herb with a musty yet fruity, lemon-rind scent and "sunny" flavor.

Caribbean Black Beans

Take your taste buds on a Caribbean cruise with these black beans flavored with chiles, tomatoes, lime, and an ample amount of the highly fragrant spices loved by the people of the islands, like allspice, cloves, and nutmeg.

Yield:	Prep time:	Cook time:	Serving size:
4 or 5 cups	10 to 15 minutes	2 to 2½ hours	1 cup

1 large red bell pepper, ribs and
  seeds removed, and diced
1 medium Anaheim chile, ribs and
  seeds removed, and finely diced
1 cup red onion, diced
1 TB. olive oil
1 TB. minced garlic
1 TB. fresh peeled and minced ginger
1 tsp. dried thyme
½ tsp. sea salt

½ tsp. ground allspice
½ tsp. ground cinnamon
⅛ tsp. ground cloves
⅛ tsp. freshly grated nutmeg
⅛ tsp. freshly ground black pepper
3 cups cooked black beans, or
  2 (15-oz.) cans black beans,
  drained and rinsed
1 (14-oz.) can crushed fire-roasted
  tomatoes
2 TB. fresh lime juice

1. In a large, nonstick skillet over medium heat, combine red bell pepper, Anaheim chile, red onion, and olive oil. Sauté, stirring often, for 3 minutes.

2. Add garlic, ginger, thyme, sea salt, allspice, cinnamon, cloves, nutmeg, and black pepper, and sauté, stirring often, for 1 minute. Remove the skillet from heat.

3. In a medium or large slow cooker, combine black beans and red bell pepper mixture. Pour in crushed fire-roasted tomatoes.

4. Cover and cook on high for 2 to 2½ hours, on low for 4 or 5 hours, or until vegetables are tender.

5. Stir in lime juice, taste and adjust seasonings, and serve hot.

Variation: For a truly authentic (and hot!) Caribbean flavor, replace the Anaheim chile with 1 habanero pepper, ribs and seeds removed, and finely diced. To turn this into a one-pot **Caribbean Black Beans and Rice,** add 2 cups cooked brown rice or other variety during the last 15 minutes of cook time.

LOW AND SLOW

Instead of using my suggested dried herbs and spices in this recipe, you can use 1 or 2 teaspoons Jerk seasoning blend instead.

Tex-Mex Pinto Beans

Tex-Mex cuisine is known for being well seasoned, and a generous amount of chili powder, cumin, and chipotle chile powder does just that to these pinto beans.

Yield:	Prep time:	Cook time:	Serving size:
4 or 5 cups	10 to 15 minutes, plus 1 hour or more soak time	3 or 4 hours	1 cup

1 lb. (about 2¼ cups) dried pinto beans, sorted and rinsed

1 large green bell pepper, ribs and seeds removed, and diced

1 cup yellow onion, diced

1 medium jalapeño pepper, ribs and seeds removed, and finely diced

1 TB. minced garlic

1 TB. nutritional yeast flakes

1 TB. chili powder

1 tsp. dried oregano

1 tsp. ground cumin

¼ tsp. chipotle chile powder or cayenne

6½ cups water

⅓ cup chopped fresh cilantro

Sea salt

Freshly ground black pepper

1. Presoak pinto beans in water for 6 hours or overnight, or quick-soak for 1 hour. Drain pinto beans in a colander, and discard soaking liquid.

2. In a medium or large slow cooker, layer, in order, soaked pinto beans, green bell pepper, yellow onion, jalapeño pepper, garlic, nutritional yeast flakes, chili powder, oregano, cumin, and chipotle chile powder. Pour in water.

3. Cover and cook on high for 3 or 4 hours, on low for 6 to 8 hours, or until pinto beans are tender.

4. Stir in cilantro, taste and season with sea salt and black pepper, and serve hot.

Variation: You can replace the dried pinto beans with anasazi beans, red beans, or black beans. For **Salsa Pinto Beans,** reduce the water to 5½ cups, and add 1 cup salsa, salsa verde, or pico de gallo.

LOW AND SLOW

These spicy beans are terrific as a filling for burritos or enchiladas, spooned over pieces of Country Cornbread (recipe in Chapter 17), or topped with diced avocado and shredded vegan cheddar cheese.

Mujadara

This *mujadara*—a lentils and rice dish enhanced with aromatic spices—is delicious, inexpensive, and so simple to make. But it's the Caramelized Onions on the top that really make this dish.

Yield:	Prep time:	Cook time:	Serving size:
5 or 6 cups	5 minutes	1½ to 2 hours	1 cup

1 cup dried brown lentils, sorted and rinsed

1 cup long-grain brown rice

1 tsp. ground cumin

½ tsp. ground allspice

½ tsp. ground cinnamon

½ tsp. sea salt

½ tsp. freshly ground black pepper

4 cups water

¼ cup chopped fresh parsley

1 cup Caramelized Onions (recipe in Chapter 7)

Vegan plain yogurt

1. Lightly coat a medium slow cooker's ceramic crock insert with vegetable cooking spray or oil of choice.

2. In the slow cooker, combine brown lentils, long-grain brown rice, cumin, allspice, cinnamon, sea salt, and black pepper. Pour in water.

3. Cover and cook on high for 1½ to 2 hours or until lentils and brown rice are tender.

4. Stir in parsley, and taste and adjust seasonings. Serve hot, garnishing individual servings with Caramelized Onions and vegan yogurt.

Variation: You can also prepare this dish with green French lentils or red lentils.

LOW AND SLOW

When it comes to cooking legumes, adding salt at the beginning of the cooking process often toughens the beans' skins, which then lengthens the cook time. To avoid this, wait to add the salt until after the beans are tender. However, you don't need to heed this advice when using lentils because they have very thin skins and cook rather quickly.

Sicilian-Style Green Beans and Chickpeas

Smoky, fire-roasted tomatoes and red wine are the perfect simmering components for green beans and chickpeas, and adding basil at the end adds that nice sweet perfume Italian cuisine is so famous for.

Yield:	Prep time:	Cook time:	Serving size:
5 or 6 cups	10 to 15 minutes	2 to 2½ hours	1 cup

1 cup yellow onion, diced

1 lb. (3 cups trimmed) fresh green beans, cut in ½ diagonally, or 1 (16-oz.) pkg. frozen whole green beans

1½ cups cooked chickpeas, or 1 (15-oz.) can chickpeas, drained and rinsed

1½ TB. minced garlic

1 TB. nutritional yeast flakes

1 tsp. dried oregano

1 tsp. crushed red pepper flakes

¾ tsp. sea salt

½ tsp. freshly ground black pepper

1 (14-oz.) can crushed fire-roasted tomatoes

¼ cup red wine (such as dry Marsala, Sangiovese, or Zinfandel)

⅓ cup fresh basil, cut chiffonade

1. In a medium or large slow cooker, layer, in order, yellow onion, green beans, chickpeas, garlic, nutritional yeast flakes, oregano, crushed red pepper flakes, sea salt, and black pepper. Pour in crushed fire-roasted tomatoes and red wine.

2. Cover and cook on high for 2 to 2½ hours, on low for 4 or 5 hours, or until beans are tender.

3. Stir in basil, taste and adjust seasonings, and serve hot.

Variation: For **Moroccan Green Beans with Eggplant and Chickpeas,** omit the basil and oregano, and add 3 cups (1 pound or ½ medium) eggplant, cut into 1-inch cubes; ½ teaspoon ground coriander; and ½ teaspoon ground cumin.

SLOW INTERESTING

Chickpeas, the cute, brain-shape beans used in this recipe, are known by various names. Italians call them *ceci;* to the Spanish, they're *garbanzos* or *garbanzo beans;* and in India, they're referred to as *chana.*

Black-Eyed Peas with Collards and Yams

It's customary to eat black-eyed peas on New Year's Day to ensure good luck in the year ahead. So start your year off right with a heaping helping of this full-flavored combination of black-eyed peas, collard greens, and yams.

Yield:	Prep time:	Cook time:	Serving size:
8 cups	15 to 20 minutes	3 or 4 hours	1 cup

1½ cups dried black-eyed peas, sorted and rinsed

3 cups (3 large) garnet yams, peeled and cut into 1-in. cubes

1 cup yellow onion, diced

1 cup celery (including inner leaves and tops), diced

1 cup green bell pepper, ribs and seeds removed, and diced

1 medium jalapeño pepper, ribs and seeds removed, and finely diced

1½ TB. minced garlic

4 cups (½ bunch) collard greens, stems removed, and cut chiffonade into 1-in. strips

2 TB. Cajun seasoning blend

1 TB. nutritional yeast flakes

1 bay leaf

4 cups water

⅓ cup green onions, white and green parts, thinly sliced

⅓ cup chopped fresh parsley

Smoked sea salt or sea salt

Freshly ground black pepper

Hot pepper sauce

1. Presoak black-eyed peas in water for 6 hours or overnight, or quick-soak for 1 hour. Drain black-eyed peas in a colander, and discard soaking liquid.

2. In a medium or large slow cooker, layer, in order, soaked black-eyed peas, garnet yams, yellow onion, celery, green bell pepper, jalapeño pepper, garlic, collard greens, Cajun seasoning blend, nutritional yeast flakes, and bay leaf. Pour in water.

3. Cover and cook on high for 3 or 4 hours, on low for 6 to 8 hours, or until black-eyed peas are tender.

4. Stir in green onions and parsley. Remove and discard bay leaf. Taste and season with smoked sea salt, black pepper, and hot pepper sauce, and serve hot.

Variation: Feel free to replace the collard greens with an equal amount of turnip greens, mustard greens, or kale. Or replace the garnet yams with sweet potatoes.

LOW AND SLOW

You can buy Cajun seasoning blend in most grocery stores, but you can make it yourself by combining 1½ tablespoons chili powder, 1½ tablespoons smoked or sweet paprika, 1 tablespoon dried thyme, 2 teaspoons dried oregano, 2 teaspoons cayenne, 1 teaspoon onion powder, and 1 teaspoon garlic powder or garlic granules. Makes approximately ⅓ cup.

Gratifying Grain Dishes

16

In This Chapter

- Rave-worthy rice dishes
- Fruit- and veggie-studded grains
- Smooth and creamy polenta
- Delicious bread stuffing

In Chapter 3, we used grains to make some yummy hot breakfast cereals. Grains make a second appearance in this chapter, but this time around, they're used for savory side dishes to help round out your meals.

It's nutritionally essential to include sources of whole grains in your daily diet because the plant-based powerhouses are loaded with fiber and protein, as well as many minerals and B vitamins. In actuality, what we call grains are really the fruit or seed of different types of grass plants, and some of the most popular varieties are wheat, rice, corn, barley, oats, rye, millet, and quinoa.

Some grains cook better in the slow cooker than others (I wouldn't recommend trying to make couscous in a slow cooker, for example), but don't be afraid to experiment with your favorite grain recipes to see if they can be prepared via your slow cooker.

For the most part, when revamping your grain recipes for preparation in the slow cooker, you don't need to do much tinkering with your original ingredient amounts. When cooking most grains the ratio of grain to liquid is 1:2, or 1 cup grain and 2 cups liquid. With these measures, you'll end up with around 3 cups cooked grains. However, liquids do evaporate at a slightly different rate in the slow cooker, and I have found that some ingredients, like quinoa, will come out better if I add a little less liquid, and so I usually use only $1\frac{1}{2}$ cups liquid per 1 cup quinoa.

Here's another helpful hint: before combining your grains with your cooking liquid or other ingredients, drizzle a little bit of oil or melted margarine over your grains and stir to coat. This helps prevent the individual grains from being sticky or clumping together. Be sure to use a gentle hand when running a fork through your slow-cooked grain dishes. You're trying to loosen the grains to eliminate any clumps, but if you overdo it, you'll end up with mushy grains that are slightly sticky and stuck together.

You'll be pleasantly surprised that your slow cooker can be used to make a creamy risotto, and unlike when you make it on the stovetop, with the slow cooker, you don't have to constantly stir and add broth to the dish. You only have to give it 5 minutes of hands-on attention, versus 30 to 40 minutes of intense labor—awesome!

Sun-Dried Tomato and Spinach Risotto

Sun-dried tomatoes impart a dramatically intense color and rich tomato flavor to Italian *arborio rice*, while spinach, basil, and parsley provide a few vibrant streaks of leafy green goodness to this luscious, creamy risotto.

Yield:	Prep time:	Cook time:	Serving size:
6 cups	7 to 10 minutes	1½ to 2 hours	1 cup as a side dish or 1½ cups as a main dish

¾ cup (2 large) shallots, finely diced

2 TB. olive oil

1¼ cups arborio rice

1½ TB. minced garlic

⅓ cup white wine (such as Chardonnay, Riesling, or Pinot Grigio)

⅓ cup sun-dried tomato pieces or (6 or 7) whole sun-dried tomatoes, cut into small pieces

1 bay leaf

1½ tsp. Italian seasoning blend or ½ tsp. each dried basil, oregano, and thyme or marjoram

1 tsp. smoked paprika

1 tsp. sea salt

½ tsp. garlic pepper

¼ tsp. freshly ground black pepper

4 cups Homemade Vegetable Broth (recipe in Chapter 8)

3 cups spinach, roughly chopped, or baby spinach, packed

¼ cup fresh basil, cut chiffonade

¼ cup chopped fresh Italian flat-leaf parsley

2 TB. nutritional yeast flakes

1 TB. nonhydrogenated margarine

1. Lightly coat a medium slow cooker's ceramic crock insert with vegetable cooking spray or oil of choice.

2. In a large nonstick skillet over medium heat, combine shallots and olive oil. Sauté, stirring often, for 2 minutes.

3. Add arborio rice and garlic, and sauté, stirring often, for 1 or 2 minutes or until rice is opaque. Remove the skillet from heat. Transfer rice mixture to the slow cooker.

4. Add white wine, sun-dried tomatoes, bay leaf, Italian seasoning blend, smoked paprika, sea salt, garlic pepper, and black pepper to the slow cooker, and stir well. Pour in Homemade Vegetable Broth.

5. Cover and cook on high for 1½ to 2 hours or until all liquid is absorbed. Start checking rice after 1½ hours to avoid overcooking (otherwise rice will get sticky).

6. Add spinach, basil, and Italian flat-leaf parsley. Cover and leave alone for 5 to 10 minutes or until spinach is wilted.

7. Remove and discard bay leaf. Add nutritional yeast flakes and nonhydrogenated margarine, and stir gently with a fork to combine. Taste and adjust seasonings, and serve hot.

Variation: For added flavor and crunch, add ¼ cup toasted pine nuts to the finished risotto.

DEFINITION

Arborio rice is a plump, short-grain, highly glutinous white rice variety grown in Italy. The rice's outer layers contain a high concentration of starch that's released when cooked, which makes it the ideal choice for making risotto.

Broccoli and Rice Casserole

Even if broccoli isn't your favorite vegetable, you'll love this creamy casserole made with brown rice and broccoli florets. The secret is adding a bit of smoky toasted sesame oil and toasted sliced almonds for some extra crunch.

Yield:	Prep time:	Cook time:	Serving size:
6 or 7 cups	8 to 10 minutes	2 to 2½ hours	1 cup

2 cups Homemade Vegetable Broth (recipe in Chapter 8)

2 cups water

1 TB. Bragg Liquid Aminos, tamari, or shoyu

3 cups (1 lb.) broccoli, cut into small florets or 1 (16-oz.) pkg. frozen broccoli florets

1½ cups short-grain brown rice

½ cup green onions, white and green parts, thinly sliced

2½ TB. nutritional yeast flakes

1 TB. minced garlic

2 tsp. dried thyme

1 tsp. seasoning salt (such as Herbamare)

½ tsp. garlic pepper or lemon pepper

½ tsp. freshly ground black pepper

⅓ cup chopped fresh parsley

1 TB. toasted sesame oil

⅓ cup toasted sliced almonds

1. In a medium saucepan over high heat, bring Homemade Vegetable Broth, water, and Bragg Liquid Aminos to a boil. Remove the saucepan from heat.

2. Lightly coat a medium slow cooker's ceramic crock insert with vegetable cooking spray or oil of choice.

3. In the slow cooker, combine broccoli, short-grain brown rice, green onions, nutritional yeast flakes, garlic, thyme, seasoning salt, garlic pepper, and black pepper. Pour in vegetable broth mixture.

4. Cover and cook on high for 2 to 2½ hours, on low for 4 or 5 hours, or until brown rice is tender.

5. Stir in parsley and toasted sesame oil. Taste and adjust seasonings, sprinkle toasted almonds over top, and serve hot.

Variation: For added color and flavor, add 1 cup red bell pepper, ribs and seeds removed, and diced. For **Cheesy Broccoli and Rice Casserole,** add ¾ cup shredded vegan cheddar cheese or other variety to the brown rice mixture, and replace the toasted almond topping with ⅔ cup crushed buttery round crackers.

LOW AND SLOW

Many of the recipes in this book call for toasted nuts or seeds. Toasting is easy: simply bake them in a pie pan at 350°F for 5 to 10 minutes. Or cook them in a small skillet over medium heat, shaking the pan occasionally, for 5 to 10 minutes or until they're lightly browned and fragrant.

Mixed Grain Medley

This filling grain dish highlights the chewy texture of barley, *wild rice*, and wheat berries. For a splash of color and texture, peas, green onions, and fresh parsley are added.

Yield:	Prep time:	Cook time:	Serving size:
6 or 7 cups	5 to 7 minutes	2 to 2½ hours	1 cup

½ cup hulled barley

½ cup wild rice

½ cup wheat berries

1 TB. nonhydrogenated margarine, melted

1 cup red or yellow onion, diced

1 cup celery (including inner leaves and tops), diced

1 TB. minced garlic

1 bay leaf

½ TB. dried basil

½ tsp. dried marjoram or oregano

¾ tsp. sea salt

½ tsp. freshly ground black pepper

3½ cups Homemade Vegetable Broth (recipe in Chapter 8)

1½ cups frozen peas, thawed

½ cup green onions, white and green parts, thinly sliced

⅓ cup chopped fresh parsley

1 TB. tamari, shoyu, or Bragg Liquid Aminos (optional)

1 TB. nutritional yeast flakes

1. Lightly coat a medium slow cooker's ceramic crock insert with vegetable cooking spray or oil of choice.

2. Place hulled barley, wild rice, and wheat berries in a fine-mesh sieve, and rinse well under running water for 1 minute.

3. In the slow cooker, combine barley, wild rice, wheat berries, and melted non-hydrogenated margarine, and stir well to coat. Add red onion, celery, garlic, bay leaf, basil, marjoram, sea salt, and black pepper. Pour in Homemade Vegetable Broth.

4. Cover and cook on high for 2 to 2½ hours or until all liquid is absorbed. Start checking grains after 2 hours, and avoid overcooking (otherwise grains will get sticky).

5. Add peas, green onions, parsley, tamari (if using), and nutritional yeast flakes. Cover and leave alone for 5 minutes. Gently stir with a fork to combine and loosen grains.

6. Remove and discard bay leaf. Taste and adjust seasonings, and serve hot.

Variation: You can replace the hulled barley with pearled barley. For **Mixed Grain and Veggie Medley,** replace the frozen peas with 1½ cups frozen mixed vegetable blend (carrots, corn, green beans, and peas), thawed.

DEFINITION

Wild rice is actually the edible seed of a grass plant. The rice has a deep-brown color and a rich, nutty flavor and makes a nutritious side dish.

Hearty Mushroom Barley

The combination of meaty crimini mushrooms and red wine provide a rich, full-bodied flavor to the cooking liquid, which soaks into the chewy barley base of this filling side dish.

Yield:	Prep time:	Cook time:	Serving size:
6 cups	20 to 25 minutes	3 to 3½ hours	1 cup

1¼ cups hulled or pearled barley

12 oz. crimini or white button mushrooms, cut in ½ and thinly sliced

1 cup carrots, diced

1 cup celery, diced (including the inner leaves and tops)

1 medium leek, washed well, cut in ½ lengthwise, and thinly sliced, or 1 cup yellow onion, diced

2 TB. tomato paste

1 TB. minced garlic

1 bay leaf

1 TB. Italian seasoning blend, or 1 tsp. each dried basil, oregano, and thyme

½ tsp. rubbed (or dried) sage

½ tsp. ground fennel seed

½ tsp. freshly ground black pepper or garlic pepper

2 cups Homemade Vegetable Broth (recipe in Chapter 8)

1½ cups water

½ cup red wine (such as Merlot, Burgundy, or Cabernet)

1 TB. tamari, shoyu, or Bragg Liquid Aminos

⅓ cup chopped fresh parsley

2 TB. nutritional yeast flakes

1. Lightly coat a medium slow cooker's ceramic crock insert with vegetable cooking spray or oil of choice.

2. Place hulled barley in a fine-mesh sieve, and rinse well under running water for 1 minute.

3. In the slow cooker, combine barley, crimini mushrooms, carrots, celery, leek, tomato paste, garlic, bay leaf, Italian seasoning blend, rubbed sage, fennel seed, and black pepper. Stir in Homemade Vegetable Broth, water, red wine, and tamari.

4. Cover and cook on high for 3 to 3½ hours, on low for 6 or 7 hours, or until barley is tender.

5. Stir in parsley and nutritional yeast flakes. Remove and discard bay leaf. Taste and adjust seasonings, and serve hot.

Variation: For a nonalcoholic version, omit the red wine and add an additional ½ cup vegetable broth or water.

> **LOW AND SLOW**
>
> Leeks, like greens, are notorious for trapping grit or dirt within their inner layers. I like to cut leeks first and then triple wash them. I place the sliced leeks in a large bowl, cover them with water, swish them around several times to loosen any dirt, lift the leek slices out of the water, and place in a colander. I dump out water and repeat the entire procedure two more times.

Confetti Quinoa

This speckled grain dish is made with a blend of white, red, and black quinoa and studded with colorful bits of red onion, red bell pepper, and zucchini. Don't forget to sprinkle the toasted pepitas over the top for an added crunch.

Yield:	Prep time:	Cook time:	Serving size:
6 cups	7 to 10 minutes	2 to 2½ hours	1 cup

1½ cups tricolor quinoa blend (white, red, and black)

1 TB. olive oil

1 cup red onion, diced

1 cup red bell pepper, ribs and seeds removed, and diced

1 cup zucchini, cut into quarters lengthwise, and thinly sliced

1½ TB. minced garlic

1½ TB. nutritional yeast flakes

½ TB. dried oregano

1 tsp. sea salt

1 tsp. crushed red pepper flakes

½ tsp. garlic pepper

¼ tsp. freshly ground black pepper

2½ cups Homemade Vegetable Broth (recipe in Chapter 8)

½ cup green onions, white and green parts, thinly sliced

⅓ cup chopped fresh cilantro

⅓ cup toasted pepitas or raw pumpkin seeds

1. Lightly coat a medium slow cooker's ceramic crock insert with vegetable cooking spray or oil of choice.

2. Place quinoa blend in a fine-mesh sieve, and rinse well under running water for 1 minute.

3. In the slow cooker, combine tricolor quinoa blend and olive oil, and stir well to coat. Add red onion, red bell pepper, zucchini, garlic, nutritional yeast flakes, oregano, sea salt, crushed red pepper flakes, garlic pepper, and black pepper. Pour in Homemade Vegetable Broth.

4. Cover and cook on high for 2 to $2\frac{1}{2}$ hours or until all liquid is absorbed. Start checking quinoa after 2 hours, and avoid overcooking (otherwise quinoa will get sticky).

5. Add green onions and cilantro, and gently stir with a fork to combine and loosen quinoa grains.

6. Taste and adjust seasonings, and serve hot, scattering toasted pepitas over top before serving.

Variation: For **Spanish-Style Quinoa,** use only white quinoa. Replace the zucchini with 1 cup green bell pepper, ribs and seeds removed, and diced, and add 2 tablespoons tomato paste and 1 teaspoon chili powder.

COOKER CAVEAT

The tiny seeds of the quinoa plant are covered with a bitter-tasting coating known as saponin, which acts as a natural insect repellent. Fortunately, you can remove this nasty-tasting coating simply by rinsing quinoa under running water. Many quinoa manufacturers sell their quinoa products prerinsed and sorted, but I still suggest you check it for bits of dirt and debris before adding quinoa to a recipe. Place it in a fine-mesh sieve and give it a good rinse.

Creamy Polenta

Polenta is a traditional Italian comfort food made from cornmeal, and this thick and creamy version is embellished with nutritional yeast flakes and margarine to give it a sensuous buttery and cheesy flavor.

Yield:	Prep time:	Cook time:	Serving size:
8 cups	5 minutes	2 to 2½ hours	1 cup

8 cups water

2 cups cornmeal (preferably medium-grind or coarse)

1½ tsp. sea salt

½ tsp. freshly ground black pepper

3 TB. nutritional yeast flakes

3 TB. nonhydrogenated margarine

1. Lightly coat a medium slow cooker's ceramic crock insert with vegetable cooking spray or oil of choice.

2. In the slow cooker, combine water, cornmeal, sea salt, and black pepper.

3. Cover and cook on high for 2 to 2½ hours or until polenta is smooth and creamy.

4. Stir in nutritional yeast flakes and nonhydrogenated margarine. Taste and adjust seasonings, and serve hot.

Variation: For added flavor, replace 2 cups water with Homemade Vegetable Broth (recipe in Chapter 8). For **Herbed Polenta,** stir in ⅓ cup fresh basil, cut chiffonade, and ¼ cup chopped fresh parsley to the finished polenta.

LOW AND SLOW

Enjoy this creamy polenta as a side dish, or elevate it to a main dish by topping it with cooked vegetables or leafy greens. It's also delicious served with the Red Wine Marinara Sauce or its Mushroom Marinara Sauce variation (recipes in Chapter 6).

Savory Bread Stuffing

This classic family favorite transforms your day-old bread into a savory side dish simply by flavoring it with a blend of sautéed aromatic vegetables and some herbs and seasoning.

Yield:	Prep time:	Cook time:	Serving size:
9 or 10 cups	15 to 20 minutes, plus overnight for air-drying bread	4 or 5 hours	1 cup

1 loaf Hearty Herb Bread or Wheat Bread (recipe and variation in Chapter 17), cut into 1-in. cubes (about 10 cups)

1¼ cups (1 large) yellow onion, diced

1¼ cups (2 or 3 large stalks) celery (including inner leaves and tops), diced

1 TB. olive oil

½ cup green onions, white and green parts, thinly sliced

2 TB. chopped fresh thyme or 2 tsp. dried

2 tsp. poultry seasoning blend

1 tsp. sea salt

¾ tsp. freshly ground black pepper

½ cup chopped fresh parsley

2 TB. nutritional yeast flakes

1 cup Homemade Vegetable Broth (recipe in Chapter 8)

1½ TB. tamari, shoyu, or Bragg Liquid Aminos

½ to 1 cup water or as needed

1. Place Hearty Herb Bread cubes on a cookie sheet, cover with a towel, and set aside to air-dry overnight. (Alternatively, bake bread cubes in a 325°F oven for 20 to 25 minutes or until lightly toasted and dry. Remove from the oven and set aside to cool.)

2. In a large, nonstick skillet over medium heat, combine yellow onion, celery, and olive oil. Sauté, stirring often, for 3 minutes.

3. Add green onions, thyme, poultry seasoning blend, sea salt, and black pepper, and sauté, stirring often, for 1 minute. Remove the skillet from heat.

4. In a large bowl, combine bread cubes, onion mixture, parsley, and nutritional yeast flakes. Gently stir in Homemade Vegetable Broth and tamari, and add water as needed to moisten bread, but don't make it soggy.

5. Lightly coat a medium or large slow cooker's ceramic crock insert with vegetable cooking spray or oil of choice. Transfer stuffing mixture to the slow cooker.

6. Cover and cook on high for 1 hour.

7. Gently stir stuffing mixture, reduce heat to low, and cook for 3 or 4 hours or until stuffing is lightly browned around the edges and slightly puffy.

8. Taste and adjust seasonings, and serve hot.

Variations: For **Savory Mushroom Bread Stuffing,** add 1½ cups (8 ounces) crimini or white button mushrooms, cut in ½ and thinly sliced, and 1 tablespoon chopped fresh rosemary or 1 teaspoon dried rosemary to the sautéing onion mixture. For **Apple-Nut Bread Stuffing,** add 1 large apple of choice, peeled, cored, and diced, and ½ cup toasted pecans or walnuts, roughly chopped, to the sautéing onion mixture.

LOW AND SLOW

If you're like me and really love the savory flavor and aroma of herbs, use the Hearty Herb Bread or its Scarborough Fair Bread variation, which are both golden brown loaves flecked with herbs. Using the Wheat Bread variation of this same recipe makes for a more traditional-style bread stuffing (recipe and variations in Chapter 17).

Sweet and Savory Breads

In This Chapter

- Sweet quick breads
- Fast, easy, and round biscuits and breads
- Steam-baked brown bread
- Yeast-risen loaves and rolls

Get ready to learn the ins and outs of baking breads in your slow cooker—or as I like to call it, slow baking. In this chapter, you'll find several recipes for sweet quick breads perfect for enjoying for breakfast or brunch, as well as biscuits and cornbread. You'll also learn how to make a classic steam-baked brown bread, an herb-flavored loaf, deliciously sweet cinnamon-swirled raisin bread, and even pull-apart rolls.

In Chapter 2, I gave you some pointers on using your slow cooker as an oven for slow-baking sweet treats and baked goods. So before tackling one of the bread recipes in this chapter, you may want to flip back and reread that information for a quick refresher.

When making breads, I find that most breads slow-bake best when they're made in a pan, rather than when the dough or batter is placed directly in the ceramic crock insert. The outer edges and bottom tend to get overbaked while the center remains underbaked … not good! Breads seem to slow-bake more evenly when I use a pan and slightly vent the lid during all or part of the cook time.

If you want to try slow-baking without a pan, liberally oil and line the ceramic crock insert with parchment paper. Check out the Pull-Apart Whole-Wheat Rolls recipe in this chapter for a more detailed explanation of this procedure.

When slow-baking using a pan or casserole dish, you'll need to use a large slow cooker (preferably an oval one), but if you opt for going pan-less, you can use a medium slow cooker. Undoubtedly, your pan-less bread will require less slow-baking time, anywhere for 30 to 60 minutes, so check its progress much earlier than suggested in the recipe.

Speaking of time, I give 1-hour time ranges for judging doneness, as exact slow-baking time depends on whether you use a loaf pan, a cake pan, or 6-cup casserole dish. Also, I've discovered that 30 minutes does make a tremendous amount of difference in the quality of my baked goods, especially breads.

Over-slow-baking a cake or steamed pudding may result in a slightly drier-textured cake than normal. However, if you over-slow-bake bread, especially the yeast-based ones, you can end up with an extremely hard, dark brown outer crust, rather than a nice chewy crust. But fear not. If your bread comes out dry or dense because you slow-baked it too long, don't despair or throw it out. You can use it to make a strata or bread pudding—see Chapters 4 and 19 for recipes.

Cinnamon-Swirl Raisin Bread

You'll impress everyone with this sweet bread that's dotted with raisins and has a cinnamon-sugar swirl in the center. Enjoy slices as is or lightly toasted for breakfast.

Yield:	Prep time:	Cook time:	Serving size:
1 (8×4×2½-inch) loaf	15 to 20 minutes, plus 1 hour rise time	3 to 3½ hours	1 slice

⅔ cup soy or other nondairy milk

½ cup water

6 TB. unbleached cane sugar

1 (.25-oz.) pkg. or 2¼ tsp. *rapid-rise active yeast*

3 cups bread flour

1 tsp. sea salt

2 TB. sunflower or other oil

1 TB. vanilla extract

¾ cup raisins

1½ TB. ground cinnamon

1. Lightly coat an 8×4×2½-inch loaf pan or 6-cup or larger casserole dish (which-ever fits a large oval slow cooker) with vegetable cooking spray or oil of choice.

2. In a small saucepan over medium heat, combine soy milk and water. Cook for 1 or 2 minutes or until liquids reach 110°F. Remove the saucepan from heat. (Alternatively, place soy milk and water in a microwave-safe bowl, and cook on high for 45 to 60 seconds or until warm.)

3. Add 3 tablespoons unbleached cane sugar and rapid-rise active yeast, and set aside for 5 to 7 minutes or until yeast is fully dissolved and mixture is very foamy.

4. In a large bowl, combine bread flour and sea salt.

5. When yeast mixture is foamy, add sunflower oil and vanilla extract, and gently stir to combine. Add raisins and wet ingredients to dry ingredients, and stir well.

6. Transfer mixture to a clean counter or work surface. Using your hands, knead mixture for 3 to 5 minutes or until a smooth and pliable ball of dough forms.

7. Drizzle a little additional sunflower oil around the outer edge of the bowl. Roll dough around in sunflower oil, and turn over dough to coat the other side. Cover bowl lightly with a clean towel or plastic wrap, and let rise in a warm place for 1 hour or until doubled in size.

8. Place a trivet or foil ring in the bottom of the slow cooker. Preheat the slow cooker to high.

9. Punch down dough, turn out onto a lightly floured work surface, and knead for 1 minute. Using your hands, flatten dough into an 8×10-inch rectangle, with the shorter side nearest you.

10. In a small bowl, stir together remaining 3 tablespoons unbleached cane sugar and cinnamon. Evenly sprinkle mixture over top of dough. Roll up dough tightly like a jelly roll cake to enclose cinnamon mixture, and firmly pinch the seam to seal. Place dough seam-side down into the prepared pan or casserole dish.

11. Place the pan or casserole dish on top of the trivet or foil ring. Cover and cook on high for 1 hour. After 1 hour, slightly vent lid with a toothpick, chopstick, or wooden spoon, and cook on high for 2 to 2½ hours or until bread is firm to the touch and lightly browned around edges.

12. Uncover and allow bread to cool inside the slow cooker for 10 minutes. Carefully remove the pan or casserole dish from the slow cooker, transfer to a rack, and cool for 10 minutes.

13. Loosen sides of bread with a spatula. Invert loaf, remove it from the pan or casserole dish, flip loaf back over onto the rack, and cool as desired. Serve warm, cold, or at room temperature.

Variations: For **Cinnamon-Pecan Swirl Bread,** replace the raisins with ¾ cup toasted pecans, roughly chopped. For **Cinnamon Cranberry-Raisin Bread,** reduce the raisins to ½ cup and add ⅓ cup dried cranberries.

> **DEFINITION**
>
> **Rapid-rise active yeast** is a variety of baker's yeast that's essentially an instant version of active dry yeast. It must be hydrated to activate the dough and cause the rise to occur.

Gluten-Free Blueberry Muffin Bread

Enjoy the great taste of blueberry muffins, but in bread form, with this blueberry polka-dotted quick bread that's covered with a sweet, cinnamon-spiced crumb topping.

Yield:	Prep time:	Cook time:	Serving size:
1 (8×4×2½-inch) loaf	8 to 10 minutes	2½ to 3½ hours	1 slice

⅓ cup plus 2¼ cups Bob's Red Mill Gluten-Free All-Purpose Baking Flour

¼ cup light brown or muscovado sugar, packed

½ tsp. ground cinnamon

6 TB. nonhydrogenated margarine, softened

½ cup unbleached cane sugar

1½ TB. aluminum-free baking powder

1½ TB. arrowroot

1 tsp. xanthan gum

½ tsp. sea salt

3 TB. water

1½ TB. Ener-G Egg Replacer

1 cup soy or other nondairy milk

½ TB. vanilla extract

¾ cup fresh or frozen blueberries (do not thaw)

1. Lightly coat an 8×4×2½-inch loaf pan or 6-cup or larger casserole dish (whichever fits a large oval slow cooker) with vegetable cooking spray or oil of choice. Place a trivet or foil ring in the bottom of the slow cooker, and preheat to high.

2. In a small bowl, combine ⅓ cup Bob's Red Mill Gluten-Free All-Purpose Baking Flour, light brown sugar, and cinnamon. Using your fingers, work 2 tablespoons nonhydrogenated margarine into dry ingredients until mixture resembles coarse crumbs, and set aside.

3. In a large bowl, whisk together remaining 2¼ cups Bob's Red Mill Gluten-Free All-Purpose Baking Flour, unbleached cane sugar, aluminum-free baking powder, arrowroot, xanthan gum, and sea salt.

4. In a medium bowl, combine water and Ener-G Egg Replacer, and whisk vigorously for 1 minute or until very frothy (like beaten egg whites). Add soy milk, remaining 4 tablespoons nonhydrogenated margarine, and vanilla extract, and whisk well.

5. Pour wet ingredients into dry ingredients, and stir well. Gently fold in blueberries.

6. Transfer batter to the prepared pan or casserole dish, and smooth top with a spatula. Sprinkle crumb topping over top and gently press into batter with your hand.

7. Place the pan or casserole dish on top of the trivet or foil ring. Cover; slightly vent lid with a toothpick, chopstick, or wooden spoon; and cook on high for 2½ to 3½ hours or until a toothpick inserted in the center comes out clean.

8. Uncover and allow bread to cool inside the slow cooker for 10 minutes. Carefully remove the pan or casserole dish from the slow cooker, transfer to a rack, and cool for 10 minutes.

9. Loosen sides of bread with a spatula. Place a large plate or cutting board on top of pan or casserole dish, invert, remove loaf from the pan or casserole dish, flip loaf back over onto the rack, and cool as desired. Serve warm, cold, or at room temperature.

Variation: Feel free to replace the blueberries with other fresh or frozen berries such as raspberries, blackberries, or sliced strawberries. For **Gluten-Free Blueberry Streusel Bread,** add ⅓ cup toasted walnuts or other nuts, roughly chopped, to the crumb topping mixture.

LOW AND SLOW

Many of the gluten-free baked goods in this book are made with Bob's Red Mill Gluten-Free All-Purpose Baking Flour, which is a mixture of chickpea/garbanzo bean flour, potato starch, tapioca flour (starch), sorghum flour, and fava flour. You can find this baking flour blend in bulk and packaged in most grocery and natural foods stores, as well as online at bobsredmill.com.

Banana Chocolate-Chip Nut Bread

Sweet and creamy bananas, rich chocolate chips, and toasted walnuts are all stellar ingredients on their own, but when combined, they're an over-the-top taste sensation. The aroma of this bread as it slow bakes will drive you bananas!

Yield:	Prep time:	Cook time:	Serving size:
1 (8×4×2½-inch) loaf	8 to 10 minutes	2½ to 3½ hours	1 slice

1½ cups whole-wheat pastry flour

½ cup unbleached cane sugar

2 tsp. baking soda

1 tsp. ground cinnamon

½ tsp. sea salt

1 large banana, peeled and broken into 3-in. pieces

½ cup water

2 TB. sunflower oil

1 TB. apple cider vinegar

½ TB. vanilla extract

½ cup vegan chocolate chips

½ cup toasted walnuts, roughly chopped

1. Lightly coat an 8×4×2½-inch loaf pan or 6-cup or larger casserole dish (whichever fits a large oval slow cooker) with vegetable cooking spray or oil of choice. Place a trivet or foil ring in the bottom of the slow cooker, and preheat to high.

2. In a large bowl, whisk together whole-wheat pastry flour, unbleached cane sugar, baking soda, cinnamon, and sea salt.

3. In a medium bowl, and using a potato masher or a fork, roughly mash banana. Add water, sunflower oil, apple cider vinegar, and vanilla extract, and stir well to combine.

4. Pour wet ingredients into dry ingredients, and stir well. Gently fold in chocolate chips.

5. Transfer batter to the prepared pan or casserole dish, and smooth top with a spatula. Sprinkle toasted walnuts over top, and gently press into batter with your hand.

6. Place the pan or casserole dish on top of the trivet or foil ring in the slow cooker. Cover; slightly vent lid with a toothpick, chopstick, or wooden spoon; and cook on high for 2½ to 3½ hours or until a toothpick inserted in the center comes out clean.

7. Uncover and allow bread to cool inside the slow cooker for 10 minutes. Carefully remove the pan or casserole dish from the slow cooker, transfer to a rack, and cool for 10 minutes.

8. Loosen the sides of bread with a spatula. Invert loaf, remove it from the pan or casserole dish, flip loaf back over onto the rack, and cool as desired. Serve warm, cold, or at room temperature.

Variation: For **Banana Split Bread,** use only ⅓ cup chocolate chips, and add ⅓ cup fresh or frozen cherries, roughly chopped, or ¼ cup dried cherries; for the top of the bread, use only ⅓ cup toasted walnuts and add 2 tablespoons toasted shredded coconut.

LOW AND SLOW

Overly ripe bananas are the best to use for baked goods. You can easily freeze peeled and broken ripe bananas for use in your baked goods whenever you need them. In this recipe, you could use a frozen banana that's been thawed rather than a fresh one.

Studded Sweet Potato Quick Bread

Fitting for the fall and winter months, golden sweet potato purée provides the perfect backdrop for the jewel-like pieces of dried fruit that stud this quick bread, and the toasted pecans add a nice crunch to its top.

Yield:	Prep time:	Cook time:	Serving size:
1 (8×4×2½-inch) loaf	8 to 10 minutes	2½ to 3½ hours	1 slice

1½ cups whole-wheat pastry flour

⅔ cup unbleached cane sugar

2 tsp. aluminum-free baking powder

2 tsp. pumpkin pie spice

½ tsp. sea salt

¾ cup Sweet Potato Purée (variation in Chapter 7) or canned sweet potato purée

½ cup water

2 TB. sunflower oil

½ TB. vanilla extract

3 TB. raisins

3 TB. dried cranberries

3 TB. dried apricots, roughly chopped

3 TB. toasted pecans, roughly chopped

1. Lightly coat an 8×4×2½-inch loaf pan or 6-cup or larger casserole dish (whichever fits a large oval slow cooker) with vegetable cooking spray or oil of choice. Place a trivet or foil ring in the bottom of the slow cooker, and preheat to high.

2. In a large bowl, whisk together whole-wheat pastry flour, unbleached cane sugar, aluminum-free baking powder, pumpkin pie spice, and sea salt.

3. In a medium bowl, whisk together Sweet Potato Purée, water, sunflower oil, and vanilla extract.

4. Pour wet ingredients into dry ingredients, and stir well. Gently fold in raisins, dried cranberries, and dried apricots.

5. Transfer batter to the prepared pan or casserole dish, and smooth top with a spatula. Sprinkle toasted pecans over the top, and gently press into batter with your hand.

6. Place the pan or casserole dish on top of the trivet or foil ring in the slow cooker. Cover; slightly vent lid with a toothpick, chopstick, or wooden spoon; and cook on high for 2½ to 3½ hours or until a toothpick inserted in the center comes out clean.

7. Uncover and allow bread to cool inside the slow cooker for 10 minutes. Carefully remove the pan or casserole dish from the slow cooker, transfer to a rack, and cool for 10 minutes.

8. Loosen sides of bread with a spatula. Invert loaf, remove it from the pan or casserole dish, flip loaf back over onto the rack, and cool as desired. Serve warm, cold, or at room temperature.

Variation: If you don't have pumpkin pie spice, you can replace it with 1 teaspoon ground cinnamon, ½ teaspoon ground ginger, ¼ teaspoon freshly grated nutmeg, and ¼ teaspoon ground cloves. For **Maple, Pumpkin, and Pecan Bread,** replace the Sweet Potato Purée with an equal amount of Pumpkin Purée (variation in Chapter 7), use only ⅓ cup water, and add 2 tablespoons maple syrup; omit the raisins, dried cranberries, and dried apricots.

SLOW INTERESTING

You have several options when it comes to storing dried fruits. Use jars with tight-fitting lids, airtight containers, or zipper-lock bags. If stored properly this way, you can keep dried fruits in a cool, dry, dark place (like your pantry) or in the refrigerator for 6 months, or in the freezer for up to 12 months. Discard them if they look odd or show signs of mold.

Biscuits in the Round

The pat-and-cut-in-the-pan technique used to slow bake these biscuits couldn't be easier. Vegan yogurt and a *clabbered* soy milk mixture give the biscuit dough a slight tang and tender, moist crumb.

Yield:	Prep time:	Cook time:	Serving size:
8 biscuits	8 to 10 minutes	1½ to 2 hours	1 biscuit

¾ cup soy or other nondairy milk

1½ TB. apple cider vinegar

2½ cups white whole-wheat or whole-wheat pastry flour

4 tsp. aluminum-free baking powder

½ tsp. sea salt

⅓ cup nonhydrogenated margarine

⅓ cup vegan plain yogurt

1. Lightly coat an 8-inch cake pan or 6-cup or larger casserole dish (whichever fits a large oval slow cooker) with vegetable cooking spray or oil of choice. Place a trivet or foil ring in the bottom of the slow cooker, and preheat to high.

2. In a small bowl, combine soy milk and apple cider vinegar, and set aside for 5 minutes to thicken.

3. In a medium bowl, combine white whole-wheat flour, aluminum-free baking powder, and sea salt.

4. Using a fork, work nonhydrogenated margarine into dry ingredients until mixture resembles coarse crumbs. Add soy milk mixture and yogurt, and stir until just combined.

5. Using your hands, gather dough into a ball. Transfer to the prepared pan or casserole dish, and gently pat to flatten and evenly fill pan. With a knife, cut dough into 8 wedge-shape pieces.

6. Place the pan or casserole dish on top of the trivet or foil ring in the slow cooker. Cover; slightly vent lid with a toothpick, chopstick, or wooden spoon; and cook on high for 1½ to 2 hours or until biscuits are dry on top and feel firm to the touch.

7. Uncover and allow biscuits to cool inside the slow cooker for 10 minutes. Carefully remove the pan or casserole dish from the slow cooker. Serve warm, cold, or at room temperature.

Variations: For **Herbed Biscuits in the Round,** add 3 tablespoons chopped fresh herbs or 2 or 3 teaspoons dried herbs—basil, dill, parsley, thyme, or rosemary, or a combination is a good option. For **Gluten-Free Biscuits,** replace the white whole-wheat flour with an equal amount of Bob's Red Mill Gluten-Free All-Purpose Baking Flour, and add ¹/₂ teaspoon xanthan gum.

> **DEFINITION**
>
> **Clabbering** is a process of combining soy or other nondairy milk with a little lemon juice or vinegar, which, when left to sit for a few minutes, causes the soy milk to sour and thicken slightly. Sometimes this mixture is referred to as soy buttermilk because it can be used as a measure-for-measure replacement for buttermilk in recipes.

Country Cornbread

The whole-grain goodness of stone-ground cornmeal dominates the savory flavor of this classic comfort food, which is an ideal accompaniment to a big bowlful of soup, chili, or slow-cooked beans.

Yield:	Prep time:	Cook time:	Serving size:
1 (8-inch) pan	8 to 10 minutes	2 to 2¹/₂ hours	1 piece

1¹/₄ cups medium-grind yellow cornmeal

1 cup whole-wheat pastry or white whole-wheat flour

2 TB. unbleached cane or light brown sugar, packed

1¹/₂ TB. nutritional yeast flakes

1¹/₂ TB. aluminum-free baking powder

¹/₂ tsp. sea salt

1¹/₂ cups soy or other nondairy milk

¹/₄ cup sunflower or other oil

1. Lightly coat an 8-inch cake pan or 6-cup or larger casserole dish (whichever fits a large oval slow cooker) with vegetable cooking spray or oil of choice. Place a trivet or foil ring in the bottom of the slow cooker, and preheat to high.

2. In a large bowl, whisk together yellow cornmeal, whole-wheat pastry flour, unbleached cane sugar, nutritional yeast flakes, aluminum-free baking powder, and sea salt.

3. Add soy milk and sunflower oil, and whisk well to combine. Transfer mixture to the prepared cake pan or casserole dish.

4. Place the pan or casserole dish on top of the trivet or foil ring. Cover; slightly vent lid with a toothpick, chopstick, or wooden spoon; and cook on high for $1^{1}/_{2}$ to 2 hours or until a toothpick inserted in the center comes out clean.

5. Uncover and allow cornbread to cool inside the slow cooker for 10 minutes. Carefully remove the pan or casserole dish from the slow cooker. Serve warm, cold, or at room temperature.

Variations: For **Chiles and Cheese Cornbread,** add $^{1}/_{2}$ cup shredded vegan cheddar cheese or other variety and 3 tablespoons canned mild green chiles to the blended cornbread mixture, and serve topped with several spoonfuls of salsa. For **Gluten-Free Cornbread,** replace the whole-wheat pastry flour with an equal amount of Bob's Red Mill Gluten-Free All-Purpose Baking Flour, and add $^{1}/_{2}$ teaspoon xanthan gum.

LOW AND SLOW

Cornbread tastes good plain or topped with a little margarine, but it tastes really delicious when topped with several spoonfuls of salsa. Give it a try!

Boston Brown Bread

Steam-cooked brown bread dates to the colonial times. Back then, it was made in a mold, which was placed in a water bath inside a covered pot and placed over the fire. Using a similar setup in your slow cooker results in a moist bread that's amply flavored with dark, rich molasses.

Yield:	Prep time:	Cook time:	Serving size:
1 loaf	5 to 7 minutes	2½ to 3 hours	1 slice

1⅓ cups soy or other nondairy milk	½ tsp. baking soda
1 TB. apple cider vinegar	½ tsp. allspice
½ cup medium-grind cornmeal	½ tsp. sea salt
½ cup rye flour	⅓ cup molasses
½ cup whole-wheat flour	⅓ cup raisins
½ tsp. aluminum-free baking powder	Hot water

1. Lightly coat a 6-cup or larger stainless-steel bowl or casserole dish (whichever fits a large oval slow cooker) with vegetable cooking spray or oil of choice. Place a trivet or foil ring in the bottom of the slow cooker, and preheat to high.

2. In a small bowl, combine soy milk and apple cider vinegar, and set aside for 5 minutes to thicken.

3. In a large bowl, whisk together cornmeal, rye flour, whole-wheat flour, aluminum-free baking powder, baking soda, allspice, and sea salt.

4. Add soy milk mixture and molasses, and whisk well to combine. Stir in raisins. Transfer mixture to the prepared bowl or casserole dish. Cover the bowl or casserole dish tightly with a layer of parchment paper and aluminum foil, and secure foil with a large rubber band or tie with kitchen twine.

5. Place the bowl or casserole dish on top of the trivet or foil ring. Carefully pour enough hot water around the outer edge to come about 1 or 2 inches up the sides of the mold, bowl, or casserole dish. Cover and cook on high for 2½ to 3 hours or until a toothpick inserted in the center comes out clean. This can be done directly through the layer of parchment paper and foil to check for doneness.

6. Uncover and allow bread to cool inside the slow cooker for 10 minutes. Carefully remove the bowl or casserole dish from the slow cooker, transfer to a rack, and cool for 10 minutes.

7. Remove aluminum foil covering. Loosen sides of bread with a spatula. Invert loaf, remove it from the bowl or casserole dish, flip loaf back over onto the rack, and cool as desired. Serve warm, cold, or at room temperature.

Variation: If you don't like the flavor of rye, you can replace the rye flour with graham flour or additional whole-wheat flour. For **Vermont Brown Bread,** replace the molasses with an equal amount of maple syrup, and add ⅓ cup toasted walnuts, roughly chopped.

SLOW INTERESTING

For a truly, traditional Bostonian meal, serve this moist brown bread with Boston Baked Beans (recipe in Chapter 15).

Hearty Herb Bread

Using more lighter white whole-wheat flour than nutty brown whole-wheat flour makes the texture of this bread less dense, while nutritional yeast flakes and Italian seasoning blend accentuate its savory aroma and flavor.

Yield:	Prep time:	Cook time:	Serving size:
1 (8×4×2½-inch) loaf	10 to 15 minutes, plus 1 hour rise time	2½ to 3 hours	1 slice

1⅓ cups warm water (110°F to 115°F)

1½ TB. light brown or unbleached cane sugar

1 (.25-oz.) pkg. or 2¼ tsp. rapid-rise active yeast

2 cups white whole-wheat or bread flour

1½ cups whole-wheat flour

3 TB. Italian seasoning blend or 1 TB. each dried basil, oregano, and thyme

2 TB. nutritional yeast flakes

1 tsp. sea salt

2 TB. olive oil

1. In a small bowl, combine warm water, light brown sugar, and rapid-rise active yeast, and set aside for 5 to 7 minutes or until yeast is fully dissolved and mixture is very foamy.

2. In a large bowl, combine white whole-wheat flour, whole-wheat flour, Italian seasoning blend, nutritional yeast flakes, and sea salt.

3. When yeast mixture is foamy, add olive oil, and gently stir to combine. Add wet ingredients to dry ingredients, and stir well.

4. Transfer dough to a clean counter or work surface. Using your hands, knead for 3 to 5 minutes or until a smooth and pliable ball of dough forms.

5. Drizzle a little additional olive oil around the outer edge of the bowl. Roll dough around in olive oil, and turn over dough to coat the other side. Cover the bowl lightly with a clean towel or plastic wrap, and let rise in a warm place for 1 hour or until doubled in size.

6. Lightly coat an 8×4×2½-inch loaf pan or 6-cup or larger casserole dish (whichever fits a large oval slow cooker) with vegetable cooking spray or oil of choice. Place a trivet or foil ring in the bottom of the slow cooker, and preheat to high.

7. Punch down dough. Turn out dough onto lightly floured work surface, and knead for 1 minute. Using your hands, flatten dough into an 8×10-inch rectangle, with the shorter side nearest you, and roll it like a jelly roll cake. Place dough seam-side down in the prepared pan or casserole dish.

8. Place the pan or casserole dish on top of the trivet or foil ring. Cover and cook on high for 1 hour. After 1 hour, slightly vent lid with a toothpick, chopstick, or wooden spoon, and cook on high for 1½ to 2 hours or until bread is firm to the touch and lightly browned around the edges.

9. Uncover and allow bread to cool inside the slow cooker for 10 minutes. Carefully remove the pan or casserole dish from the slow cooker, transfer to a rack, and cool for 10 minutes.

10. Loosen sides of bread with a spatula. Invert loaf, remove from the pan or casserole dish, flip loaf back over onto the rack, and cool as desired. Serve warm, cold, or at room temperature.

Variations: For **Wheat Bread,** replace the unbleached cane sugar with 2 tablespoons maple syrup and omit the Italian seasoning blend. For **Scarborough Fair Bread,** replace the Italian seasoning blend with 2 tablespoons chopped fresh parsley, 1½ tablespoons chopped fresh sage, 1½ tablespoons fresh rosemary, and 1½ tablespoons thyme. Or use 1 teaspoon each dried sage, rosemary, and thyme.

Pull-Apart Whole-Wheat Rolls

Using a combination of bread and whole-wheat flours, along with a little wheat bran, gives these rolls a nice soft texture and a slightly nutty flavor.

Yield:	Prep time:	Cook time:	Serving size:
8 rolls	10 to 15 minutes	2 to 2½ hours	1 roll

1 cup warm water (110°F to 115°F)

5 TB. turbinado or unbleached cane sugar

1 (.25-oz.) pkg. or 2¼ tsp. rapid-rise active yeast

1½ cups *bread flour*

1 cup whole-wheat flour

¼ cup wheat bran

2 TB. nutritional yeast flakes

¾ tsp. sea salt

3 TB. olive oil

1. Lightly coat a large oval slow cooker's ceramic crock insert with vegetable cooking spray or oil of choice. Cut a 13×16-inch piece of parchment in ½ lengthwise, and place pieces in a criss-cross pattern, creasing paper as necessary, to cover the bottom and sides of the ceramic crock insert. Lightly oil parchment paper.

2. In a small bowl, combine warm water, 1 tablespoon turbinado sugar, and rapid-rise active yeast, and set aside for 5 to 7 minutes or until yeast is fully dissolved and mixture is very foamy.

3. In a large bowl, combine bread flour, whole-wheat flour, remaining 4 tablespoons turbinado sugar, wheat bran, nutritional yeast flakes, and sea salt.

4. When yeast mixture is foamy, add olive oil, and gently stir to combine. Add wet ingredients to dry ingredients, and stir well.

5. Transfer dough to a clean counter or work surface. Using your hands, knead for 3 to 5 minutes or until a smooth and pliable ball of dough forms. Roll dough into a log, and divide into 8 pieces. Roll each piece into a ball, and place in the slow cooker, spacing them 1 or 2 inches apart (depending on shape of slow cooker).

6. Cover and cook on high for 1 hour. After 1 hour, slightly vent lid with a toothpick, chopstick, or wooden spoon, and cook on high for 1 to $1\frac{1}{2}$ hours or until rolls are firm to the touch and lightly browned around the edges.

7. Uncover and allow rolls to cool inside the slow cooker for 10 minutes. Carefully lift the parchment paper to remove rolls from the slow cooker, and transfer to a rack. Serve warm, cold, or at room temperature.

Variations: For **Golden Pull-Apart Rolls,** replace the whole-wheat flour with an additional 1 cup bread flour and omit the wheat germ. For **Seeded Pull-Apart Whole-Wheat Rolls,** sprinkle 2 tablespoons sesame seeds over the top of the shaped rolls.

DEFINITION

Bread flour has a high gluten/protein content, which helps give yeasted baked goods a higher rise than you typically get from using all-purpose or unbleached flour. It's often used in combination with whole-wheat or other whole-grain flours. Bread flour is commonly used in making sweet and savory breads, rolls, and pizza dough.

Sweet Endings

I've saved the best for last, and this may be the most popular part of the book, especially among those with a sweet tooth. Part 7 shows you how to transform your slow cooker into a mini-oven to slow bake some delicious desserts and other sweet treats. You also learn how to make fabulous stewed, poached, stuffed, and topped fruit-filled desserts. Once you've got those down, you're ready to move on to making creamy grain-based puddings, classic steamed pudding, and puddinglike cakes.

After mastering all those recipes, you'll be pleasantly surprised at how easy it is to use your baking pans and casserole dishes inside your slow cooker to create moist cakes and cheesecakes.

Fruity Desserts

In This Chapter

- Stewed fruit desserts
- Elegant and alcohol-enhanced fruit desserts
- Spiced and stuffed apples
- Terrific topped fruit-filled treats

Fruit is so good for you, and you should strive to include a wide variety of fruits in your diet—including dessert! The easiest way to do this is to take the seasonal approach, eating the fruits ripest and in season throughout the year. For instance, fresh berries and rhubarb are at their flavorful peak and most readily available in the spring and summer, so that's when you should be gobbling them up. If you crave out-of-season berries in the winter, you're better off using frozen berries in your recipe.

Slow cookers really come in handy for preparing desserts and other sweet treats during the spring and especially the hot summer months when you don't want to heat up your kitchen by turning on the oven. They can turn fresh berries, cherries, rhubarb, and even stone fruits such as peaches and plums into classic comfort foods like cobblers and crisps or more sophisticated desserts like flambéed Cherries Jubilee.

You'll find recipes for all these, plus a few more that make use of dried fruits and the autumnal favorites apples and pears, which are presented spiced, stuffed and sauced, and even poached in a mulled wine.

Cherries Jubilee

This show-stopping dessert is a luscious blend of syrup-coated cherries doused with brandy, dramatically flambéed, and served with nondairy ice cream or cake.

Yield:	Prep time:	Cook time:	Serving size:
4 cups	5 minutes	1 to 1½ hours	⅔ cup

4 cups fresh sweet or sour cherries, pitted, or 2 (16-oz.) pkg. frozen sweet or sour cherries (do not thaw)

⅔ cup unbleached cane sugar

8 TB. water

Zest of 1 large orange

Juice of 1 large orange

1½ TB. cornstarch

½ cup brandy

1. In a medium slow cooker, combine cherries, unbleached cane sugar, 5 tablespoons water, orange zest, and orange juice.

2. Cover and cook on high for 1 to 1½ hours, on low for 2 or 3 hours, or until cherries are very soft.

3. In a small bowl, stir together cornstarch and remaining 3 tablespoons water. Add to the slow cooker, and cook for 5 to 10 minutes or until sauce thickens slightly.

4. Uncover and turn off slow cooker. Stir in brandy, flambé (ignite) the brandy with a long match, and let flame subside. Serve immediately.

Variation: For **Sugar-Free Cherries Jubilee,** replace unbleached cane sugar with ⅓ cup agave nectar. This dessert can also be used as a topping for nondairy ice cream, cakes, and your other favorite desserts.

COOKER CAVEAT

When preparing any type of flambéed dish, be very careful to avoid getting burned, or worse yet, causing a fire! Avoid wearing long sleeves, be very cautious of dangling or long hair, and if you're wearing a tie, tuck it in. You should also have an appropriate lid nearby, just in case something goes awry and you need to quickly snuff out the flame. Lastly, know where the fire extinguisher is located!

Spiced Apples

This apple recipe is quick and easy. From minimal effort comes a great reward, and you can fill your house with the alluring aroma of apple pie with this delightful combination of apples, muscovado sugar, and spices.

Yield:	Prep time:	Cook time:	Serving size:
5 or 6 cups	7 to 10 minutes	1½ to 2 hours	¾ cup

4 or 5 large Fuji, Rome, Gala, or Golden Delicious apples, peeled, cored, and cut into wedges

½ cup light or dark muscovado sugar, packed

1 tsp. ground cinnamon

½ tsp. freshly ground cardamom

¼ tsp. freshly grated nutmeg

½ cup apple juice or apple cider

1 tsp. vanilla extract

1. In a medium slow cooker, combine Fuji apples, light muscovado sugar, cinnamon, cardamom, and nutmeg. Pour in apple juice.

2. Cover and cook on high for 1½ to 2 hours, on low for 3 or 4 hours, or until apples are tender.

3. Stir in vanilla extract. Serve hot or cold as a dessert, side dish, or topping for pancakes, waffles, and cakes.

Variation: Feel free to replace the apples with an equal amount of pears, peaches, or nectarines. For **Maple-Cinnamon Apples,** replace the muscovado sugar with ⅓ cup maple syrup and omit the cardamom and nutmeg.

LOW AND SLOW

If you're an apple lover like I am, I suggest buying an apple corer and wedge slicer. With one strong downward push on this handy gadget, you can quickly and easily core your apples and cut them into 8 wedges all at once.

Baked Caramel Apples

Choose the largest and firmest baking apples you can find for this recipe so they'll hold their shape. Then stuff them with a sweetened and spiced raisin-date filling, and when they're tender, ladle on the Butterscotch Sauce.

Yield:	Prep time:	Cook time:	Serving size:
4 baked apples	7 to 10 minutes	1½ to 2 hours	1 baked apple

4 large Fuji, Rome, or Granny Smith apples

¼ cup raisins

¼ cup date pieces coated with oat flour or pitted dates, roughly chopped

2 TB. brown rice syrup

1 tsp. vanilla extract

½ tsp. ground cinnamon

1 batch Butterscotch Sauce (recipe in Chapter 6)

1. Lightly coat a medium or large slow cooker's ceramic crock insert with vegetable cooking spray or oil of choice.

2. Using a knife or vegetable peeler, remove core from each Fuji apple, not going all the way through the apple, and discard core. Remove a 1-inch strip of peel from the top of each apple.

3. In a small bowl, combine raisins, dates, brown rice syrup, vanilla extract, and cinnamon. Fill each apple cavity with raisin-date mixture, and place apples in the slow cooker.

4. Cover and cook on high for 1½ to 2 hours, on low for 3 or 4 hours, or until apples are tender and easily pierced with the tip of a knife.

5. Uncover and allow apples to cool inside the slow cooker for 5 minutes. Using a slotted spoon, carefully remove apples from the slow cooker. Serve hot or warm, drizzled with Butterscotch Sauce.

Variation: For a nutty version, add ¼ cup toasted pecans, roughly chopped, to the filling mixture.

LOW AND SLOW

You don't want to go all the way through the apple from top to bottom, so it's best to use a paring knife or vegetable peeler to remove the apple's inner core.

Mulled Wine Poached Pears

This recipe is so simple! Large, firm pears are peeled and *poached* in robustly spiced (or *mulled*) red wine to create an elegant dessert. Serve them topped with some of the poaching liquid or with the vegan alternative to crème fraîche—vanilla yogurt.

Yield:	Prep time:	Cook time:	Serving size:
4 poached pears	7 to 10 minutes	1½ to 2 hours	1 poached pear

2½ cups Burgundy, Merlot, or Cabernet Sauvignon

¼ cup maple syrup or light brown sugar, packed

Large zest of ½ orange

1 (3-in.) cinnamon stick

3 whole allspice or ¼ tsp. ground allspice

3 whole cloves

¼ tsp. ground ginger or freshly grated nutmeg

4 large Bosc, Comice, or D'Anjou pears

Vanilla vegan yogurt (optional)

1. In a medium bowl, combine Burgundy, maple syrup, orange zest, cinnamon stick, allspice, cloves, and ginger.

2. Peel Bosc pears, leaving stems intact, and place in a medium slow cooker. Pour in wine mixture, and tilt pears on their sides to submerge them as much as possible.

3. Cover and cook on high for 1½ to 2 hours, on low for 3 or 4 hours, or until pears are tender and easily pierced with the tip of a knife.

4. After 1 hour of cook time, baste pears with wine mixture, and continue to baste every 30 minutes after that as needed.

5. Uncover and allow pears to cool inside the slow cooker for 5 minutes. Using a slotted spoon, carefully remove pears from the slow cooker. Serve hot or warm, drizzled with remaining wine cooking liquid and topped with dollops of vanilla vegan yogurt (if using). You can also slice the poached pears and serve them on top of salads.

Variation: For an easier preparation, you can cut the pears in half and remove their cores. You can also poach the pears in your favorite red wine instead. For a nonalcoholic **Fruit Juice–Poached Pears,** poach pears in 2½ cups cranberry-raspberry or cherry juice, ⅓ cup light brown sugar, and ½ teaspoon ground cinnamon.

> **DEFINITION**
>
> **Poach** is a cooking technique that entails cooking a food in a simmering liquid, such as water, fruit juice, wine, or broth. **Mulled** (or to mull) refers to the heating of a liquid, such as apple cider, fruit juice, water, or wine, along with a blend of spices and/or dried or fresh herbs, and sometimes with a small amount of sugar or other sweetener as well.

Stone Fruit Crisp

Slices of nectarines, peaches, and plums are tossed with a generous dose of turbinado sugar and spices and then blanketed with a sweet and crumbly rolled-oat topping.

Yield:	Prep time:	Cook time:	Serving size:
6 cups	15 minutes	1½ to 2 hours	1 cup

2 cups (4 medium) fresh nectarines, pitted and cut into ½-in. slices, or 1 (16-oz.) pkg. frozen sliced nectarines	⅔ cup turbinado sugar
	1 tsp. ground cinnamon
	½ tsp. ground ginger
2 cups (4 medium) fresh peaches, pitted and cut into ½-in. slices, or 1 (16-oz.) pkg. frozen sliced peaches	⅛ tsp. freshly grated nutmeg
	1½ cups old-fashioned rolled oats
	½ cup white whole-wheat or whole-wheat pastry flour
2 cups (5 or 6 medium) plums, pitted and cut into ½-in. slices	6 TB. nonhydrogenated margarine
½ cup water	½ tsp. vanilla extract

1. Lightly coat a medium slow cooker's ceramic crock insert with vegetable cooking spray or oil of choice.

2. In the slow cooker, combine nectarines, peaches, plums, and water. Cover and cook on high while preparing topping.

3. In a medium bowl, combine turbinado sugar, cinnamon, ginger, and nutmeg. Sprinkle ½ of spiced-sugar mixture over fruit in the slow cooker, stir well to combine, and cover.

4. Add old-fashioned rolled oats and white whole-wheat flour to remaining spiced-sugar mixture, and stir well to combine. Using your fingers, work non-hydrogenated margarine and vanilla extract into dry ingredients until mixture resembles coarse crumbs. Sprinkle mixture over fruit in the slow cooker.

5. Cover; slightly vent lid with a toothpick, chopstick, or wooden spoon; and cook on high for 1½ to 2 hours, on low for 3 or 4 hours, or until stone fruit filling is tender and easily pierced with the tip of a knife. (Alternatively, tent the lid by placing a clean kitchen towel across the top of the slow cooker, just under the lid, to help capture the steam and prevent it from falling back down.)

6. Uncover and allow crisp to cool inside the slow cooker for 5 minutes. Serve hot or warm, plain or with nondairy ice cream or vegan whipped topping.

Variations: Feel free to make this crisp using only one variety of stone fruit. For **Stone Fruit and Berry Crisp,** replace the sliced plums with 2 cups fresh or frozen blueberries or raspberries. For **Gluten-Free Stone Fruit Crisp,** use gluten-free rolled oats, and replace the white whole-wheat flour with an equal amount of sorghum or oat flour.

> **SLOW INTERESTING**
>
> Stone fruits such as apricots, peaches, plums, and nectarines are available in two varieties—freestone, or those not connected to the stone pit, or clingstone, the kind connected to the inner stone pit of the fruit, making them more challenging to consume and slice. Feel free to peel these fruits or leave the skin on.

Strawberry-Rhubarb Brown Betty

A brown Betty is a rather humble, old-fashioned dessert that's basically cooked fruit layered with sweetened breadcrumbs or cubes. This springtime Betty is a lovely, blushing pink-red combination of strawberries and rhubarb with alternating layers of an almond-studded breadcrumb topping.

Yield:	Prep time:	Cook time:	Serving size:
5 or 6 cups	10 minutes	1½ to 2 hours	1 cup

1 lb. (6 or 8 large stalks) fresh rhubarb, cut into 1-in. pieces (about 4 cups), or 1 (16-oz.) pkg. frozen sliced rhubarb

1 pt. strawberries, hulled and cut in ½, or 1 (16-oz.) pkg. frozen whole strawberries

½ cup unbleached cane sugar

Zest of 1 large lemon

Juice of 1 large lemon

2 cups fresh breadcrumbs

¼ cup light brown sugar, packed

1 tsp. ground cinnamon

½ cup toasted almonds or other nuts, roughly chopped

2 TB. nonhydrogenated margarine, melted

1. Lightly coat a medium or large slow cooker's ceramic crock insert with vegetable cooking spray or oil of choice. Preheat the slow cooker to high.

2. In a large bowl, combine rhubarb, strawberries, unbleached cane sugar, lemon zest, and lemon juice.

3. In a medium bowl, combine breadcrumbs, light brown sugar, and cinnamon. Add toasted almonds and nonhydrogenated margarine, and stir gently to combine.

4. In the slow cooker, place ½ of strawberry-rhubarb filling. Pour in water. Sprinkle ½ of breadcrumb topping over top. Repeat layering procedure with remaining strawberry-rhubarb filling and breadcrumb topping mixtures.

5. Cover; slightly vent lid with a toothpick, chopstick, or wooden spoon; and cook on high for 1½ to 2 hours, on low for 3 or 4 hours, or until fruit filling is tender.

6. Uncover and allow brown Betty to cool inside the slow cooker for 5 minutes. Serve hot or warm, plain or with nondairy ice cream or vegan whipped topping.

Variation: For a slightly different flavor, replace the lemon zest and juice with the zest and juice of 1 large orange. For the classic **Apple Brown Betty,** replace the sliced rhubarb and strawberries with 6 cups (2 pounds or 3 or 4 large) apples of choice, peeled, cored, and sliced; in the breadcrumb topping mixture, replace the almonds with an equal amount of toasted walnuts.

COOKER CAVEAT

Only eat the slender stalks of the rhubarb plant. Never eat the leaves because they're considered poisonous. Even ingesting a small amount could be toxic.

Mixed Berry Cobbler

Cobblers are synonymous with comfort food, and this homey dessert features a sweet, biscuitlike topping that's slow baked on top of a colorful mix of plump, juicy berries.

Yield:	Prep time:	Cook time:	Serving size:
6 cups	7 to 10 minutes	1½ to 2 hours	1 cup

7 cups each fresh mixed blueberries, blackberries, strawberries, and red raspberries, or 2 (16-oz.) pkg. frozen mixed berries

⅔ cup unbleached cane sugar

2 TB. plus 1 cup whole-wheat pastry or white whole-wheat flour

1 tsp. aluminum-free baking powder

½ cup soy or other nondairy milk

2 TB. sunflower or other oil

1 tsp. vanilla extract

1. Lightly coat a medium or large slow cooker's ceramic crock insert with vegetable cooking spray or oil of choice.

2. In the slow cooker, combine mixed berries, ⅓ cup unbleached cane sugar, and 2 tablespoons whole-wheat pastry flour.

3. In a medium bowl, combine remaining ⅓ cup unbleached cane sugar, remaining 1 cup whole-wheat pastry flour, and aluminum-free baking powder. Add soy milk, sunflower oil, and vanilla extract, and stir well. Drop spoonfuls of mixture over top of berry mixture.

4. Cover; slightly vent lid with a toothpick, chopstick, or wooden spoon; and cook on high for 1½ to 2 hours, on low for 3 or 4 hours, or until fruit filling is tender and a toothpick inserted in cobbler topping comes out clean. (Alternatively, tent lid by placing a clean kitchen towel across the top of the ceramic crock insert, just under the lid, to help capture the steam and prevent it from falling back down.)

5. Uncover and allow cobbler to cool inside the slow cooker for 5 minutes. Serve hot or warm, plain or with nondairy ice cream or vegan whipped topping as desired.

Variations: For **Black and Blue Cobbler,** prepare the fruit filling using half blueberries and half blackberries. For **Cherry Cobbler,** replace mixed berries with 6 cups fresh sweet or sour cherries, pitted, or 2 (16-ounce) packages frozen cherries.

LOW AND SLOW

Several brands of vegan whipped topping are now available. The makers of Soyatoo offer both Soy Whip and soy-free Rice Whip in convenient pressurized cans, as well as Soy Whip in small cartons, which you beat with an electric mixer until fluffy. Another whip-it-yourself option is Healthy Top by MimicCreme. Look for these items in the refrigerated case of your local grocery or natural foods stores.

Pleasing Puddings

In This Chapter

- Creamy tapioca and rice puddings
- Classic steamed puddings
- Boozy bread pudding
- Self-saucing pudding cakes

The term *pudding* is used to describe many different styles of dessert. If you live in the United States, *pudding* probably makes you think of the creamy vanilla, tapioca, or rice puddings your mother and grandmother made on the stovetop. If you live across the pond, you might be hoping for a sticky date or steamed pudding. In between lies bread pudding, made by slow baking custard-coated bread cubes. And then there's the mystifying pudding cake. They're all called pudding, but they're all very different, and they're all featured in this chapter.

Some of these tasty puddings can be cooked or slow baked directly in the slow cooker, but others need the confines of a bowl or casserole dish, and even some hot water to help them achieve their desired shape and degree of doneness. In this chapter, you learn how to cook each type.

Whichever pudding you choose, rest assured it will have them all saying, "More pudding, please!"

Chai Rice Pudding

The exotic flavors of Indian chai tea are infused into fragrant jasmine rice to create a sumptuous and lightly spiced rice pudding delicious warm or cold.

Yield:	Prep time:	Cook time:	Serving size:
4 or 5 cups	5 minutes	1½ to 2 hours	1 cup

1 pt. vegan vanilla coconut creamer or coconut milk beverage

2 cups freshly brewed chai tea

¾ cup jasmine or arborio rice

⅓ cup brown rice syrup or agave nectar

Pinch sea salt

2 tsp. vanilla extract

Ground cinnamon

Raisins (optional)

Toasted unsweetened shredded coconut (optional)

1. Lightly coat a small or medium slow cooker's ceramic crock insert with vegetable cooking spray or oil of choice.

2. In the slow cooker, combine vanilla coconut creamer, chai tea, jasmine rice, brown rice syrup, and sea salt.

3. Cover and cook on high for 1½ to 2 hours, on low for 3 or 4 hours, or until most of liquid is absorbed and rice is tender.

4. Uncover, stir in vanilla extract, and allow rice pudding to cool inside the slow cooker for 5 minutes. (Rice pudding will thicken as it cools.)

5. Serve warm, or transfer to a bowl and refrigerate. Garnish individual servings with a little cinnamon, raisins (if using), and toasted shredded coconut (if using).

Variation: For **Chai Kheer** (Indian rice pudding), replace the jasmine rice with white basmati rice, add ½ teaspoon ground cardamom, and garnish individual servings with raisins (or golden raisins) and toasted pistachios.

SLOW INTERESTING

Chai tea is one of the most popular beverages served in India and is believed to offer many health benefits, like increasing circulation, relaxing the mind and muscles, and improving digestion. The particular blend of spices used in this fragrant brew differs from region to region, but the most commonly used spices include cardamom, cinnamon, cloves, ginger, and black peppercorns. Some also add fennel seeds.

Vanilla-Almond Tapioca Pudding

Tapioca is a great thickening agent, and the tiny, *tapioca pearls* are just the thing for making a creamy, slightly sweet pudding. This tasty treat is enhanced with the floral undertones of vanilla extract and vanilla almond milk.

Yield:	Prep time:	Cook time:	Serving size:
4 cups	5 minutes	1½ to 2 hours	1 cup

4 cups vanilla almond or other nondairy milk

½ cup tapioca pearls

⅓ cup unbleached cane sugar or agave nectar

Pinch sea salt

1 TB. vanilla extract

Toasted sliced almonds (optional)

Diced fresh fruit or berries (optional)

1. Lightly coat a small or medium slow cooker's ceramic crock insert with vegetable cooking spray or oil of choice.

2. In the slow cooker, combine vanilla almond milk, tapioca pearls, unbleached cane sugar, and sea salt.

3. Cover and cook on high for 1½ to 2 hours, on low for 3 or 4 hours, or until most of liquid is absorbed and tapioca pearls are soft and transparent.

4. Uncover, stir in vanilla extract, and allow tapioca pudding to cool inside the slow cooker for 5 minutes. (Tapioca pudding will thicken as it cools.)

5. Serve warm, or transfer to a bowl and refrigerate. Garnish individual servings with toasted sliced almonds (if using) or diced fruit or berries (if using).

Variations: For **Rich Vanilla Bean Tapioca Pudding,** replace 2 cups almond milk with 1 pint vanilla soy or coconut creamer, and replace the vanilla extract with 1 teaspoon raw vanilla bean powder. For **Chocolate Tapioca Pudding,** replace the vanilla almond milk with chocolate almond milk or other nondairy milk, and garnish individual servings with a little chopped vegan dark chocolate bar or cacao nibs.

DEFINITION

Tapioca pearls are made from tapioca starch (tapioca flour) that's soaked, cooked, shaped, and dried into assorted sizes of pellets or pearls. You can find both the small, white tapioca pearls and the quick-cooking (granulated) tapioca in most grocery and natural foods stores.

Sticky Date Toffee Pudding

One taste of this classic British dessert will make you swoon! Using the traditional steamed pudding technique gives this dried date and muscovado sugar–sweetened sponge a melt-in-your-mouth moist texture that's complemented by Butterscotch Sauce topping.

Yield:	Prep time:	Cook time:	Serving size:
5 or 6 cups	20 to 25 minutes	2½ to 3 hours	1 cup, plus sauce

1¼ cups pitted dates, roughly chopped

1¼ cups water

1 tsp. baking soda

2 TB. ground flaxseeds or flaxseed meal

¾ cup light or dark muscovado sugar, packed

¼ cup nonhydrogenated margarine

½ TB. vanilla extract

1¼ cups whole-wheat pastry or *white whole-wheat flour*

1 tsp. aluminum-free baking powder

½ tsp. allspice, or ¼ tsp. each ground ginger and freshly grated nutmeg

½ tsp. sea salt

Hot water

1 batch Butterscotch Sauce (recipe in Chapter 6)

1. Lightly coat a 6-cup or larger stainless-steel bowl or casserole dish (whichever fits your large oval slow cooker) with vegetable cooking spray or oil of choice. Place a trivet or foil ring in the bottom of the slow cooker, and preheat the slow cooker to high.

2. In a medium saucepan over high heat, combine dates and 1 cup water. Bring to a boil, and boil for 1 minute. Remove the saucepan from heat. Add baking soda (mixture will foam up), and set aside for 10 minutes to cool.

3. In a small bowl, combine remaining ¼ cup water and flaxseeds, and let sit for 5 minutes.

4. Add flaxseed mixture, light muscovado sugar, nonhydrogenated margarine, and vanilla extract to date mixture, and stir well. Add whole-wheat pastry flour, aluminum-free baking powder, allspice, and sea salt, and stir well.

5. Transfer mixture to the prepared bowl or casserole dish. Cover the bowl or casserole dish tightly with a layer of parchment paper and aluminum foil, and secure foil with a large rubber band or tie with kitchen twine.

6. Place the bowl or casserole dish on top of the trivet or foil ring. Carefully pour enough hot water around the outer edge to come about 1 or 2 inches up the sides of the mold, bowl, or casserole dish. Cover and cook on high for 2½ to 3 hours or until pudding feels firm to the touch and a toothpick inserted in the center comes out clean. (This can be done directly through the layer of parchment paper and foil.)

7. Uncover and allow pudding to cool inside the slow cooker for 10 minutes. Carefully remove the bowl or casserole dish from the slow cooker.

8. Serve warm or at room temperature, drizzling Butterscotch Sauce over individual servings.

Variation: For **Sticky Date-Almond Toffee Pudding,** add ½ cup toasted almonds, roughly chopped.

> **DEFINITION**
>
> **White whole-wheat flour** is ground from white wheat, which was developed by cross-breeding strains of red wheat, the most commonly used wheat variety in the United States. Unlike red wheat, which has 3 bran colors, white wheat has no major genes for bran color and is lighter in color and milder in flavor. White wheat flour can be used in place of all-purpose or unbleached white flour in recipes. It's more nutritious than heavily refined flours because it still contains the beneficial bran, germ, and endosperm of the white wheat kernel.

New Orleans Bread Pudding with Bourbon Street Sauce

This dessert is divine. Cubes of Cinnamon-Swirl Raisin Bread are covered and slow baked in a sweet, soy creamer–based custard that's spiked with bourbon, vanilla, and cinnamon and then topped with Boozy Butterscotch Sauce.

Yield:	Prep time:	Cook time:	Serving size:
8 cups	10 to 15 minutes, plus 1 hour for air-drying bread	3 or 4 hours	1½ cups

8 cups Cinnamon-Swirl Raisin Bread (recipe in Chapter 17), or store-bought bread, cut into 1-in. cubes

1 pt. vegan vanilla soy or coconut creamer

2 cups soy or other nondairy milk

¾ cup unbleached cane sugar

¼ cup bourbon

1 TB. vanilla extract

1 tsp. ground cinnamon

1 batch Boozy Butterscotch Sauce (variation in Chapter 6)

1. Place Cinnamon-Swirl Raisin Bread cubes on a cookie sheet, and set aside to air-dry for 1 hour. (Alternatively, bake bread cubes in a 325°F oven for 20 to 25 minutes or until lightly toasted and dry. Remove from the oven and set aside to cool.)

2. Lightly coat a 10-cup or larger casserole dish (whatever fits your large oval slow cooker) with vegetable cooking spray or oil of choice. Place a trivet or foil ring in the bottom of the slow cooker, and preheat the slow cooker to high.

3. In a large bowl, whisk together vanilla soy creamer, soy milk, unbleached cane sugar, bourbon, vanilla extract, and cinnamon.

4. Place bread cubes in the prepared casserole dish, pour in wet ingredients, and gently push down on bread cubes to moisten them evenly.

5. Place the casserole dish on top of the trivet or foil ring. Cover and cook on high for 2½ hours. Slightly vent lid with a toothpick, chopstick, or wooden spoon, and cook on high for 30 to 60 minutes or until most of liquid is absorbed and bread is puffed up.

6. Uncover and allow bread pudding to cool inside the slow cooker for 10 minutes. Carefully remove the casserole dish from the slow cooker. Serve warm, cold, or at room temperature, drizzled with Boozy Butterscotch Sauce.

Variation: For a nonalcoholic **Sweet Cinnamon-Raisin Bread Pudding,** omit the bourbon, and drizzle Butterscotch Sauce (recipe in Chapter 6) over individual servings. You can also top servings of this bread pudding with nondairy ice cream or vegan whipped topping. For a pan-less version or a more golden brown and crispy bread pudding, assemble the bread pudding directly in the oiled ceramic crock insert of a medium slow cooker. You may need to reduce the cook time by 30 to 45 minutes to avoid overbrowning the bread cubes.

COOKER CAVEAT

Some manufacturers use activated charcoal from animal-based sources (known as bone-char) to filter impurities and bleach cane sugar. You can easily find vegan-friendly sugar. Wholesome Sweeteners, Florida Crystals, and Hain Pure Foods all sell many varieties of vegan-friendly sugars. Look for products such as unbleached cane sugar, evaporated cane juice (or cane sugar), turbinado or raw sugar, Sucanat, beet sugar, muscovado sugar, etc.

Peanut Butter Cup Pudding Cake

This pudding cake is magical. A peanut butter–flavored cake batter lines the bottom of your slow cooker, topped with a dusting of cocoa powder and sugar, and covered with boiling water. The result? A cake floating on top of a chocolate fudge sauce.

Yield:	Prep time:	Cook time:	Serving size:
6 cups	10 minutes	2 to 2½ hours	1½ cups

1 cup whole-wheat pastry flour

⅔ cup unbleached cane sugar

2 tsp. aluminum-free baking powder

¼ tsp. sea salt

⅔ cup soy or other nondairy milk

½ cup smooth or chunky peanut butter

2 TB. sunflower or other oil

2 tsp. vanilla extract

⅓ cup dry-roasted peanuts

⅓ cup cocoa powder

⅓ cup light brown sugar, packed

1½ cups boiling water

1. Lightly coat a medium slow cooker's ceramic crock insert with vegetable cooking spray or oil of choice. Preheat the slow cooker to high.

2. In a large bowl, whisk together whole-wheat pastry flour, $^{1}/_{3}$ cup unbleached cane sugar, aluminum-free baking powder, and sea salt.

3. In a medium bowl, whisk together soy milk, peanut butter, sunflower oil, and vanilla extract.

4. Add wet ingredients to dry ingredients, and whisk well. (Batter will be thick.) Stir in dry-roasted peanuts, and transfer batter to the slow cooker.

5. In a small bowl, combine cocoa powder, remaining $^{1}/_{3}$ cup unbleached cane sugar, and light brown sugar. Sprinkle cocoa-sugar mixture over batter. Carefully pour boiling water over top. Do not stir.

6. Cover and cook on high for 2 to $2^{1}/_{2}$ hours, on low for 4 or 5 hours, or until a toothpick inserted in center of pudding cake comes out clean.

7. Uncover and allow pudding cake to cool for 10 minutes. Serve warm or at room temperature, drizzled with chocolate fudge sauce.

Variation: If you're allergic to peanuts, replace the peanut butter with almond or cashew butter and the dry-roasted peanuts with roughly chopped almonds or cashews. You can also top servings with nondairy ice cream or vegan whipped topping.

LOW AND SLOW

You can easily make your own homemade nut and seed butters using a food processor fitted with an S blade. Simply place 1 or 2 cups raw, roasted, or pan-toasted nuts or seeds into the food processor, process for 3 to 5 minutes or until desired consistency. Store it in an airtight container in the refrigerator for up to 2 months.

Black Forest Pudding Cake

This rich chocolate, chocolate-chip, and cherry pudding–like cake creates its own gooey chocolate fudge sauce as it cooks. An additional garnish of vegan whipped topping and Cherries Jubilee makes this a truly memorable dessert.

Yield:	Prep time:	Cook time:	Serving size:
6 cups	10 minutes	2 to 2½ hours	1½ cups

1 cup whole-wheat pastry flour

⅔ cup unbleached cane sugar

9 TB. cocoa powder

2 tsp. aluminum-free baking powder

¼ tsp. sea salt

⅓ cup chocolate soy or other nondairy milk

3 TB. kirsch (cherry brandy)

2 TB. sunflower or other oil

2 tsp. vanilla extract

⅔ cup fresh or frozen sweet dark cherries, cut in ½

½ cup vegan chocolate chips

⅓ cup light brown sugar, packed

1½ cups boiling water

Vegan whipped topping

1 batch Cherries Jubilee (recipe in Chapter 18)

1. Lightly coat a medium slow cooker's ceramic crock insert with vegetable cooking spray or oil of choice. Preheat the slow cooker to high.

2. In a large bowl, whisk together whole-wheat pastry flour, ⅓ cup unbleached cane sugar, 5 tablespoons cocoa powder, aluminum-free baking powder, and sea salt.

3. In a medium bowl, whisk together chocolate soy milk, kirsch, sunflower oil, and vanilla extract.

4. Add wet ingredients to dry ingredients, and whisk well. (Batter will be thick.) Stir in sweet dark cherries and chocolate chips, and transfer batter to the slow cooker.

5. In a small bowl, combine remaining 4 tablespoons cocoa powder, remaining ⅓ cup unbleached cane sugar, and light brown sugar, and stir well. Sprinkle cocoa-sugar mixture over batter. Carefully pour boiling water over top. Do not stir.

6. Cover and cook on high for 2 to 2½ hours, on low for 4 or 5 hours, or until a toothpick inserted in center of pudding cake comes out clean.

7. Uncover and allow pudding cake to cool for 10 minutes. Serve warm or at room temperature, drizzled with chocolate fudge sauce and garnished with vegan whipped topping and Cherries Jubilee.

Variation: For **Hot Fudge Brownie Pudding Cake,** omit the kirsch, use $\frac{1}{2}$ cup chocolate soy milk, and replace the chopped cherries with $\frac{1}{2}$ cup toasted walnuts, roughly chopped. Top individual servings with chocolate fudge sauce and vegan whipped topping, but omit Cherries Jubilee.

LOW AND SLOW

If you love dark chocolate, feel free to replace the chocolate chips in this recipe with 2 (1.4-ounce) or 1 (3-ounce) dark chocolate with cherries–flavored bar, roughly chopped.

Cakes for All Occasions

In This Chapter

- Streusel-topped coffeecake
- Old-fashioned maple- and molasses-sweetened cakes
- Frosted and glazed cakes
- Mouthwatering marbled cheesecake

Slow-cooked cakes? You bet! As with the bread recipes in Chapter 17, rather than placing your cake batter directly in the ceramic crock insert, all the cake recipes in this chapter are slow-baked in pans or casserole dishes placed inside the slow cooker.

These cakes do take a little longer to prepare in your slow cooker than in your oven. But because you slow bake them on high, you can still enjoy them in about 3 hours. So if you get your cake going in the slow cooker and then make dinner (or breakfast or lunch), by the time you've finished eating your meal and cleared away the dishes, your freshly made, slow-baked cake will be ready to dig into.

Yes, you can slow bake your cake, and eat it, too!

Sweet Potato Streusel Coffeecake

Sweet potato purée adds moisture and flavor, but also provides a nice orange tint to this coffeecake's batter, which is nestled beneath a sweet, cinnamon and nutmeg–spiced streusel-crumb topping.

Yield:	Prep time:	Cook time:	Serving size:
1 (8-inch) coffeecake	15 minutes	2½ to 3½ hours	1 slice

2½ cups whole-wheat pastry flour

1 cup *turbinado sugar*

1 tsp. ground cinnamon

¼ tsp. freshly grated nutmeg

¼ cup nonhydrogenated margarine

1 TB. aluminum-free baking powder

¼ tsp. sea salt

¾ cup Sweet Potato Purée (recipe in Chapter 7) or canned sweet potato purée

⅔ cup soy or other nondairy milk

1 tsp. vanilla extract

Confectioners' sugar

1. Lightly coat an 8-inch cake pan or 6-cup or larger casserole dish (whichever fits your large oval slow cooker) with vegetable cooking spray or oil of choice. Place a trivet or foil ring in the bottom of the slow cooker, and preheat the slow cooker to high.

2. In a small bowl, combine ½ cup whole-wheat pastry flour, ⅓ cup turbinado sugar, ½ teaspoon cinnamon, and nutmeg. Using your fingers, work 2 tablespoons nonhydrogenated margarine into dry ingredients until mixture resembles coarse crumbs.

3. In a large bowl, whisk together remaining 2 cups whole-wheat pastry flour, remaining ⅔ cup turbinado sugar, remaining ½ teaspoon cinnamon, aluminum-free baking powder, and sea salt.

4. In a medium bowl, whisk together Sweet Potato Purée, soy milk, and vanilla extract. Pour wet ingredients into dry ingredients, and stir well.

5. Transfer batter to the prepared pan or casserole dish, and smooth top with a spatula. Sprinkle streusel topping over top, and gently press into batter with your hand.

6. Place the pan or casserole dish on top of the trivet or foil ring. Cover; slightly vent the lid with a toothpick, chopstick, or wooden spoon; and cook on high for 2½ to 3½ hours or until a toothpick inserted in the center comes out clean.

7. Uncover and allow coffeecake to cool inside the slow cooker for 10 minutes. Carefully remove the pan or casserole dish from the slow cooker, transfer to a rack, and cool for 10 minutes. Loosen sides of coffeecake with a spatula. Sprinkle top of coffeecake with a little confectioners' sugar, and serve warm or at room temperature.

Variation: For **Pumpkin-Pecan Streusel Coffeecake,** to the streusel topping, add ⅓ cup toasted pecans, roughly chopped, and in the batter, replace Sweet Potato Purée with an equal amount of Pumpkin Purée (variation in Chapter 7).

> **DEFINITION**
>
> **Turbinado sugar** is sugar made from the juice extracted from unrefined raw cane sugar, which is then spun in a centrifuge or turbine (hence its name). It has a very fine texture and a slight molasses flavor. It can also be used to replace light brown sugar. You might be familiar with the most commonly sold brand of turbinado sugar, Sugar in the Raw.

Applesauce Cake

The natural sweetness of apples is deliciously showcased in this quick-and-easy, super-moist cake that's sweetened with an ample amount of applesauce, apple juice, and agave nectar.

Yield:	Prep time:	Cook time:	Serving size:
1 (8-inch) cake	7 to 10 minutes	2½ to 3 hours	1 slice

2 TB. water

1 TB. ground flaxseeds or flaxseed meal

1 cup Apple Juice–Sweetened Applesauce (recipe in Chapter 6)

½ cup apple juice or apple cider

⅓ cup agave nectar or maple syrup

1½ TB. sunflower or other oil

½ TB. vanilla extract

2 cups whole-wheat pastry flour

1 TB. aluminum-free baking powder

1 tsp. baking soda

1 tsp. ground cinnamon

¼ tsp. sea salt

1. Lightly coat an 8-inch cake or springform pan, or 6-cup or larger casserole dish (whichever fits your large oval slow cooker) with vegetable cooking spray or oil of choice. Place a trivet or foil ring in the bottom of the slow cooker, and preheat the slow cooker to high.

2. In a medium bowl, combine water and flaxseeds, and let sit for 5 minutes.

3. Add Apple Juice–Sweetened Applesauce, apple juice, agave nectar, sunflower oil, and vanilla extract, and whisk well to combine.

4. In a large bowl, whisk together whole-wheat pastry flour, aluminum-free baking powder, baking soda, cinnamon, and sea salt.

5. Pour wet ingredients into dry ingredients, and stir well. Transfer mixture to the prepared cake pan or casserole dish.

6. Place the pan or casserole dish on top of the trivet or foil ring. Cover; slightly vent lid with a toothpick, chopstick, or wooden spoon; and cook on high for 2½ to 3 hours or until a toothpick inserted in the center comes out clean. (Alternatively, tent the lid by placing a clean kitchen towel across the top of the slow cooker, just under the lid, to help capture the steam and prevent it from falling back down.)

7. Uncover and allow cake to cool inside the slow cooker for 10 minutes. Carefully remove the pan or casserole dish from the slow cooker. Loosen sides of cake with a spatula. Serve warm or at room temperature.

Variations: For **Apple Butter Spice Cake,** replace the Apple Juice–Sweetened Applesauce with an equal amount of Sugar-Free Apple Butter (variation in Chapter 7), and add ½ teaspoon allspice. For **Maple-Walnut Applesauce Cake,** prepare the batter using maple syrup and add ½ cup toasted walnuts, roughly chopped (add ¼ cup to batter and sprinkle remaining ¼ cup on top). You can also top servings of this cake with Spiced Apples (recipe in Chapter 18), nondairy ice cream, or vegan whipped topping.

LOW AND SLOW

Due to their high oil content, whole and ground flaxseeds, as well as the prepackaged flaxseed meal, should be stored in an airtight container either in the fridge, or for longer storage, in the freezer. Otherwise, they'll go rancid.

Old-Fashioned Gingerbread

Gingerbread has been a cherished dessert for centuries, and rightfully so, as its tantalizing zing and dark, moist texture is due to a generous blend of ground ginger, other spices, and iron-rich *blackstrap molasses*.

Yield:	Prep time:	Cook time:	Serving size:
1 (8-inch) cake	7 to 10 minutes	2½ to 3 hours	1 slice

1½ cups whole-wheat pastry flour

⅓ cup turbinado or light brown sugar, packed

1 tsp. aluminum-free baking powder

½ TB. ground ginger

1 tsp. ground cinnamon

½ tsp. allspice

½ tsp. freshly grated nutmeg

½ tsp. baking soda

¼ tsp. sea salt

⅔ cup water

⅓ cup blackstrap molasses

3 TB. sunflower or other oil

1 tsp. vanilla extract

1. Lightly coat an 8-inch cake pan or 6-cup or larger casserole dish (whichever fits your large oval slow cooker) with vegetable cooking spray or oil of choice. Place a trivet or foil ring in the bottom of the slow cooker, and preheat the slow cooker to high.

2. In a large bowl, whisk together whole-wheat pastry flour, turbinado sugar, aluminum-free baking powder, ginger, cinnamon, allspice, nutmeg, baking soda, and sea salt.

3. In a medium bowl, whisk together water, blackstrap molasses, sunflower oil, and vanilla extract.

4. Pour wet ingredients into dry ingredients, and stir well. Transfer mixture to the prepared cake pan or casserole dish.

5. Place the pan or casserole dish on top of the trivet or foil ring. Cover; slightly vent the lid with a toothpick, chopstick, or wooden spoon; and cook on high for 2½ to 3 hours or until a toothpick inserted in the center comes out clean. (Alternatively, tent the lid by placing a clean kitchen towel across the top of the slow cooker, just under the lid, to help capture the steam and prevent it from falling back down.)

6. Uncover and allow gingerbread to cool inside the slow cooker for 10 minutes. Carefully remove the pan or casserole dish from the slow cooker. Loosen sides of gingerbread with a spatula, and serve warm or at room temperature.

Variations: You can also top with nondairy ice cream or vegan whipped topping. For **Maple Gingerbread,** replace the blackstrap molasses with an equal amount of maple syrup. For **Double-Ginger Gingerbread,** add ⅓ cup crystallized ginger, finely chopped.

> **DEFINITION**
>
> **Blackstrap molasses** is one of several varieties of molasses, a dark, thick, bittersweet syrup that results from the production of sugar. It contains several B vitamins, calcium, magnesium, potassium, iron, copper, and manganese. It does have a slightly bitter flavor, and if you prefer a sweeter flavor, you can replace it with unsulphured Barbados molasses.

Lemon Berry Cake

Vegan yogurt greatly adds to the moistness and also helps cut the fat content of this sunny yellow, lemony cake that's dotted with juicy, sweet berries.

Yield:	Prep time:	Cook time:	Serving size:
1 (8-inch) cake	7 to 10 minutes	2½ to 3 hours	1 slice

1½ cups whole-wheat pastry or white whole-wheat flour

¾ cup unbleached cane sugar

½ TB. baking soda

¼ tsp. sea salt

⅔ cup soy or other nondairy milk

½ cup vanilla or plain vegan yogurt

Zest of 1 large lemon

Juice of 1 large lemon

2 TB. sunflower or other oil

1 tsp. vanilla extract

⅔ cup fresh or frozen blueberries, blackberries, or red raspberries

1. Lightly coat an 8-inch cake pan or 6-cup or larger casserole dish (whichever fits your large oval slow cooker) with vegetable cooking spray or oil of choice. Place a trivet or foil ring in the bottom of the slow cooker, and preheat the slow cooker to high.

2. In a large bowl, whisk together whole-wheat pastry flour, unbleached cane sugar, baking soda, and sea salt.

3. In a medium bowl, whisk together soy milk, vanilla yogurt, lemon zest, lemon juice, sunflower oil, and vanilla extract.

4. Pour wet ingredients into dry ingredients, and whisk well. Stir in berries. Transfer mixture to the prepared cake pan or casserole dish.

5. Place the pan or casserole dish on top of the trivet or foil ring. Cover; slightly vent lid with a toothpick, chopstick, or wooden spoon; and cook on high for 2½ to 3 hours or until a toothpick inserted in the center comes out clean. (Alternatively, tent the lid by placing a clean kitchen towel across the top of the slow cooker, just under the lid, to help capture the steam and prevent it from falling back down.)

6. Uncover and allow cake to cool inside the slow cooker for 10 minutes. Carefully remove the pan or casserole dish from the slow cooker. Loosen sides of cake with a spatula. Serve warm or at room temperature.

Variation: This cake is delicious served topped with Warm Mixed Berry Sauce (recipe in Chapter 6). You can omit the berries for a plain lemon cake. For **Orange-Cranberry Cake,** replace the lemon zest and juice with the zest and juice of 1 large orange, and instead of the other suggested berries, add ⅔ cup fresh or frozen cranberries.

DEFINITION

Zest is the small slivers of peel, usually from citrus fruits such as lemon, lime, or orange, that adds extra flavor to foods without adding excess moisture. You can remove the zest from citrus fruit using a fine grater, Microplane, or zester.

Pumpkin-Pecan Cake with Maple-Buttercream Frosting

This fantastic fall-inspired treat will impress your loved ones. This luscious pumpkin cake is covered in a rich maple buttercream frosting and embellished with maple-glazed pecans.

Yield:	Prep time:	Cook time:	Serving size:
1 (8-inch) cake	10 to 15 minutes	2½ to 3 hours	1 slice

1 cup toasted pecan halves

2 cups whole-wheat pastry or white whole-wheat flour

⅔ cup unbleached cane sugar

1 TB. pumpkin pie spice

2 tsp. baking soda

¼ tsp. sea salt

1¼ cups Pumpkin Purée (variation in Chapter 7) or canned pumpkin purée

⅔ cup plus 1 TB. almond or other nondairy milk

2 TB. sunflower or other oil

1½ TB. apple cider vinegar

½ TB. vanilla extract

3 TB. nonhydrogenated margarine

1½ TB. maple syrup

1½ cups vegan confectioners' sugar

1. Lightly coat an 8-inch springform pan or 6-cup or larger casserole dish (whichever fits your large oval slow cooker) with vegetable cooking spray or oil of choice. Place a trivet or foil ring in the bottom of the slow cooker, and preheat the slow cooker to high.

2. Set aside 8 pecan halves, and roughly chop remaining pecans.

3. In a large bowl, whisk together whole-wheat pastry flour, unbleached cane sugar, pumpkin pie spice, baking soda, and sea salt.

4. In a medium bowl, whisk together Pumpkin Purée, ⅔ cup almond milk, sunflower oil, apple cider vinegar, and vanilla extract.

5. Pour wet ingredients into dry ingredients, and whisk well to combine. Stir in chopped pecans, and transfer mixture to the prepared cake pan or casserole dish.

6. Place the pan or casserole dish on top of the trivet or foil ring. Cover; slightly vent lid with a toothpick, chopstick, or wooden spoon; and cook on high for 2½ to 3 hours or until a toothpick inserted in the center comes out clean. (Alternatively, tent the lid by placing a clean kitchen towel across the top of the slow cooker, just under the lid, to help capture the steam and prevent it from falling back down.)

7. Uncover and allow cake to cool inside the slow cooker for 10 minutes. Carefully remove the pan or casserole dish from the slow cooker, transfer to a rack, and cool for 10 minutes. Loosen sides of cake with a spatula. Leave cake in the pan or invert onto a plate, and completely cool cake before frosting.

8. Meanwhile, in a medium bowl, and using an electric mixer on medium speed, or with a whisk, beat or whisk nonhydrogenated margarine, remaining 1 tablespoon almond milk, and maple syrup for 1 minute.

9. Add confectioners' sugar, and beat or whisk well for 1 or 2 minutes or until light and fluffy.

10. Using a small spatula or knife, spread frosting on top of cooled cake, decoratively arrange reserved pecan halves in a ring around outer edge of cake, and serve.

Variation: If you don't have pumpkin pie spice, use ½ teaspoon ground cinnamon, 1 teaspoon ground ginger, and ½ teaspoon freshly grated nutmeg. For a slightly different-flavored cake, replace the Pumpkin Purée with an equal amount of Pumpkin Patch Butter, Wonderful Winter Squash Purée, or Sweet Potato Purée (recipes and variation in Chapter 7).

LOW AND SLOW

If you'd prefer to top your cake with a Vanilla Buttercream Frosting, omit the almond milk and maple syrup, and replace them with 2½ tablespoons soy milk and 1 teaspoon vanilla extract.

Mexican Hot Chocolate Cake with Almonds

If you love chocolate and spicy food, you'll love the rich, dark flavor of this oil-free cake with its tingling fiery heat that's created by combining cocoa powder, cinnamon, and cayenne.

Yield:	Prep time:	Cook time:	Serving size:
1 (8-inch) cake	10 to 15 minutes	2½ to 3 hours	1 slice

2 cups whole-wheat pastry or white whole-wheat flour

1 cup unbleached cane sugar

½ cup cocoa powder

½ TB. baking soda

2 tsp. ground cinnamon

¼ tsp. cayenne

¼ tsp. sea salt

1¼ cups chocolate almond or other nondairy milk

½ cup vanilla or plain vegan yogurt

1½ TB. balsamic or apple cider vinegar

1 tsp. vanilla extract

½ cup toasted sliced almonds

1. Lightly coat an 8-inch springform pan or 6-cup or larger casserole dish (whichever fits your large oval slow cooker) with vegetable cooking spray or oil of choice. Place a trivet or foil ring in the bottom of the slow cooker, and preheat the slow cooker to high.

2. In a large bowl, whisk together whole-wheat pastry flour, unbleached cane sugar, cocoa powder, baking soda, cinnamon, cayenne, and sea salt.

3. In a medium bowl, whisk together chocolate almond milk, vanilla yogurt, balsamic vinegar, and vanilla extract.

4. Pour wet ingredients into dry ingredients, and whisk well. Transfer mixture to the prepared cake pan or casserole dish. Sprinkle toasted sliced almonds over top, and gently press into batter with your hand.

5. Place the pan or casserole dish on top of the trivet or foil ring. Cover; slightly vent lid with a toothpick, chopstick, or wooden spoon; and cook on high for 2½ to 3 hours or until a toothpick inserted in the center comes out clean. (Alternatively, tent the lid by placing a clean kitchen towel across the top of the slow cooker, just under the lid, to help capture the steam and prevent it from falling back down.)

6. Uncover and allow cake to cool inside the slow cooker for 10 minutes. Carefully remove the pan or casserole dish from the slow cooker, transfer to a rack, and cool for 10 minutes. Loosen sides of cake with a spatula. Leave cake in the pan or invert onto a plate before serving warm or at room temperature.

Variation: Try this cake plain or topped with Hot Fudge Sauce or Mocha-Almond Fudge Sauce (recipe and variation in Chapter 6). For **Mocha Java-Almond Cake,** omit the cinnamon and cayenne, use only ½ cup chocolate almond milk, and add ¾ cup freshly brewed coffee and ½ teaspoon almond extract. Top individual servings with Mocha-Almond Fudge Sauce (variation in Chapter 6).

COOKER CAVEAT

If your cocoa powder is all clumped together rather than light and fluffy, sift it into your other dry ingredients to avoid having these bits remaining intact in your finished baked goods.

Marvelous Marble Cheesecake

This luscious two-tone taste sensation is comprised of a chocolate cookie crust filled with an ultra-creamy combination of chocolate and vanilla cream cheese and tofu-based batters decoratively swirled together.

Yield:	Prep time:	Cook time:	Serving size:
1 (8-inch) cheesecake	15 minutes, plus several hours or more chill time	3 to 3½ hours	1 slice

1¼ cups chocolate wafer cookie crumbs (about 20 wafers)

2 TB. plus ⅔ cup unbleached cane sugar

¼ cup nonhydrogenated margarine

2 (8-oz.) pkg. vegan cream cheese

1 (12-oz.) pkg. extra-firm silken tofu

⅓ cup cornstarch

1 TB. lemon juice

1 TB. vanilla extract

1⅓ cups vegan chocolate chips

1. Lightly coat an 8-inch springform pan or 6-cup or larger casserole dish (whichever fits your large oval slow cooker) with vegetable cooking spray or oil of choice. Place a trivet or foil ring in the bottom of the slow cooker, and preheat the slow cooker to high.

2. In a food processor fitted with an S blade, process chocolate wafer cookie crumbs, 2 tablespoons unbleached cane sugar, and nonhydrogenated margarine for 1 minute. Using your hands, firmly press mixture into the prepared springform pan, and refrigerate crust. Wipe out the food processor with a towel.

3. In the food processor, process cream cheese, extra-firm silken tofu, remaining ⅔ cup unbleached cane sugar, cornstarch, lemon juice, and vanilla extract for 2 minutes. Scrape down the sides of the container with a spatula, and process for 30 seconds.

4. In a medium microwave-safe glass bowl, place chocolate chips. Microwave on high for 1 or 2 minutes or until chips just begin to soften. Add 1¼ cups cream cheese mixture, and whisk well to combine.

5. Gently spread ½ of vanilla cream cheese mixture over crust, drop spoonfuls of chocolate cream cheese mixture on top, and drop spoonfuls of remaining vanilla cream cheese mixture on top. Run a knife through both mixtures in a swirl pattern to marble cheesecake.

6. Place the pan or casserole dish on top of the trivet or foil ring. Cover; slightly vent lid with a toothpick, chopstick, or wooden spoon; and cook on high for 3 to 3½ hours or until top of cheesecake feels set and is no longer jiggly. (Alternatively, tent the lid by placing a clean kitchen towel across the top of the slow cooker, just under the lid, to help capture the steam and prevent it from falling back down.)

7. Uncover and allow cheesecake to cool inside the slow cooker for 1 hour. Carefully remove the pan or casserole dish from the slow cooker, transfer to a rack, and cool cheesecake to room temperature. Loosen sides of cheesecake with a spatula. Chill cheesecake for several hours or overnight or until firm.

8. Loosen sides of cheesecake again with a spatula, and remove the ring from the springform pan. Cut into pieces and serve.

Variation: For an extra treat, serve topped with Hot Fudge Sauce (recipe in Chapter 6) or Cherries Jubilee (recipe in Chapter 18). For a plain **Vanilla Cheesecake,** prepare the crust using vanilla wafer cookie crumbs (about 20 wafers). Then, in the cream cheese mixture, omit chocolate chips, and replace with 2 tablespoons vanilla extract.

LOW AND SLOW

You can vary the flavor of your cheesecake simply by using different varieties of cookie crumbs for the crust, like cinnamon, lemon, or gingersnaps. Traditionally, graham crackers are used when making a cheesecake crust, and several vegan varieties are available. (I like the amaranth ones.)

Glossary

al dente   Italian for "against the teeth," this term refers to pasta or rice that's neither soft nor hard but just slightly firm against the teeth.

all-purpose flour   Flour that contains only the inner part of the wheat grain. It's suitable for everything from cakes to gravies.

allspice   A spice named for its flavor echoes of several spices (cinnamon, cloves, nutmeg) used in many desserts and in rich marinades and stews.

amaranth   A member of the pigweed family, this plant's tiny seeds are widely used. Amaranth can be cooked in liquid much like quinoa, or ground into flour for use in making pancakes, pasta, breads, and other baked goods.

anasazi bean   A small, kidney-shape bean that has a unique deep red-and-white swirled appearance. This tasty heirloom bean is also referred to as the Aztec bean, cave bean, New Mexico Appaloosa, or Jacob's cattle bean. After cooking, it has a mild, sweet flavor and a slightly mealy texture.

arborio rice   A plump, short-grain, highly glutinous white rice variety grown in Italy. The rice's outer layers contain a high concentration of starch that's released when cooked, which makes it the ideal choice for making risotto.

arrowroot   A gluten-free binder and thickening agent that has a neutral taste and can be used in place of flour or cornstarch in baking, as well as to thicken gravies, sauces, soups, stews, and dessert recipes.

artichoke heart   The center part of the artichoke flower, often found canned in grocery stores.

arugula   A spicy-peppery green with leaves that resemble a dandelion and have a distinctive and very sharp flavor.

bake   To cook in a dry oven. Dry-heat cooking often results in a crisping of the exterior of the food being cooked. Moist-heat cooking, through methods such as steaming, poaching, etc., brings a much different, moist quality to the food.

baking powder   A dry ingredient used to increase volume and lighten or leaven baked goods.

balsamic vinegar   A vinegar produced primarily in Italy from a specific type of grape and aged in wood barrels. It's heavier, darker, and sweeter than most vinegars.

basil   A flavorful, almost sweet, resinous herb, delicious with tomatoes and used in all kinds of Italian- and Mediterranean-style dishes.

baste   To keep foods moist during cooking by spooning, brushing, or drizzling with a liquid.

beat   To quickly mix substances.

blackstrap molasses   One of several varieties of molasses, blackstrap is a dark, thick, bittersweet syrup that results from the production of sugar. It does have a slightly bitter flavor, so if you prefer a sweeter flavor, you can replace it with unsulphured Barbados molasses.

blanch   To place a food in boiling water for about 1 minute or less to partially cook the exterior and then submerge in or rinse with cool water to halt the cooking.

blend   To completely mix something, usually with a blender or food processor, slower than beating.

boil   To heat a liquid to the point where water is forced to turn into steam, causing the liquid to bubble. To boil something is to insert it into boiling water. A rapid boil is when a lot of bubbles form on the surface of the liquid.

bok choy   A member of the cabbage family with thick stems, crisp texture, and fresh flavor. It's perfect for stir-frying.

Bragg Liquid Aminos   A condiment and flavor enhancer made from soybeans and water with a salty, rich flavor similar to tamari or other soy sauce. It contains large amounts of dietary essential and nonessential amino acids.

braising   A cooking technique in which foods are slowly cooked in a small amount of liquid (such as broth, water, or wine) in a tightly covered pot, Dutch oven, or slow cooker. This moist-heat method prevents foods from drying during the cooking process.

bread flour   A flour with a high gluten/protein content, which helps give yeasted baked goods a higher rise than you typically get from using all-purpose or unbleached flour. Bread flour is often used in combination with whole-wheat or other whole-grain flours for making sweet and savory breads, rolls, and pizza dough.

broil   To cook in a dry oven under the overhead high-heat element.

broth *See* stock.

brown To cook in a skillet, turning, until the food's surface is seared and brown in color to lock in the juices.

brown rice A whole-grain rice, including the germ, with a characteristic pale brown or tan color. It's more nutritious and flavorful than white rice.

brown rice syrup A liquid sweetener made from fermenting brown rice with special enzymes until its natural starches begin to break down. It's then strained and cooked down until it reaches a syrupy consistency. It's mildly sweet with a light caramel flavor and color and is available in gluten-free and several flavored varieties in most grocery and natural foods stores.

brown rice vinegar A vinegar popular in Asian-style dishes produced from fermented brown rice, water, and koji (a beneficial type of mold), or from unrefined rice wine (sake) and water.

bulgur A wheat kernel that's been steamed, dried, and crushed and is sold in fine and coarse textures.

capers The flavorful buds of a Mediterranean plant, ranging in size from nonpareil (about the size of a small pea) to larger, grape-size caper berries produced in Spain. Capers are most commonly sold in jars packed in brine but are also available in tins packed in salt.

caramelize To cook sugar over low heat until it develops a sweet caramel flavor, or to cook vegetables (especially onions) in butter or oil over low heat until they soften, sweeten, and develop a caramel color.

caraway A distinctive spicy seed used for bread, pork, cheese, and cabbage dishes. It's known to reduce stomach upset, which is why it's often paired with foods like sauerkraut.

cardamom An intense, sweet-smelling spice used in baking and coffee and common in Indian cooking.

carob A tropical tree that produces long pods from which the dried, baked, and powdered flesh—carob powder—is used in baking. The flavor is sweet and reminiscent of chocolate.

cayenne A fiery spice made from hot chile peppers, especially the cayenne, a slender, red, and very hot chile.

chickpea (or **garbanzo bean**) A roundish yellow-gold bean used as the base ingredient in hummus. Chickpeas are high in fiber and low in fat.

chiffonade   French for "made from rags," a technique for slicing herbs and vegetables into long, thin, ribbonlike strips. This reference is usually applied to basil or mint leaves or leafy green vegetables. To chiffonade leaves, stack and roll a small pile of leaves; slice the roll crosswise into fine, thin strips; and gently toss the strips with your fingers to separate them.

chile (or **chili**)   Any one of many different "hot" peppers, ranging in intensity from the relatively mild ancho pepper to the blisteringly hot habanero.

chili powder   A warm, rich seasoning blend that includes chile pepper, cumin, garlic, and oregano.

chive   A member of the onion family, chives grow in bunches of long leaves that resemble tall grass or the green tops of onions and offer a light onion flavor.

chop   To cut into pieces, usually qualified by an adverb such as "*coarsely* chopped" or by a size measurement such as "chopped into ½-inch pieces." "Finely chopped" is much closer to mince.

chutney   A thick condiment often served with Indian curries made with fruits and/or vegetables with vinegar, sugar, and spices.

cider vinegar   A vinegar produced from apple cider, popular in North America.

cilantro   A member of the parsley family used in Mexican cooking (especially salsa), as well as in some Indian and Asian dishes. Use cilantro in moderation, as some find the flavor of cilantro overwhelming.

cinnamon   A rich, aromatic spice commonly used in baking or desserts. Cinnamon can also be used for delicious and interesting entrées.

clabbering   A method of souring soy milk by combining soy or another nondairy milk with a little lemon juice or vinegar, which, when left to sit for a few minutes, causes the soy milk to sour and thicken slightly. Sometimes this mixture is referred to as soy buttermilk because it can be used as a measure-for-measure replacement for buttermilk in recipes.

clove   A sweet, strong, almost wintergreen-flavor spice used in baking.

coriander   A rich, warm, spicy seed used in all types of recipes, from African to South American, from entrées to desserts.

corn grits   A coarsely ground cornmeal. Cooking in liquid transforms the corn grits into a porridgelike hot cereal. They're also used to make Italian polenta.

cornstarch   A thickener used in baking and food processing. It's the refined starch of the endosperm of the corn kernel. To avoid clumps, it's often mixed with cold liquid to make into a paste before adding to a recipe.

couscous   Granular semolina (durum wheat) that's cooked and used in many Mediterranean and North African dishes.

crimini mushroom   A relative of the white button mushroom that's brown in color and has a richer flavor. The larger, fully grown version is the portobello. *See also* portobello mushroom.

crudité   Fresh vegetables served as an appetizer, often all together on one tray.

cumin   A fiery, smoky-tasting spice popular in Middle Eastern and Indian dishes. Cumin is a seed; ground cumin seed is the most common form used in cooking.

curry   Rich, spicy, Indian-style sauces and the dishes prepared with them. A curry uses curry powder as its base seasoning.

curry powder   A ground blend of rich and flavorful spices used as a basis for curry and many other Indian-influenced dishes. Common ingredients include hot pepper, nutmeg, cumin, cinnamon, pepper, and turmeric. Some curry can also be found in paste form.

dash   A few drops, usually of a liquid, released by a quick shake.

dice   To cut into small cubes about ¼-inch square.

Dijon mustard   A hearty, spicy mustard made in the style of the Dijon region of France.

dill   A herb perfect for many foods, including vegetables like pickles.

dollop   A spoonful of something creamy and thick, like sour cream or whipped cream.

double boiler   A set of two pots designed to nest together, one inside the other, and provide consistent, moist heat for foods that need delicate treatment. The bottom pot holds water (not quite touching the bottom of the top pot); the top pot holds the food to be heated.

dredge   To coat a piece of food on all sides with a dry substance such as flour or cornmeal.

drizzle   To lightly sprinkle drops of a liquid over food, often as the finishing touch to a dish.

edamame   Fresh, plump, pale green soybeans, similar in appearance to lima beans, often served steamed and either shelled or still in their protective pods.

emulsion   A combination of liquid ingredients that don't normally mix well (such as a fat or oil with water) that are beaten together to create a thick liquid. Creating emulsions must be done carefully and rapidly to ensure the particles of one ingredient are suspended in the other.

Ener-G Egg Replacer   A commercial egg replacer that contains potato starch, tapioca starch, and leavening agents. It can be used as a substitute for eggs in your baked goods and other sweet and savory dishes. Look for it packaged and in bulk in most grocery and natural foods stores.

entrée   The main dish in a meal.

escarole   A variety of endive that has very broad, bitter-tasting leaves. A medium head of escarole usually yields about 7 cups torn leaves. It can be eaten raw in salads, blanched or boiled in water, or sautéed.

extra-virgin olive oil   *See* olive oil.

extract   A concentrated flavoring derived from foods or plants through evaporation or distillation that imparts a powerful flavor without altering the volume or texture of a dish.

fennel   In seed form, a fragrant, licorice-tasting herb. The bulbs have a mild flavor and a celery-like crunch and are used as a vegetable in salads or cooked recipes.

flour   Grains ground into a meal. Wheat is perhaps the most common flour, but oats, rye, buckwheat, soybeans, chickpeas, etc., can also be used. *See also* all-purpose flour; bread flour; white whole-wheat flour; whole-wheat flour.

fold   To combine a dense and light mixture with a circular action from the middle of the bowl.

frittata   A skillet-cooked mixture of eggs and other ingredients that's not stirred but is cooked slowly and then either flipped or finished under the broiler. Vegan frittata recipes often use blended tofu in place of eggs.

fry   *See* sauté.

garam masala   Literally "hot spice" in Hindi, garam masala is a seasoning blend commonly used in Indian and Southern Asian cuisines made of pungent and warming spices like cardamom, cinnamon, coriander, cumin, cloves, and black pepper, although blends vary by brand. It doesn't necessarily have a hot flavor like cayenne or chile powder.

garlic   A member of the onion family, a pungent and flavorful vegetable used in many savory dishes. A garlic bulb contains multiple cloves. Each clove, when chopped, provides about 1 teaspoon garlic.

ginger   A flavorful root available fresh or dried and ground that adds a pungent, sweet, and spicy quality to a dish.

handful   An unscientific measurement, it's the amount of an ingredient you can hold in your hand.

herbes de Provence   A seasoning mix of basil, fennel, marjoram, rosemary, sage, and thyme common in the south of France.

hominy grits   Grits made from coarsely ground, dried hominy. Hominy is dried white or yellow corn that's been soaked in an alkali solution (like baking soda or lye), which causes the corn kernels to soften and swell to nearly double their size. The hull and germ are then removed, and the hominy is dried once again before being ground into hominy grits.

hors d'oeuvre   French for "outside of work" (the "work" being the main meal), an hors d'oeuvre can be any dish served as a starter before a meal.

hummus   A thick, Middle Eastern spread made of puréed chickpeas, lemon juice, olive oil, garlic, and often tahini.

infusion   A liquid in which flavorful ingredients such as herbs have been soaked or steeped to extract their flavor into the liquid.

instant oatmeal   Oats that are precooked, dried, and rolled to make very thin, fine flakes. Some brands also add sugar, salt, and other ingredients to the finished product. Although instant is the fastest-cooking variety of oats, it's the least nutritious.

Italian seasoning   A blend of dried herbs, including basil, oregano, rosemary, and thyme.

julienne   A French word meaning "to slice into very thin pieces."

kalamata olive   Traditionally from Greece, a medium-small, long black olive with a rich, smoky flavor.

Key lime   A very small lime grown primarily in Florida known for its tart taste.

knead   To work dough to make it pliable so it holds gas bubbles as it bakes. Kneading is fundamental in the process of making yeast breads.

lacinato kale   An heirloom variety of kale with tender, dark blue-green leaves that have a slightly sweeter and more delicate taste than curly green kale. It's also referred to as Tuscan, Italian, or comically as dinosaur kale because the extremely wrinkled leaves have a somewhat prehistoric look.

lemon pepper   A seasoning made from grinding together dried lemon zest and cracked black peppercorns, which infuses the black pepper with the flavorful and extremely fragrant essential oil contained within the lemon zest. Try using lemon pepper instead of black pepper to season your favorite soups, vegetables, grains, and pasta dishes.

lentil   A tiny lens-shape pulse used in European, Middle Eastern, and Indian cuisines.

marinate   To soak a food in a seasoned sauce (a marinade) that's high in acid content.

marjoram   A sweet herb, cousin of and similar to oregano, popular in Greek, Spanish, and Italian dishes.

meld   To allow flavors to blend and spread over time. Melding is often why recipes call for overnight refrigeration and is also why some dishes taste better as leftovers.

mesclun   Mixed salad greens, usually containing lettuce and other assorted greens such as arugula, cress, and endive.

millet   A tiny, round, yellow-colored, nutty-flavored grain often used as a replacement for couscous.

mince   To cut into very small pieces, smaller than diced, about $\frac{1}{8}$ inch or smaller.

miso   A fermented, flavorful soybean paste, key in many Japanese dishes.

mouthfeel   The overall sensation in the mouth resulting from a combination of a food's temperature, taste, smell, and texture.

mulled (or to mull)   Heating a liquid such as apple cider, fruit juice, water, or wine along with a blend of spices or dried or fresh herbs, and sometimes with a small amount of sugar or other sweetener. After a few hours of cooking, you'll have a flavorful, fragrant, and warming drink.

muscovado sugar (or Barbados sugar)   A type of cane sugar with a moist texture and a pronounced molasses flavor that's produced in Barbados, Mauritius, and the Philippines. Muscovado sugar is available in both light and dark varieties, and both are an excellent substitute for light or dark brown sugar in breads and baked goods.

nutmeg   A sweet, fragrant, musky spice used primarily in baking.

nutritional yeast flakes   An inactive yeast that has a nutty, almost cheeselike flavor, which is why it's commonly used as an imitation cheese flavoring for foods and in the production of nondairy cheese products. It's an excellent product for vegans to use to attain their recommended daily dose of vitamin B_{12}. Do not confuse with active yeast, the type used for making breads and baked goods.

old-fashioned (or regular) rolled oats   Oat groats that have been steamed and then rolled between rollers (or flattened) into flakes.

olive   The fruit of the olive tree commonly grown on all sides of the Mediterranean. Black olives are also called ripe olives. Green olives are immature, although they're also widely eaten. *See also* kalamata olive.

olive oil   A fragrant liquid produced by crushing or pressing olives. Extra-virgin olive oil—the most flavorful and highest quality—is produced from the first pressing of a batch of olives; oil is also produced from later pressings.

oregano   A fragrant, slightly astringent herb used in Greek, Spanish, and Italian dishes.

orzo   A rice-shape pasta used in Greek cooking.

oxidation   The browning of fruit flesh that happens over time and with exposure to air. Minimize oxidation by rubbing the cut surfaces with lemon juice.

oyster mushroom   A variety of mushroom with a slightly puffy, oyster-shape cap and practically no stem that grows in clusters on dead logs. Many people claim oyster mushrooms have a similar taste and smell as their namesake.

paprika   A rich, red, warm, earthy spice that lends a rich red color to many dishes.

parsley   A fresh-tasting green leafy herb, often used as a garnish.

pesto   A thick spread or sauce made with fresh basil leaves, garlic, olive oil, pine nuts, and Parmesan cheese.

pilaf   A rice dish in which the rice is browned in a fat and then cooked in a flavorful liquid such as a broth, often with the addition of vegetables. The rice absorbs the broth, resulting in a savory dish.

pinch   An unscientific measurement for the amount of an ingredient—typically, a dry, granular substance such as an herb or seasoning—you can hold between your finger and thumb.

pine nut   A nut that's rich (high in fat), flavorful, and a bit pine-y. Pine nuts are a traditional ingredient in pesto and add a hearty crunch to many other recipes.

pita bread   A flat, hollow wheat bread often used for sandwiches or sliced pizza style. They're also terrific soft with dips or baked or broiled as a vehicle for other ingredients.

poach   To cook a food in simmering liquid such as water, wine, or broth.

polenta   A mush made from cornmeal that can be eaten hot or cooked until firm and cut into squares.

portobello mushroom A mature and larger form of the smaller crimini mushroom. Brown, chewy, and flavorful, portobellos are often served as whole caps, grilled, or as thin sautéed slices. *See also* crimini mushroom.

preheat To turn on an oven, broiler, or other cooking appliance in advance of cooking so the temperature will be at the desired level when the assembled dish is ready for cooking.

purée To reduce a food to a thick, creamy texture, typically using a blender or food processor.

quick-cooking rolled oat A steel-cut oat that's been steamed and then rolled and flattened into flakes.

quinoa A nutty-flavored seed that's extremely high in protein and calcium.

rapid-rise active yeast A variety of baker's yeast that's essentially a faster-working, instant version of active dry yeast. It must be hydrated to activate the dough and cause the rise to occur.

raw cacao powder A powder made from raw cacao beans that have gone through a cold-pressing process to remove the fat (cacao butter) and are then finely ground into a powder, much like cocoa powder (which is made from roasted cacao beans). It has a deep, dark, almost coffeelike flavor. Raw foodists and others often use it as a replacement for cocoa powder in recipes.

red curry paste A spicy, thick paste made by grinding together red chiles, lemon grass, shallots, garlic, ginger, kaffir lime, oil, salt, and several spices. It's used as a condiment and flavoring for curries, soups, stews, stir-fries, and noodle dishes.

reduce To boil or simmer a broth or sauce to remove some of the water content, resulting in more concentrated flavor and color.

reserve To hold a specified ingredient for another use later in the recipe.

risotto A popular Italian rice dish made by toasting arborio rice in a fat and then slowly adding liquid to cook the rice while slowly releasing its starches, resulting in a creamy texture.

roast To cook something uncovered in an oven, usually without additional liquid.

rosemary A pungent, sweet herb. A little goes a long way.

roux A mixture of a fat and flour used to thicken sauces and soups.

sage An herb with a musty yet fruity, lemon-rind scent and "sunny" flavor.

sauté To pan-cook over lower heat than what's used for frying.

savory A popular herb with a fresh, woody taste, which is often compared to marjoram. There are two major types of savory—summer and winter. Many chefs prefer summer savory because it's lighter-tasting than the winter variety but still has the characteristic minty-peppery flavor.

scant An ingredient measurement directive not to add any extra, perhaps even leaving the measurement a tad short.

sea vegetable An edible plant that grows in the ocean. Some commonly used varieties include arame, dulse, kelp, kombu, hijiki, nori, and wakame. Sea vegetables provide beneficial sources of iodine, iron, magnesium, calcium, vitamin K, and several B vitamins.

sear To quickly brown the exterior of a food over high heat.

seitan (a.k.a. wheat meat or gluten) An amazing meat replacement made by rinsing and kneading whole-wheat flour under water to help remove its starch and leave behind only the protein-rich gluten. Many people still make seitan this way, but for a faster preparation, vital wheat gluten, a flour product that already has the starch and bran removed, can be used.

sesame oil An oil made from pressing sesame seeds. It's tasteless if clear and aromatic and flavorful if brown.

shallot A member of the onion family that grows in a bulb somewhat like garlic but has a milder onion flavor. When a recipe calls for shallot, use the entire bulb.

shiitake mushroom A large, dark brown mushroom with a hearty, meaty flavor. It can be used fresh or dried, grilled, as a component in other recipes, and as a flavoring source for broth.

short-grain rice A starchy rice popular in Asian-style dishes because it readily clumps, making it perfect for eating with chopsticks.

silken tofu A type of tofu with a velvety-smooth and creamy texture. The process for making silken tofu differs slightly from regular tofu in that the soy milk curds and excess water are not separated during production. Depending on the silken tofu's final texture, it's labeled soft, firm, or extra firm. Silken tofu is often blended for making sauces, salad dressings, beverages, desserts, and baked goods.

simmer To boil a liquid gently so it barely bubbles.

skillet (also **frying pan**) A generally heavy, flat-bottomed, metal pan with a handle designed to cook food over heat on a stovetop or campfire.

smoked paprika A variety of Spanish paprika. Smoked paprika is made from mature pimento peppers that are dried; naturally smoked over oak wood fires; and stone-ground to a fine, powdery consistency. It has a deep red color, with a slightly smoky and bittersweet flavor.

smoked sea salt Sea salt that's been slow smoked for several hours over various types of wood, such as hickory, mesquite, or alder. It has a full-bodied, very intense, smoky flavor and aroma and is often used as a replacement for liquid smoke flavoring to add a bit of smokiness to barbecue sauces, marinades, and grilled or oven-roasted items.

steam To suspend a food over boiling water and allow the heat of the steam (water vapor) to cook the food. This quick-cooking method preserves a food's flavor and texture.

steel-cut oat Oat groats that have been coarsely cut into several pieces using steel blades, resulting in a chewy and slightly nutty texture.

steep To let sit in hot water, as in steeping tea in hot water for 10 minutes.

stew To slowly cook pieces of food submerged in a liquid. Also, a dish prepared by this method.

stir-fry To cook small pieces of food in a wok or skillet over high heat, moving and turning the food quickly to cook all sides.

stock A flavorful broth made by cooking vegetables with seasonings until the liquid absorbs these flavors. The liquid is strained, and the solids are discarded. Stock can be eaten alone or used as a base for soups, stews, etc.

strata A dish commonly made with layers of bread cubes, veggies, and often cheese, which are covered with a rich, custardlike blend of eggs and other ingredients, but vegan versions are often tofu-based instead.

super-firm tofu An extremely densely textured tofu from which most of the water has been pressed out prior to packaging. Super-firm tofu can be used in many dishes, especially in recipes that call for marinating, grilling, baking, or frying the tofu.

tapioca pearl Tapioca starch (a.k.a. tapioca flour) that's soaked, cooked, shaped, and dried into assorted sizes of pellets or pearls.

tarragon A sweet, rich-smelling herb. It's perfect with vegetables (especially asparagus).

tempeh A cultured food product made by mixing partially cooked soybeans with a beneficial mold (*Rhizosporus oligosporus*) and fermenting it. The result is a firm soybean cake with a marbled appearance, which is why tempeh is often classified as the bleu cheese version of tofu.

teriyaki A Japanese-style sauce composed of soy sauce, rice wine, ginger, and sugar.

thyme A minty, zesty herb.

tofu A cheeselike substance made from soybeans and soy milk.

turbinado sugar Sugar made from the juice extracted from unrefined raw cane sugar, which is then spun in a centrifuge or turbine (hence its name). It has a very fine texture and a slight molasses flavor and can be used to replace light brown sugar. You might be familiar with the most commonly sold brand of turbinado sugar—Sugar in the Raw.

turmeric A spicy, pungent yellow root used in many dishes, especially Indian cuisine, for color and flavor. Turmeric is the source of the yellow color in many prepared mustards.

vegetable steamer A metal insert pan with tiny holes in the bottom designed to fit on or in another pot to hold food to be steamed above boiling water. *See also* steam.

vinegar An acidic liquid widely used as a dressing and seasoning, often made from fermented grapes, apples, or rice. *See also* balsamic vinegar; brown rice vinegar; cider vinegar; wine vinegar.

vital wheat gluten (a.k.a. instant gluten flour or gluten flour) A powdered form of dehydrated pure wheat gluten. It's often mixed with liquid and seasonings to make seitan and its many meat analog variations, in addition to being added to breads and other baked goods. Find it in bulk bins or packaged in most grocery and natural foods stores.

water chestnut A white, crunchy, and juicy tuber popular in many Asian dishes. It holds its texture whether cool or hot.

whisk To rapidly mix, introducing air to the mixture.

white mushroom A button mushroom. When fresh, white mushrooms have an earthy smell and an appealing soft crunch.

white whole-wheat flour A flour ground from white wheat, which was developed by cross-breeding strains of red wheat. Unlike red wheat, which has three bran colors, white wheat has no major genes for bran color, and therefore is lighter in color and milder in flavor. White whole-wheat flour can be used in place of all-purpose or unbleached white flour in recipes, but it's more nutritious than these heavily refined flours because it still contains the beneficial bran, germ, and endosperm of the white wheat kernel.

whole grain   A grain derived from the seeds of grasses, including rice, oats, rye, wheat, wild rice, quinoa, barley, buckwheat, bulgur, corn, millet, amaranth, and sorghum.

whole-wheat flour   Wheat flour that contains the entire grain.

wild rice   Not a rice at all, this grass has a rich, nutty flavor and serves as a nutritious side dish.

wine vinegar   Vinegar produced from red or white wine.

yeast   Tiny fungi that, when mixed with water, sugar, flour, and heat, release carbon dioxide bubbles, which, in turn, cause the bread to rise.

zest   Small slivers of peel, usually from citrus fruits such as lemon, lime, or orange, that adds extra flavor without adding excess moisture to foods.

Resources

Now that you've begun your adventure into vegan slow cooking, many other books and websites can provide additional information that may prove helpful. This appendix is meant to help you find any additional information you might need.

Vegan Products

Bob's Red Mill
bobsredmill.com
(Gluten-free flours, starches, grains, etc.)

Daiya Foods
daiyafoods.com
(Vegan cheeses.)

Endangered Species Chocolate
chocolatebar.com

Ener-G Foods
ener-G.com

Follow Your Heart
followyourheart.com
(Vegan cheeses, cream cheese, sour cream, Vegenaise, and salad dressings.)

Lundberg Family Farms
lundberg.com

Mountain Rose Herbs
mountainroseherbs.com

So Delicious Dairy Free (Turtle Mountain)
turtlemountain.com
(Lots of yummy vegan nondairy milks, yogurt, ice creams and other frozen novelties, etc.)

Theo Chocolate
theochocolate.com

Vegan Essentials
veganessentials.com

Wildwood
wildwoodfoods.com
(Tofu, especially sprouted and super firm; soy-based products; and yogurt.)

Vegan Information/Support

Beverly Lynn Bennett
veganchef.com

Forks Over Knives
forksoverknives.com

**Physicians Committee for
Responsible Medicine (PCRM)**
pcrm.org

Plant-Based Dietitian
plantbaseddietitian.com

Vegetarian Resource Group
vrg.org

VegNews **Magazine**
vegnews.com

VegSource
vegsource.com

Slow Cooker Manufacturers

All-Clad
all-clad.com

CorningWare
corningware.com

Cuisinart
cuisinart.com

Hamilton Beach
hamiltonbeach.com

KitchenAid
kitchenaid.com

Proctor Silex
proctorsilex.com

Rival
crockpot.com

West Bend
westbend.com

Vegan Books and Cookbooks

Atlas, Nava. *Vegan Express*. New York, NY: Clarkson Potter, 2008.

———. *Vegan Holiday Kitchen: More Than 200 Delicious, Festive Recipes for Special Occasions*. New York, NY: Sterling, 2011.

Bennett, Beverly Lynn. *Vegan Bites*. Summertown, TN: Book Publishing Company, 2008.

Bennett, Beverly Lynn, and Julieanna Hever, MS, RD, CPT. *The Complete Idiot's Guide to Gluten-Free Vegan Cooking*. Indianapolis, IN: Alpha Books, 2011.

Bennett, Beverly Lynn, and Ray Sammartano. *The Complete Idiot's Guide to Vegan Cooking*. Indianapolis, IN: Alpha Books, 2008.

————. *The Complete Idiot's Guide to Vegan Living, Second Edition*. Indianapolis, IN: Alpha Books, 2012.

Campbell, T. Colin, and T. M. Campbell. *The China Study*. Dallas, TX: Benbella Books, 2006.

Davis, Brenda, and Vesanto Melina. *Becoming Vegan*. Summertown, TN: Book Publishing Company, 2000.

Grogan, Bryanna Clark. *World Vegan Feast: 200 Fabulous Recipes from Over 50 Countries*. Woodstock, VA: Vegan Heritage Press, 2011.

Hever, Julieanna. *The Complete Idiot's Guide to Plant-Based Nutrition*. Indianapolis, IN: Alpha Books, 2011.

Robbins, John. *The Food Revolution*. Boston, MA: Conari Press, 2010.

————. *Healthy at 100*. New York, NY: Ballantine Books, 2007.

Robertson, Robin. *1,000 Vegan Recipes*. Hoboken, NJ: Wiley, 2009.

————. *Vegan Planet: 400 Irresistible Recipes with Fantastic Flavors from Home and Around the World*. Boston, MA: Harvard Common Press, 2003.

Stepaniak, Jo. *The Vegan Sourcebook*. New York, NY: McGraw Hill, 2000.

Index